FROM ACADEMIA TO ENTREPRENEUR

FROM ACADEMIA TO ENTREPRENEUR

Lessons from the Real World

EUGENE KHOR, PhD (VIRGINIA TECH)

Chiticore Enterprises Inc.
209-1095 McKenzie Avenue
Victoria, BC, Canada, V8P 2L5
ekhor@chiticore.com

AMSTERDAM • BOSTON • HEIDELBERG • LONDON
NEW YORK • OXFORD • PARIS • SAN DIEGO
SAN FRANCISCO • SINGAPORE • SYDNEY • TOKYO

Academic Press is an imprint of Elsevier

Academic Press is an imprint of Elsevier
32 Jamestown Road, London NW1 7BY, UK
225 Wyman Street, Waltham, MA 02451, USA
525 B Street, Suite 1800, San Diego, CA 92101-4495, USA

Notice
No responsibility is assumed by the publisher for any injury and/or damage to persons
or property as a matter of products liability, negligence or otherwise, or from any use or
operation of any methods, products, instructions or ideas contained in the material herein.
Because of rapid advances in the medical sciences, in particular, independent verification of
diagnoses and drug dosages should be made.

British Library Cataloguing-in-Publication Data
A catalogue record for this book is available from the British Library

Library of Congress Cataloging-in-Publication Data
A catalog record for this book is available from the Library of Congress

ISBN: 978-0-12-410516-4

For information on all Academic Press publications
visit our website at www.store.elsevier.com

Typeset by MPS Limited, Chennai, India
www.adi-mps.com

Contents

Preface

ABOUT ENTREPRENEURS

There are countless ways to define what entrepreneurs are. In this book, an entrepreneur is either an individual who runs a business concern or someone who takes on the risk of starting an enterprise that, when providence favors, brings the venture to success. In the vernacular of business at the street level, the term entrepreneur can be further refined into two species, the *jet-stream* entrepreneur and the *runway* entrepreneur.

The term *jet-stream* entrepreneur insinuates an established corporate setting where the enterprise is perceived to be performing at a high and efficient level, much like a big jet airliner cruising at 35,000 feet above sea level progressing smoothly, the odd turbulence notwithstanding, to its destination. The entrepreneur in this instance is visualized as business savvy, self-confident, visionary, most likely MBA equipped, an industry mover and shaker on a big stage. In some cases, this is the *anointed* one, who made all the right moves, said all the right things, strategized and planned (at times schemed may be more suitable) all the way to the top of the *pecking order*. Some less complimentary allusions may imply a chosen one with less than impeccable credentials placed there by merit of birthright, or through other less professional and/or ethical maneuverings. However one views this breed, the *jet-stream* entrepreneur is not the subject of this book.

A *runway* entrepreneur in all probability conjures up images of a naïve but determined novice trying to make it in the entrepreneurial world. Picture a trainee pilot trying to qualify for his pilot's license strapped in his seat at the controls of a small plane taking off from the *runway* on his first solo flight. The view is from the ground up. Every aspect is felt in close proximity: the cramped cockpit, the instruments panel, the control column, the throttle, the payload, the vibrations from the single propeller turns and the tarmac. Once in the air there is no autopilot to engage, no radar and at a typical altitude of between 2000–5000 feet AGL,[i] the pilot has to pretty much lookout for surrounding air-traffic. It is a highly

---

[i] Above Ground Level.

charged *hands-on* situation, where many things have to be dealt with simultaneously.[ii]

The decision to do something distinct once commenced leads to a long and arduous effort with undefined challenges surfacing, depleting finite resources at a more rapid rate than planned. Each and every factor regardless of whether small or big, can influence whether the enterprise will takeoff and reach the heavenly heights or crash into a burning inferno.

This is the *true* environment of a *start-up enterprise* and how they come about:

From the *runway* up

The *runway* entrepreneur is the one who sizes up an opportunity and, weighing the odds as acceptable, embarks on a course of action that can eventually lead to a Fortune 500 listing, attain a more modest yet creditable existence or end up as a non-descript memory of what could have been. The *runway* entrepreneur may eventually metamorphose into the *jet-stream* entrepreneur, but that is a story for another day. This book focuses on the *runway* entrepreneur going from nothing to something.

ABOUT BIOMEDICAL ENTERPRISES

Setting up a business is a relatively straightforward, albeit a non-trivial, exercise. Figure out what you want to do, dream up a name for the company, pay a few dollars to incorporate the enterprise and you're in the game. But starting up a ***biomedical enterprise*** is not as simple as emulating orthodox business models. Biomed[iii] is more than just identifying the right medical product or service, building it into a business plan, raising the capital, putting the plan into action and seeing it through to success. The ingredients to success for biomed extend beyond conventional intuition, cash, luck and wit.

Biomed is also something you do not want to start in a garage or the comfort of your air-conditioned bedroom. Biomed is not about a couple of computer geniuses putting software and/or hardware together from the garage to success as legends of the dot.com era have spawned; or anecdotes of the more conservative bespectacled accountant, teacher, or the smartly dressed real-estate agent bringing entities from the bedroom

---

[ii] The contrast between the *jet-stream* and *runway* entrepreneurs is illustrative only. Flying is a serious matter that includes comprehensive ground school training and a minimum number of flying hours with an instructor before a solo flight. Similarly, flying commercial jetliners requires specialized training.

[iii] Biomed is used in this book as an abbreviation for biomedical, biomedical science, or a biomedical business/enterprise depending on the context.

to thriving small and medium enterprises (SMEs). There are requirements specific to biomed that make these start-up approaches improbable. In other words, biomed is not something you create in a small space, surviving on the little cash you obtained after pawning your last earthly possession of value and "living on soy sauce and rice"[1] for several months, at the end of which your first concept is ready for launch. Biomed is a whole new ballgame that can be daunting to even those who have the skills. What am I talking about?

ABOUT ACADEMIA'S RELEVANCE TO BIOMED AND ENTERPRISE

Biomed businesses are not normally something you dream up and put together in a moment of inspiration. In most instances (disregarding large biomed corporations), the knowledge and skills biomed requires are more commonly found in the realms of academia that probably has taken several years of research by lead scientists[iv] and their research teams to define. Getting this knowledge out from academia to the marketplace is complicated at best, and practically impossible to replicate in the constraints of a garage or bedroom, as the work had probably been developed in the confines of controlled specialized laboratories and engineering workshops.

The first tremendous hurdle is that academic knowledge rarely comes pre-packaged for utilization. In academia, researchers are trained to come up with ideas, execute the laboratory or practical work, draw conclusions from their results, and publish their work, thereby advancing scientific knowledge. Taking it to the next level of methodically developing a prospective product or service that can ultimately result in financial and social benefits is usually *someone else's concern* that need not be traversed. The task of utilizing the knowledge generated, innovating and creating products was the domain of others such as government agencies, industry and other commercial entities to sort out. Today, there are extensive and diverse interactions between industry and academia. Therefore, further effort (translated as more funds, work and time needed for a defined purpose) before the research results can be reasonably assessed for it's commercial feasibility is now more mainstream.

Equally important, when results denote exploitation as a worthwhile undertaking, is how this can be achieved. Licensing to an established entity and looking forward to royalties is one option. This channel excites bureaucrats and makes lawyers very busy. The person(s) behind the invention is normally rewarded a share of the royalty fees, the

---

[iv]Denotes a medical, dental, engineering or science academic.

quantum dependent on the institution's prevailing administrators. The other is to progress to creating an enterprise.

One trendy approach for starting-up biomed enterprises that have been "endowed" with substantial funds is to find a suitable brand name transplant, i.e. someone with a track record of running or related management involvement in a related technology business to head the start-up. This is more in tune with the *jet-stream* approach. Unfortunately, a brand name is unlikely to accept a *runway* biomed start-up challenge. Three reasons are offered. The first is costs. Brand name individuals command salaries that are likely prohibitive for a *runway* start-up on a shoestring budget, unless they willingly undertake a personal financial risk for deferred and unsure rewards. Second, while these persons may comprehend business and science, their focus is likely the business end, delegating the scientific aspects of the undertaking to others. It may be contended that as long as the principal academic is there to provide the necessary input to resolve concerns that may arise, the situation is manageable. Possibly, but this reasoning is subject to many uncertainties, key among them being the availability of the principal academic and their adeptness to orientate on commercial instead of academic facets. Furthermore, recognizing subtleties in the science when issues are confronted, then maneuvering around them within a specified timeline, may be what makes or breaks a commercial endeavor. Third, the entrepreneur of a *runway* start-up is the first to see the light; and has to infect and convert others such as helpers, sponsors and customers with belief; forcing solutions by sheer willpower in order for the enterprise to have a chance to move beyond the *concept in the head* phase. Therefore, unless the biomed enterprise setting is well defined, the "trendy approach" is less likely for *runway* start-ups.

The default then would be to consider coaxing a champion from the source. Barring the occasional maverick, this automatically begs the question, why would an academic in medicine, dentistry, engineering or the sciences, having spent several years establishing a credible academic career, want to start a business enterprise? Why forgo the safe ground of a steady stream of journal publications, international peer recognition and the status of a professorship? Even if they were prompted by interest and circumstances, how would they get started in becoming biomed entrepreneurs? What does an academia-based physician, dentist, engineer or scientist know about starting or running a business? Is there such a thing as an *academic biomed entrepreneur*? If they asked their graduating students to run the business, would the student still be beholden to the mentor to the extent that can stifle the enterprise's chances to succeed? Certainly in Asia, this can be a concern in a setting that can be at times rather hierarchical and parochial. In a nutshell, how do you approach starting a biomed type business based on academic research results in such a way that the chances for success are improved?

These were some of the questions that confronted me in the late 1980s when I first went down a road less traveled by academics in general, that of satisfying my innate preference for creating knowledge to be applied in practical terms. A direction that led to developing a research methodology more streamlined for commercial exploitation and concurrently, success in starting-up a premier medical technology *runway* enterprise.

FROM ACADEMIA TO ENTREPRENEUR

These continue to be invigorating times to talk about starting-up biomed around the world, including Singapore, the country of domicile during my work-life, where biomedical research and enterprise has been an expressed government initiative since the year 2000.[2] Today, when one meets many business people, academics, students and government officials, the enthusiasm to do something that combines biomed with entrepreneurship is there, and at times, overwhelming. There are now also many resources that have appeared almost instantly, that a budding biomed entrepreneur can access, such as assistance from specific government agencies; consultants; angel investors and venture capitalists. With research being performed at break-neck speed and intensity in academia among countless institutions globally, there appears no lack of possibilities for results to form the basis for start-up biomed enterprises from academia. *But, excitement without direction does not take one very far; nor do means without insight an enterprise make.*

Obviously, when contemplating turning a medical, engineering or scientific academic foundation into a biomed-type business proposition, some form of evaluation to estimate realistically the chances for success must take place. What is intuitive to seasoned businesspersons probably is not apparent to novices confronted with *an opportunity of a lifetime* scenario. How does one go about initiating this exercise in appraising these opportunities pragmatically? What are the indicators one looks for? What can and should be done while in academia prior to entering the *real world*?[v] How do you overcome the key reservations in offsetting the risks involved, to find a balance that will persuade you and others to move the venture forward? And most important, why should you be the one to do it?

And if the decision were to attempt, what would await you when you take your academic results and start a *runway* biomed company from scratch with it? What would the processes to go about this be like? This is the subject of this book, to inform the reader of one approach, peppered with *frontline* accounts, in starting-up a *runway* biomed enterprise

---

[v] Defined as anything *outside academia*.

from concept to reality. *The emphasis is from the perspective of an individual or a small team of like-minded associates starting from academia with nothing more than instinct, utilizing primarily personal resources and ingenuity.* You do not have to be the possessor of diverse and extensive skill sets or have undergone specialized commando-style business training to qualify. All that is necessary is a good biomed foundation and a willingness to try.

In the ensuing pages, specific issues and processes one has to work through in creating a potentially successful *runway* biomed enterprise from the ground-up will be expounded. An overview chapter sets the stage, followed by a chapter providing a snapshot of academic research and some thoughts on how this can be business-nized. Next is a chapter exemplifying the process of starting applied biomed research in academia that can progress into the real world to reach the patient. This leads into the decision-making process a person or a group with suitable scientific qualifications and knowledge either from academia and/ or other relevant background can draw from to evaluate whether they should start a *runway* biomed enterprise, concluding the background portion. Chapters on business potential evaluation, business plans and raising funds, follow. A topic specific to biomed and another on experts, complete the buildup phase. Subsequently, two chapters inform the reader what should take place after the decision to start-up is made. The entrepreneur is very much involved from the get-go. How she[vi] responds to the never-ending stream of decisions to be made in a perpetual risk environment, defining her own clarity while the picture is still hazy and honing her business intuition skills along the way are paramount to the venture succeeding. The final two chapters advocate some of the ethereal common sense attitudes one should adopt to emerge from the endeavor not only successful in achievement and financial terms, but retaining one's sensibilities and perspectives towards life.

The *runway* enterprise is where you can experience exhilaration, encounter frustration, be filled with panic, receive reprieve, and end up with a great dose of reality.

WHY THIS BOOK?

This book was conceived with the many in academia, business and government who have an interest in biomed and S&T-based[vii] start-ups from academia in mind. Specifically, clinicians,[viii] dentists, engineers

---

[vi] *Runway* entrepreneurs are not defined by their gender.

[vii] S&T: science and technology

[viii] This book adopts a narrow definition for the term *clinician* to mean a *licensed medical doctor* and is used interchangeably with the term *physician*.

and scientists in academia pursuing biomed and associated research pondering turning their knowledge, results and experience into starting an enterprise; persons considering supporting one financially or otherwise; or persons who are trying to find a reason to say *no* to sponsoring a persistent yet possibly ill-conceived prospect. Students at all levels and disciplines in the sciences, engineering, medicine, law and business; institutional administrators, members of research grant bodies; entrepreneurs; and other professionals and pertinent parties may also find the contents of this book useful.

From Academia to Entrepreneur (as "FATE" would have it), is about taking suitable academic biomed research results to starting-up a *runway* enterprise. FATE is based primarily on lessons I learnt from performing my academic biomaterials research in an applied/product development manner and starting my first company Biomedical Research And Support Services Private Limited (BRASS) since 1997; bringing it to and maintaining financial profit; revitalizing and positioning it for growth in a dynamic business environment (Brass P.L. from November 2011); interspersed with insights garnered from participation with other ventures, as well as discussions with founders and observations of other medical device companies. While the example used is a Medical Technology services company, and therefore a service (less product) orientation, the principles can be applied to the broader spectrum of turning an academia-derived technology concept into an enterprise. The context is unavoidably Asian, but learning has no borders.

To the reader, a few words of preview are appropriate. This book **is not:**

1. Intended as a step-by-step guide on how to start a biomed-type business.
2. Neither is this a book on theories and practices of how to run biomed-type enterprises or businesses in general.

There are enough fine business, entrepreneur and *how to start-up* books flooding the bookstores both in physical and electronic forms. Most explain and teach the technical, mechanics and procedural aspects of starting-up quite well. The author has read and learnt from many of these *gurus*, a selection of which are referenced throughout this book.[3]

Rather, this book attempts to share with the reader a *feel* for the considerations and decision-making process one is likely to confront and should work through in starting-up a *runway* biomed enterprise from academia based on an idea and nothing much more. The "if only I had known this ......", or "I wished someone had told me about ......" type of perspective.

The case for initiating preparation as early as possible in academia, leveraging as many advantages as possible prior to actual start-up is offered. The types of tasks, common difficulties and the handling of particular situations novices with a technical background but lacking entrepreneurial experience will face, are presented. The presentation style of using examples, explanations and thinking points throughout this book where appropriate are illustrative, not all-inclusive; meant as primers for further assessment by the reader on individual topics. The opinions and insights are from a *runway* entrepreneur who started several biomed enterprises in (or from) Asia from scratch while in academia. The present achievement record as of this writing stands at 1:1:1 for success, stillborn and to-be-continued. The lessons were obtained through *real world* initiation and fighting in the *trenches*, with accompanying battle scars and no medals. These experiences are shared with whoever wishes to learn from one who has been through it thrice (and counting) and survived to write about it.

Naturally, the situations an individual intent on starting-up a biomed enterprise encounters, as in life, will be different. But many lessons can be agonizing when learnt first hand. It is always judicious to profit from the experiences of others to mitigate the distress. Counsel from anonymous sources in most instances are best, as they are non-intrusive and can be adopted without fanfare, or discarded without condemnation or remorse. Best of all, there are no expectations placed on the reader to set on a defined course of action. Readers are free to extract and assimilate into their own thought processes and actions, as they deem relevant. Of course this pre-supposes that you also take on the sole responsibility for your subsequent decisions and actions however you may use the information presented in this book. If this fits what you feel has been missing in your contemplations, read on. I wish you every success.

Eugene Khor PhD, Virginia Tech

April 30, 2013

References

[1] Quoted from: Kawasaki G. *The art of the start*. Portfolio/Penguin; 2004. p. 79.
[2] Search: <www.edb.gov.sg>; <www.a-star.gov.sg>.
[3] For example: Kolchinsky P. The entrepreneur's guide to a biotech startup. 4th ed. 2004. Download at: <www.evelexa.com>; Shimasaki CD. *The business of bioscience: what goes into making a biotechnology product*. Dordecht: Springer; 2009.

Acknowledgments

I began forming the ideas for *From Academia to Entrepreneur* after my first scientific book *Chitin: Fulfilling a Biomaterials Promise* was published in late 2001. The interim years were necessary for me to bring BRASS to where it is today, evaluate what was done and refine my thoughts. Here, I put down what I tried and learnt, and hopefully my experiences may help you if you choose to take a similar path.

In any endeavor, no one does it alone. No matter how difficult my circumstances were, my God, the God of the Bible has always been my rock, blessing me through family, friends, colleagues, acquaintances, and the kindness of many others, a reflection of His love and care for me. Exemplified by:

J.N. (accountant by training) who declared the writing in my draft chapters were comprehensible for a layman with little scientific background.

The unsung heroes of academia, the men and women collectively known as librarians and their associated staff, who played an instrumental role in my academic research program.

For those I name below, thank you for being pivotal in my life.

To Rosa Kang, your behind the scenes effort paved the way for BRASS through the NUS system. And for making this novice realize that for BRASS to succeed, he had to develop a SOLID BRASS constitution. I trust you take pleasure and gain satisfaction in BRASS succeeding.

To P.C., for your friendship and wise counsel in hard times and for always celebrating each small victory along the way.

To V.K., steadfast by me through the vagaries of this life, and for correcting what I drafted, kindly yet firmly, in order for what is written to make better sense.

A dog she may have been, but *Sprite*, the abandoned mongrel puppy whose sad eyes paved her way into my heart and life, showered me for 17 years with her love and faithfulness. I treasure the memory of her each day.

About the Author

Dr Eugene Khor is the principal co-founder of Biomedical Research And Support Services Private Limited (BRASS), a Singapore Medical Technology Tests Services company. BRASS was founded in 1997 when Dr Khor was in academia. He guided BRASS from its humble beginnings to profit in 2005. He relinquished his responsibilities at BRASS in January 2007 but returned briefly in mid-2009 to November 2010, at the request of his major shareholders, to steer the company forward in a changed business environment. He updated the company's name to its acronym BRASS P.L. and put in place a strong Board of Directors and management team that has resulted in progressive and continual growth in revenue, profit and market presence (www.brass-asiapacific.com). He is presently the strategic consultant to the Board of Directors, BRASS P.L.

Dr Khor received his BSc in Chemistry from Lakehead University, Thunder Bay, Ontario, Canada in November 1979 and his PhD in Chemistry from Virginia Tech, Blacksburg, Virginia, USA, in December 1983. He joined the National University of Singapore (NUS) in April 2004 as a member of the Academic Staff in the Department of Chemistry. At NUS, Dr Khor's research program was in biomaterials, specifically on the durability of the bioprosthetic heart valve and chitin materials: their production, characterization and biomedical applications. He is the co-inventor of five NUS patents and has contributed extensively in publications to the biomaterials field. He has been an associate editor of the journal *Biomaterials* and a reviewer of manuscripts for many reputable scientific journals. He has served as a member of the Medical Technology Standards Committee of Singapore. He was a technical committee member for the Singapore Accreditation Council–Singapore Laboratory Accreditation Scheme (SAC–Singlas) that approved laboratories in Singapore to ISO 17025. After 27 years of service to NUS, Dr Khor retired from academia at the end of November 2011, trading in his chemistry lab coat for a fishing vest to fulfill a work-long ambition to go fishing.

Dr Khor's scientific career has been shaped by his interest in applied research that leads to practical applications. As an academic researcher, he performed research that embraced product development and entrepreneurship. Dr Khor believes that sharing the understanding gained from these experiences would benefit a broad readership. In the

process, like-minded scientists may be encouraged to consider break-
ing away from the safe haven of traditional practices that could result in
more innovation and products in the biomedical field. It is hoped that
this would ultimately benefit the patient, both in treatment and cost
containment.

CHAPTER

1

Entrepreneuring Academic Biomedical Science

From Academia to Entrepreneur.
DOI: http://dx.doi.org/10.1016/B978-0-12-410516-4.00001-X

1

1.1 THE BIOMEDICAL BUZZ AND ITS ECONOMIC POTENTIAL

In July 1897, the discovery of *gold* in the remote Canadian Yukon was reported in the media, setting off the Klondike gold rush.[1] Many were attracted by the "outrageous claims of wealth to be had for all who could get there to stake a claim". Most could not differentiate real gold from iron pyrite or *fool's gold*, let alone had any gold prospecting experience. But once the *bandwagon or herd mentality* started, nothing could stop a number of otherwise rational people from taking a chance for a *roll of the dice* to the wealth that lay in the barren ground. Within 6 months, a massive rush of 100,000 "stampeders" to the Yukon took place. Many perished on the way. For the survivors of the treacherous journey to the *gold fields* of the Yukon, they found that the expectation of instant fortune was nothing more than conjecture. The *stampeders* were late to the party, as those who were there before word got out had already been granted the deeds to the most promising *gold bearing* real estate. For the *stampeders* who persevered, they found that to recover the *gold* from the land was very hard work, as most of the *gold* was buried and not on stream surfaces as they were led to believe. Fortune seekers beware; instant riches are never straightforward, and typically end in heartache and disappointment to the un-initiated. Finally it is beguiling to note, there was one other cohort that profited from the gold rush, the "outfitters" and "suppliers" of goods to the *stampeders*. There will always be those shrewd enough to do well with calculated effort in any circumstance.

Fast-forward roughly seven decades. In the shadow of the *Silicon Valley* electronics boom, biomedical research in a branch of the life sciences called recombinant DNA technology was coupled with entrepreneurship into a start-up called Genentech. Genentech eventually blossomed into a new generation of biomed[i] companies that spearheaded new ways of treating human diseases and disorders.[2] Genentech's scientific and technological achievements are without question. But it is the **financial success** of Genentech and its select group of contemporaries, specifically Amgen, that have seized the world's attention. Welcome to the late twentieth century equivalent of a *gold rush* that can be termed **biomed rush**.

Seemingly overnight, the rest of the world buzzed with the impression that the life sciences are a tremendous hotbed of activity and opportunity. News reports on television and radio, articles in newspapers and magazines, and the countless websites one can surf through on the Internet heralded a new era of technological revolution permeating across the world at the speed of a mouse click. Include the potential for

---

[i]Biomed is used in this book as an abbreviation for biomedical, biomedical science or a biomedical business/enterprise depending on the context.

generating a high financial dividend and a compelling concoction is created that should not be missed. Have all the winners been taken? Will the bonanza of opportunities in the life sciences end up the same way, as was the case for the *stampeders* of the *gold rush*? Certainly many politicians and scientists do not think so. Curious? Read on.

1.2 A PIECE OF THE ACTION

Just as in the Klondike *gold rush*, there are those like Genentech and Amgen who arrived ahead of the pack. More conspicuously in this instance, there are and will continue to be a steady stream of *stampeders*, *outfitters* and *suppliers* as the saga unfolds. *Why?* The *gold rushes* of eras long-gone were about finding a precious metal that was physically deposited in the ground eons ago according to the geological timescale and whose abundance has ultimately been predetermined. The now twenty-first century parallel is unique in that the *gold field*, i.e. the scientific expertise and knowledge, are found in *the gray matter between the ears* of mobile individuals. Therefore, unlike *gold*, scientific knowledge is not confined by physical boundaries. The know-how and imagination of trained clinicians,[ii] dentists, engineers and scientists can be acquired, nurtured and transformed into biomed products generating sought-after fortunes anywhere in the world. As long as there continue to be individuals who come forward to be trained and subsequently generate new science or improve on existing understanding, the *gold assets* appear limitless.

Consequently, the profile of the *prospectors* and the *goldmines* are different. The *goldmine* in this instance is the infrastructure that goes to support the on-going R&D that can be designed and built almost instantaneously, and the subsequent enterprises to be set-up. Considering the costs, governments, reputable global enterprises and wealthy entrepreneurs are obvious *prospector* candidates who can establish *goldmines* advantageously in their own backyard. Relocating the *gold fields* from their places of origin to the *goldmines* is the tricky part. Fortunately, in this age of globalization, highly talented individuals can be enticed with an open check for research incentive for example, to move to these potential goldmines. Governments, corporations and wealthy individuals, who collectively are the modern day equivalent of stampeders, can potentially do very well financially translating scientific discoveries into technology and successful businesses, provided the right lode is found and mined. Finally, today's scientific research and associated businesses are technology intensive and require sophisticated instruments, equipment and assorted high-end lab-wares, reagents

[ii]This book adopts a narrow definition for the term *clinician* to mean a *licensed medical doctor* and is used interchangeably with the term *physician*.

and chemicals. This has provided the opportunity for a broad spectrum of present day outfitters and suppliers to sprout up to meet the demand for new generation scientific tools and equipment, and related services and supplies.

What's the catch? For all intents and purposes, life sciences, while broad in scope, in reality is only defined as biomed in most interested parties' eyes. Doubtless, biomed is a huge pie scientifically and financially. But it is a pie that contains only a small number of cherries on top, i.e. only a limited number of findings will turn into spectacular blockbusters, the billion dollar winners. With many national, regional and even local governments from the first to third world countries placing a bet in the biomed economic potential, the field appears very crowded. The premise that when sufficient funding is provided to do the necessary research, the next moneymaking marvel is almost certain is not reassuring. Often the road to these riches is a complex maze speckled with intricacies so that getting there is nowhere near as easy as said and done. A key impediment is the longer length of time that has to be spent on R&D. The other obvious roadblock is that much of the useful science will be under some form of intellectual property (IP) protection, and maneuvering the legal quagmire to end up with the rights to develop and produce will not be straightforward. Sanguinely, patience will prevail and less scrupulous players, pursuing questionable shortcuts to get to market quickly, do not surface.

Are there better bets? Awareness of global warming, an increasing detrimental eco-system and a (perceived) move from oil dependence suggests environment and energy can be equally profitable, and undeniably are being pursued.

Regardless, biomed persists as the preferred *goldmine*. The current obsession with *biomed is mesmerizing*. Biomed impacts individuals at a personal and emotional level, subconsciously tugging at their own mortality, making the decision to incur multi-million dollar financial outlays more palatable. And while the biotech aspect of biomed has been in the spotlight, other areas such as bioengineering and tissue engineering, among many others, are equally relevant. The *biomed rush* is here to stay. This is especially obvious in Asia. Take a look at my stomping ground when I was an active participant, Singapore, as an illustration.

1.3 SINGAPORE'S BIOMEDICAL ENDEAVOR

Singapore is a country in Asia that came into being in 1965. At the turn of the twenty-first century, after just a little over 35 years, Singapore had transformed from its British colonial past into a first world country. A modern miracle as some international watchers have observed, and no longer just a mere speck of real estate on the globe located at the bottom tip of the Malayan peninsular in South East Asia.[3]

In the year 2000, the biomed gambit erupted in Singapore when the Singapore Government publicly announced the push into the life sciences as part of a broad national economic agenda.[4] A key emphasis was developing a credible research base in the life sciences. It soon became clear that in the Singapore context at least, life sciences equated to endeavors aimed at benefiting humans, i.e. *biomedical* science. To this end, a sizable financial investment was used to develop infrastructure primarily to house research institutes and centers; the tapping of international scientific talent to relocate and establish in Singapore; and the dispensation of research grants to academic institutions, research centers and institutes throughout Singapore. The *raison d'être* was to build an internationally respected capability especially in new and select areas of biomed science and technologies to springboard Singapore to the forefront of biomed research excellence. Today Singapore boasts an international array of clinical, engineering and scientific talent, with Biopolis as the centerpiece of the biomed hub infrastructure completing one component of the biomed economic jigsaw.

An expected outcome sought was for research results to become convertible into real life applications in order for Singapore to benefit economically from this endeavor. Licensing, collaborations and joint-ventures with the big boys is one likely channel. Results that may generate blockbusters leading to clinical and financial successes will likely be top-down driven. But big-ticket items are rare, and successful ones even more remote. More importantly, an assortment of indigenous biomed enterprises that hold their own on the global stage should also preferably emerge. Obviously, strategies are being conceived and implemented to realize this eventuality. How this aspect plays out over the coming years may determine whether a country such as Singapore that has staked a respectable fraction of its GDP[iii] in this endeavor, made the right decisions regarding biomed research and enterprise. When competition from around Asia and the world in life sciences is factored in, the survival of a natural-resource deficient island country in an ever changing global economy could well depend on how well this *bet* (among others) is driven.

1.4 ADVANTAGE ASIA?

Singapore represents but a mere microcosm of the *economic-sphere* that is Asia. To truly take in the enthusiasm that is going on, a closer look at Asia is worthwhile.

[iii] Gross Domestic Product.

What's so special about Asia? Everything! It is common knowledge that the two most populous countries in the world today are China and India, and they are Asian. Economic progress since the latter part of the twentieth century has been growing steadily in China, India and most of Asia. The twenty-first century is fast becoming known as the Asian century. The forecast is for future spectacular growth in Asia, the occasional global economic downturns notwithstanding. There is a sense of inevitability that from Beijing to Bangalore interspersed by the ASEAN nations and the established economies of South Korea and Taiwan, Asia is in on the action. How does this impact biomed rush?

A huge population base with increasing spending power is what is fixing global attention on Asia. Newfound wealth is often accompanied by expectations for a better quality of life. An emphasis for better healthcare is one aspect. In addition, many Asian countries have their share of an increasing aging population with an associated anticipation for more medical and related needs. Therefore, the potential for expenditure on biomed products, and more importantly, the prospects to create biomed products to meet that need is enormous. Consequently, it is reasonable to suggest that the opportunity to be a biomed entrepreneur in Asia is bright.

This proposal is even more believable when the parallels in the scientific, engineering and manufacturing sectors accompanying the shift in economic prowess to Asia are noted. What are the indicators? Since the turn of the twenty-first century, holding scientific meetings in Asia is *in vogue*. A noted example is China, where more and more international scientific, engineering and medical conferences and conventions are held. There has also been an increase in international collaborations between established scientists, universities and research centers from North America, Europe and within Asia with their Chinese counterpart institutions and colleagues.

There is vibrant biomed research in Asia where governments are placing a huge emphasis in this sector. Singapore is but one example. China is another, where a sizable fraction of the action will likely be focused.[5] Will this mean an advantage for Asian biomed research and enterprises? This is most plausible. There are ample business opportunities in the biomed field even if you disregard the *next big thing* items. However, you will always have competition because biomed appears to be where much of the attention is and will be for quite some time. Some time back, it was amusing to observe at biotech conventions the many countries, provinces, states and even cities occupying booths to entice businesses to start in their own neck of the woods with claims of good environment, educated workforce, preferential tax breaks, etc. Definitely, Asia is one of *the places* to be for biomed in the foreseeable future.

Last, the human resource availability cannot be ignored. My personal observation from my vantage perch when I was in academia permitted a unique view of changes in Asian graduate student attitudes. Beginning in the early 1990s, an influx of graduate students primarily from China came to NUS (The National University of Singapore). Some in that early cohort, where opportunity arose, proceeded to other destinations such as the USA. Others stayed and completed their studies in Singapore and this outlook became increasingly common in what can be termed the second wave of students around the late 1990s. Many stayed after graduation, finding jobs and the way of life in Singapore acceptable. These days, students who make up what can be termed the third wave, consider the prospect of returning to China after completing their education as a possible course of action that cannot be dismissed outright.[6] This attitude is quite the same for students coming to NUS from the other big populace Asian country, India.

Succinctly, the market, the available funds, and an eager human resource to embark on the biomed juggernaut suggest that Asia has an advantage. But this disregards other notable markets such as the South American continent, where similarities with what is happening in Asia are surfacing. And the established markets of North America, Europe and Japan cannot be ignored, as they remain leaders of the biomed industry, primary centers of innovation where premium-pricing positions should not be overlooked. Furthermore, already in the second decade of the twenty-first century, the cost advantage of manufacturing in China in some sectors may be beginning to display erosion. "Re-shoring", i.e. the repatriation of some (and maybe eventually all) manufacturing capacity back into advanced economies is a term that is beginning to make sense and can become fashionable. Finally, biomed serves humankind, not regions or countries. Therefore, a global strategy should be the only approach in contemplating a response to address the biomed rush.

1.5 THE BIOMEDICAL INDUSTRY IN TRANSITION

Why is there a fixation on the life sciences as it pertains to the biomed industry? To comprehend this, we first have to look at where the biomed industry has been and where it is headed.

Fact: the biomed industry is a high value-add industry that generates yearly revenues in the US$ billions. Just glance at the annual Fortune 500 list in Fortune magazine to note several pharmaceutical companies in the listing. There are also medical devices and associated healthcare companies on this list. Legal drugs, medical gadgets and healthcare are big businesses. But what have *Big Pharma* (as the giant pharmaceutical industry is commonly referred to) and other associated biomed and healthcare companies to do with life sciences?

The twentieth century pharmaceutical industry was primarily based on *small* molecules of distinct chemical formula and structure, produced by a chemical process and packaged in a distinct tablet or pill (the delivery medium) to be swallowed by the patient.[iv] The effectiveness of the drug was based on the premise that a defined drug amount in the delivery medium when prescribed correctly would be effective for the majority of patients. *Big Pharma* ostensibly invests years and billions of dollars in R&D, manufacturing and clinical trials, to bring these drugs to market.[7] This investment is protected by a series of patents and other proprietary information and processes. This accords *Big Pharma* the exclusivity to command a price premium for the duration the patent is enforced. It is common industry knowledge that the patent life of many *cash cow* drugs of the twentieth century pharmaceutical industry has lapsed or is near the end of their exclusivity cycle.[8] Upon patent expiry, generic manufacturers offering lower cost alternatives can enter, undercutting and depleting *Big Pharma's* high-margin profits.[v] The M&A[vi] consolidation seen in this industry sector in recent decades (and continuing) can partly be attributed to this factor. The purpose is to acquire patents with years to go before expiry and pipeline products on the way.

Similarly, the medical device industry's focus was on using *off-the-shelf* artificial body parts to replace a diseased or badly injured human organ or tissue. Metals, ceramics, plastics and some animal derived materials are used to make these artificial body parts. The primary consideration when using these materials is that they be inert and do no harm to the body. Since the mid-1980s, increasing understanding of the interactions between the human body and medical devices have challenged this concept of inertness where new terms such as bioactive and regeneration have taken root. Innovations such as *tissue engineering* have shown that combining a mixture of materials and biology can give more *realistic body parts*.

Finally in the latter twentieth century, nascent scientific advances and comprehension in the life sciences, physical sciences and engineering were leading to the better understanding of the complexity of the human body, unraveling functions at the cell and molecular level. All these activities dovetail into the promise that the twenty-first century's answer of treating and healing diseases and other ills will be more sophisticated than just popping a pill or using *off-the-shelf* artificial body parts.

[iv] Author's note: This is an oversimplified illustration. There are many other ways of introducing drugs into the human body.

[v] Author's note: It is not necessarily wrong or immoral to charge a premium. The process of bringing a discovery from the laboratory bench finally to market is reported to be very costly. Many candidates do not make it and the subsequent profits garnered from a success in the market must consider in perspective the whole process of drug discovery that screens hundreds of candidates at a substantial cost. Detractors (the rational ones) challenge the quantum of the premium, as well as what constitute R&D costs.

[vi] M&A: Mergers & Acquisition.

There is no doubt that both the *small* molecules and *off-the-shelf* artificial body parts resources will continue to be used well into the twenty-first century and beyond. However, the progressive introduction of truly revolutionary approaches using methods derived from molecular biology, nanotechnology and related fields to treat ailments are taking place. The new biomed harvest that is biotech led is happening. Search the web and you will find an endless list of companies, both leaders and start-ups (and of course those that ran out of steam), that have sprung up in the past 30 years. One key differentiation feature is that they are more life sciences-than chemistry-based.[9] These applications will intensify with time despite some early flops, possibly eventually displacing many present methods. It only takes the imagination of scientists, engineers and clinicians coupled with good business judgment and there will be many biomed innovations that will come on-line in the not too distant future.

1.6 CONFRONTING SOME COMMONLY HELD BELIEFS

The above section is the "background story" behind the "buzz" of *biomed rush* that many vocal advocates refer to. Realize that hype can be an ingredient in many of these expositions, mixing potential with reality into the excitement of the moment to demonstrate that the proponents are spot-on and farsighted. Simply put, facts can be perked up, refined or otherwise placed in a more agreeable light to change mindsets, generate momentum, drum up support and finances. Granted, the new technologies are more exclusive and target sites more specific, and the new treatments should work better. Nevertheless, once the sensationalism and fuzzy impressions surrounding biomed and other healthcare promises take on a life of their own, myths and misconceptions (discussed below) about biomed research as they relate to economic returns, are born. Consequently, it is still best to be cautious. The parallels between the Klondike *gold rush* and today's *buzz* about biomed research and enterprise are important and should not be dismissed. Remember, the same lessons can be drawn (and more importantly applied) from an era when the impact of science and technology was non-existent or minimal, so as not to end up eventually as a *stampeder* casualty in this twenty-first century *gold rush* equivalent.

Therefore, it is prudent to sift through the plethora of possibilities, to discern what the true opportunities are. How do you elucidate reality from fiction? You question some of the assertions and assumptions. In the process you separate the fantasy and fallacies surrounding the promise of the biomed phenomenon to gain a perspective that will set you on the course to start-up and succeed. The following are a collection of the more common suppositions about starting biomed enterprises. No means exhaustive, it is intended to prime the reader to deliberate carefully before acting.

1.6.1 Biomed Enterprises are Mega Bucks Return Ventures

This misconstrued impression, while neither wrong nor dishonest, is at the heart of the matter. Much like the *stampeders* of the Klondike *gold rush*, most prospects focus on the upside to participating in an exclusive opportunity that is not to be missed. It was stated earlier that the biomed pie is huge while the cherries on top of the pie are scarce. The *hard sell* spotlights the cherries. In other words, the likelihood of having a blockbuster in hand that will generate billions of dollars is remote. In the introduction of an article reported in *Fortune* magazine dated May 26, 2003, for biotech-based ventures that have been around since the 1970s, only two ventures, Amgen & Genentech, have successfully made it to the *Billion Dollar* club.[10] Two in 30 years! While there are several others in the more than one hundred *Million Dollar* club, most prospects do not want to deal with the fact that their probability of joining the *Billion Dollar* club is probably more than one in a million. Regardless of how you assess it, these are unfavorable odds. This fact is indisputable.

For a person wanting to start a potential *runway* enterprise and join this club, you're probably out of luck. It is important to have bold aspirations. But ensure that these dreams are based on sound foundations in the clear light of day and you are awake. So, if you plan to venture into setting up a biomed enterprise in anticipation that you will end up a billionaire, be forewarned. No matter what science is in your bag, chances are not in your favor. And if you are using this as a pitch to raise funds, it is a certainty that those who may grant you an audience know this fact. Therefore, if money is your primary or only motivation, be very certain that your end reality is really what it promises. Otherwise, embarking on your undertaking is probably futile. In essence, be aware that there is loose talk out there that can lead to (your) unsubstantiated expectations.

1.6.2 Going Biomed is Sound as it has Potential for Good Profit, can have Fast Growth and is Recession Proof

The promotion of biomed business opportunities in Asia has impacted several Asian businessmen that I know and they want to participate. The common story line is that biomed is a good value-add industry with a lot of prospect for growth, evoking a sure thing and get rich quick mentality. Again, these impressions are not new or incorrect. However, these street-smart seasoned businesspersons catch on quickly when I tell them that the biomed industry is not straightforward and has some peculiarities that can trip them up that immediately temper their enthusiasm.

It is true that there is good potential profit in biomed. People fall ill; their instincts are to survive and most are willing to (and can) pay for treatment. Product proliferation can also be good and at times even fast. Therefore, biomed can be so-called recession proof. However, as will be introduced in Section 1.8, the biomed industry is a highly regulated industry. There are many rules and requirements that have been established by health regulators that bog down the average entrant trying to meet the seemingly endless regulatory issues. Rarely are they circumvented but rather, have to be satisfied. This means that the great potential good profit and fast growth come only after the many regulatory hurdles have been met head-on and effectively resolved. This can take many months, but more commonly, years!

Figure 1.1 illustrates a typical plot for the lifecycle of a product. The solid black line represents any ordinary product a normal business would produce to obtain revenue. Sales start once the product is made even in the induction phase, as product introduction is normally clearcut. The dotted line depicts a medical product. No sales are generated during the induction period, and revenue growth is negative. This is the phase where start-up funds are used to make the product. Only when the product is approved (that can stretch from the induction phase well into the growth phase) do sales really commence. If the product is successful, there follows a period of exponential growth when the product catches *fire* and can do no wrong. Eventually, the product will hit a peak or plateau and sales will flatten out. Finally, the product will reach obsolescence, competition surpasses it, or a replacement emerges. Most products that do not make it will fail at the induction phase that can span

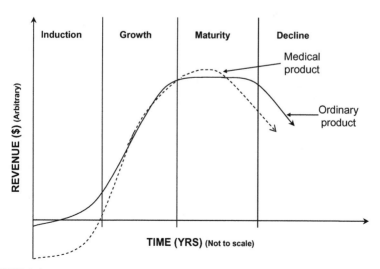

FIGURE 1.1 Life cycle of a product: ordinary (solid line); medical (dotted line).

anywhere from (on average) 2 years upwards. Therefore, while all the features of an upside are true, this only manifests itself when the product makes it past the regulatory approval process.

Finally, the biomed industry, like all businesses, is highly competitive. Once a first-to-market product is introduced and starts acquiring user adoption, two main occurrences can take place. *Me-too* products can appear, focusing on a lower price as the edge. Alternatively, a more and/or new features product to try and better the leader will be developed. Albeit, in both instances, it will take a while for the competition to introduce their product, but once the *path* has been laid out, following the leader is not that difficult. Even the regulatory approval process may be easier, as there is a product in the market as a reference. In other words, getting there first gives only a temporary advantage that must be protected by your ingenuity.

1.6.3 All You Need is the Right Science!

Credence of researchers can be that great science is paramount in any technological advancement. Researchers can after many years of chasing an elusive idea be obsessed with their science. This may become precarious when good scientific results begin to take form as product ideas. When involved in enterprises, strong-minded researchers can be impediments by insisting on perfecting the science, confident that when transformed into a product, they will inevitably succeed. For any enterprise, financial success happens because good products make money. Incontrovertibly, downstream processes are based on the upstream scientific and/or engineering accomplishments. But the only important aspect once the science transcends into technology is to respect product development dictates and do what is practical to realize a product.

A common impression from the business perspective is that getting the science and engineering concept right approximates the starting 10% of the whole product development process that may provide a head start. After that, well that is where all the trouble begins. What trouble? An illustration is appropriate. Every year, a mainstream university produces hundreds of graduates. Each is (presumably) equipped with the knowledge of their particular field of study. What becomes of each graduate, however, depends on many other factors beyond the educational institution's control, such as personal drive, communication skills, EQ,[vii] etc., as well as the opportunity each graduate meets and how they respond. Great science is much like a fresh graduate. What becomes of the science depends on the many other factors, such as the business opportunity window, the start-up capital raised, the founder's drive, etc. Be wary that good science is only the beginning and that the end of the road is long and winding, and

[vii] EQ: Emotional Quotient.

arriving in one piece, let alone successfully, is never a foregone conclusion. Therefore, do not be overly preoccupied with great science but follow the business demands.

1.6.4 All You Have to do is Make the Product!

A companion to the great science attitude is the beautiful product concept. Sometimes the science or engineering concept becomes the centerpiece around which all activity revolves. Time, energy and funds are spent making and perfecting the product. Little or no market entry preparation has been done to ascertain the best method to introduce the product. If this neglect goes unchecked for a long period, it may result in the eventual demise of the enterprise.

No business takes off only because of a wonderful product, barring some extraordinary exceptions. Marketing is the normal way stuff is going to get sold. Without marketing and subsequent sales, little if any of the product will be going out the door. Without sales, you do not have revenue and we know where that leads! So while the product is slowly taking shape, an equal or more amount of effort should be spent on the marketing strategy and how sales are to be accomplished. Remember, business is eventually about making money, regardless how fancy your product may be.

1.6.5 All you Have to do is Sell!

The biomed industry is a regulated industry (refer to Section 1.8). Pharmaceuticals and medical devices are not sold like commodity goods. Therapeutic drugs are only prescribed by a licensed physician and dispensed by a licensed pharmacist. Critical care medical devices utilize surgeons and medical specialists for their placement into patients. The method of introducing, marketing and selling regulated medical products are somewhat unique. Familiar business models such as retail outlets, mail order catalogs and Internet sales cannot be adopted wholesale in this industry. Only very simple medical devices such as syringes, superficial wound dressings, etc. and select pharmaceuticals that have been deemed safe for OTC[viii] sales are available for purchase by the average patient.

The primary distinction is that selling to doctors, nurses and other healthcare experts for the purpose of treating patients involves educating these professionals on the product, sometimes training them on product features and use; demonstrating and convincing them on the efficacy, safety and advantage over competitors. While rocket science know-how is not required of the sales person, some level of technical knowledge and

---

[viii]OTC: Over The Counter.

competency are often times necessary. The sales are to a conservative group that is averse to change from what they know works. It is a tough sell.

1.7 THE ACADEMIC DILEMMA

As stated in the preface, much of the knowledge and skills required for biomed is concentrated in academia. The goals of academic research as universally practiced are to answer questions about phenomena, to offer new insights on a multitude of issues, or even to generate new discoveries. The academic scientist has independence to pursue what they believe is important, with the emphasis on addressing the scientific aspect. It is usually an afterthought whether the outcome or discovery is useful or could be subsequently applied. This practice has more or less been the basis of academic research, especially since the end of World War II, when access to relatively liberal funding from many sources permitted generally unimpeded research and scientific pursuits. Even in today's environment where it is becoming more convoluted to determine whether funding sources are driving certain research agendas, this time-honored academic research methodology persists, albeit with present-day adaptations.

Whether this state of affairs can or should continue is a matter best dealt with elsewhere by others, except for the few comments made throughout this book as a former academic. Can the system be tweaked to favor more applied orientation in research and better potential for commercialization of research outcomes? It will always be a matter of balance. The Singapore initiative presented above is one example of an attempt to shift towards a more directed approach. Concentrating on producing useful results leads to the probability that non-obvious but potentially crucial aspects are missed. Conversely, too much emphasis on fundamental research could make identifying commercial winners difficult. And it will be challenging to change the academic mentality steeped in traditions of freedom to choose research areas and topics, autonomy in the way the research is performed, and proclaiming findings at the earliest possible opportunity. Fortunately, this prevailing attitude will not deter entrepreneurial aspirants from coming forward, and in the end that is what matters.

1.8 THE REGULATORY IMPERATIVE

Globalization has occurred. What this means for any entrant to the biomed endeavor to be treated as a member of this "world club" is that they have to play by the rules. To be accepted in the global market place, your products have to meet the legal requirements of the target countries' health authorities. This is the regulatory imperative.

Pharmaceutical products have the longest history in this regard that would now extend to biopharmaceuticals. Medical devices differ in requirements and for many of the new technologies, such as tissue engineering and nanotechnology, new rules will progressively appear.

Individual countries differ in specific requirements. Their health authorities publish documents and procedures to detail how to make medical products acceptable from their conception, design, manufacture, testing to demonstrate products are safe and effective, and after their approval for sales, continued vigilance of the product when in use. Many countries also utilize International Standards such as the ISO 13485 as part of their requirements for meeting regulatory approval. This topic is extensive and at times cumbersome. Further comment is deferred until Chapter 8.

In 1996 when I first started going down the biomed entrepreneurial path, the issue of meeting regulatory requirements was a matter we pondered over how to reconcile. Handling regulatory issues is time-consuming and costly to achieve and maintain. Even until very recently (early 2000s), I was still asked by some of my contacts involved in biomed why they have to pay for this to be done and at a price that is considerable to their operating budget. I shall not enter into this hornet's nest. What I want to make clear is that if you are going to do biomed, you will have to deal with and prevail over this challenge.

1.9 BIOMED BUSINESSES

As stated in the preface, the basis for biomed businesses is the science. Almost all science-based processes can be turned into business ventures with the limitation being whether there is money to be made, and if so, whether it will be worth the effort. While the popular vote goes to biomed applications defined primarily as biotech, medical devices and diagnostics, the possibly better returns in the cosmetics and health supplements domains that are loosely healthcare related should not be ignored, although they may be somewhat less puritanical for biomed zealots to consider. Each scientific proposition that surfaces requires a rigorous evaluation of true business promise. Remarks such as *this work is a potential winner* or *this process can really make money* that habitually pops up in the minds of would be scientists-wannabe-entrepreneurs who really only see the potential of their fascinating science and not the further hard work required, should be avoided.

When the talk about biomed comes up, most people's mental radar automatically attenuate to topics such as bioinformatics, biopharmaceuticals, cloning, genomics and its cousin proteomics, gene therapy, tissue engineering, stem cells, etc. These *buzzwords* are catchy and the focus of the *next big thing* watchers. Any breakthroughs here will likely attract big money and be difficult for *runway* entrepreneurs to access. Look beyond the immediate and you will see a whole assortment of opportunities, especially as *outfitters* and *suppliers*, that are nothing to spurn and very suitable for *runway* entrepreneurs. After all, a first triumph can (should you decide in favor of) springboard you to the next level when you have the experience and better financial prowess to do something bolder. And just as a reminder, a quote from another (California) *gold rush*:

> "The people who made the real money in the gold rush were those who sold maps, the tools, and the clothing (it's where Levi's started). Most of the folks who rushed off to get rich never did. And what's worse, a fair percentage didn't make it back alive".[11]

What are good areas where your scientific background may be relevant for starting a biomed products or services business? Examples of what biomed products are include Class I, IIa, IIb and III medical devices, non-obvious[ix] pharmaceuticals and biopharmaceuticals, TCM (Traditional Chinese Medicine), medical instruments and equipment, diagnostic reagents, kits and tools. A case in point is the advent of rapid microbiological technology that has resulted in kits that facilitate easier, in-house testing of bioburden and bacteria identification. Even the traditional rabbit endotoxin test has progressed to the qualitative test-tube gel clot method through quantitative assays and now to a portable rapid analysis system.

Biomed services may comprise synthesizing potential pharmaceutical intermediates and/or active agents, various types of assays, testing and characterization, consultancy and training. You will find that the biomed industry from global companies, mid-sized entities, and of course start-ups, outsource regularly. Companies outsource for various reasons, for example to reduce the high HR (human resource) payroll cost, capital equipment and facilities costs; to focus on their strengths and leave the rest to reliable sub-contractors and vendors, etc. This is quite relevant today, where a consequence of the end of patent life mentioned earlier is leading to a contraction in the pharmaceutical industry. Many traditional drug companies are looking at outsourcing to reduce in-house testing costs as they seek to focus their finances and efforts on core competencies. Even the new frontier biopharmaceutical companies (dealing with monoclonal antibodies, etc.) see outsource testing as a viable alternative to having it done in-house. Therefore, services are definitely something to consider and starting with a service does not negate you from doing a product or *vice versa*.

In selecting what to work on, two details should be noted. First, no matter what you settle on, the choice normally distills down to a **specialization versus volume** game. Using medical devices as example, a Class III medical device is typically a sophisticated, disease-targeted and critical-use product that is based on the (presumed) best science and engineering. This justifies

[ix] i.e. something no one you know is thinking about or working on.

the higher cost. However, the specialist nature of the product limits their proliferation, i.e. the number of units sold. A lower class device, for example a customized disposable tube in a sterile pack or a sterile disposable syringe set, usually falls into a volume sales category at an affordable cost. But a lower class equals less regulatory scrutiny, quicker to market and as long as your sales team is performing, revenue and profits are more likely.

Looking at this from another perspective, **elegance is not a necessity**. An implant may have a mystical attractiveness based perhaps on the perception of its use, but its development is comparatively more complex, therefore harder to realize. A short-term use device, on the other hand, has all the pluses going for it as it is easier to achieve and should not be laughed at no matter what its application or the lack of appeal because of the body part where it will end up being in (short-term) contact with![x] You do not have to be stylish to make money, just a good product backed up by great marketing.[xi] Don't be enticed by the attraction of sophistication. Avoid the pitfalls of working on an area just because it is the *in-thing*, grand, or earth shattering. Follow your instincts and always choose the path that makes for good biomed science-based business sense if you wish to be a *runway* biomed entrepreneur.

The other important aspect of biomed businesses is about the time required to transform the science into a product. This is no simple task and will be elaborated in subsequent chapters. For now, suffice to say that a biomed product that can traverse the design, manufacturing and testing hurdles, as well as other legal and financial obstacles that you will confront, will take some time. Time scale is usually measured in months that are two digits with the first number greater than zero or 1 and maybe even 2. Be sure to tell yourself to be patient, and impress on those you bring on board, staff, investors, etc. that this is the reality.

Finally, by perception biomed enterprises are innovation enterprises. As presented in Section 1.6.2, you are unlikely to see revenue in the first few years and steady revenue or exponential growth year-on-year expectations only occur after product introduction. What is important is that the value of the enterprise is growing. You do this by meeting milestones set. So focus on completing events according to schedule to build your enterprise's value especially for the *founding* investors.

1.10 ENTER THE BIOMED *RUNWAY* ENTREPRENEUR

When the term *technopreneur* initially appeared, a first impression would be to construe the term as an oxymoron. This was because the two

[x] I am referring to anatomy locations where the sun doesn't shine!
[xi] Great marketing/positioning of a good enough product can beat a great R&D/bells & whistles products ineffectively marketed/positioned.

modes from which the word is derived appear distinct opposites. A scientist/technologist is trained and works in a disciplined manner to primarily explain and increase knowledge. An entrepreneur, on the other hand, is someone who exploits that scientific knowledge for monetary gains. However, with further reflection, combining the two into the term *technopreneur* does make sense. Coined originally to describe entrepreneurs in the information technology field, the term these days has broad application including biomed. This is the era of the technopreneur, but it involves hard work that has to be done by someone, "many someones" in actuality, who have to assume the challenge and turn a rallying call into profitable cold hard cash.

But where do you go to find a pool of biomed-type entrepreneur success wannabes wanting to stake a claim based on whatever *discoveries* or ideas appear in their minds? The partial answer is that one source of such people do exist in academia throughout Asia and the rest of the world. But how can they be enticed to breakaway from their relatively blissful existence in the ivory towers of academia and exchange it for something as grueling as being a biomed entrepreneur in the knowledge-based economy of this twenty-first century?

There are those who assert that entrepreneurs can be created when the right environment to inspire, foster and handhold them to success exists. But can individuals handpicked based on academic excellence and enthusiasm, who are given some guidance with a little start-up funding succeed as entrepreneurs? Perhaps. But, the majority of stories of successful entrepreneurs have not followed this route and even when they have, there is normally an underlying undisclosed tale or two behind that success. They are mostly *self-made*, starting from scratch. *Self-made* entrepreneurs usually are those born out of an innate need to be different, to prove themselves, or from adversity, and atypically exude commitment, passion and enthusiasm. The driving force comes from deep within them. Their "fire in the belly" and take on situations are different, and their solutions at times border on absurdity that defies convention. It is important to encourage entrepreneur wannabes with every incentive possible, but ultimately, make or break is very much an individual matter.

Add the term *biomed* to entrepreneur and the difficulty escalates. For *biomed*, the first hurdle is how to unlock the scientific potential, turning the possible into probable. This is the process of transiting a scientific promise into a technology. The second hurdle is about encouraging anyone suitably qualified scientifically and/or technically, such as academics, students and local entrepreneurs, to come forward to take up the biomed entrepreneur challenge.

Attracting indigenous entrepreneurs for biomed to surface is no cakewalk as biomed generates reservations for many. Why? A biomed entrepreneur has to have the technological savvy of an (preferably) established clinician, dentist, scientist or engineer, combined with the streetwise *savoir faire* of a business person to maneuver, survive and eventually thrive in the wheel and deal world of the private sector. Academic researchers by training and experience can discriminate good from bad research ideas. But can they better distinguish the potential winners from the masses when financial prospects are included in the equation? Undoubtedly, a few veterans will spot opportunities and profit.

But why would the rest consider participating, since the odds are that only a few will succeed while disappointment awaits the horde? Even if a few stood up to be counted, the obvious question is when and how should one go about starting a company in the biomed sector from academia. There are no easy answers. One thing is certain. This is a situation where no amount of fancy talk and coaxing alone can persuade an individual to step forward. It requires each individual to contemplate long and hard to ascertain if they have the right mix of talent and desire to take a shot at it. Starting from ground zero to a successful biomed entrepreneur can be achieved, but it requires tenacity and every ounce of willpower the individual can muster. You have to have an unwavering resolve to succeed despite the self-doubt, the warning by others, and the temptation to settle for safer ground. You will surely suffer setback upon setback, and at times plead for mercy. None will be given. Business can be unforgiving. But if you learn to survive, persist and endure, you will find the right mixes of boldness, hard work and the occasional dose of good fortune to succeed.

This is where a concept such as a *runway* strategy to becoming an entrepreneur may help. The *runway* strategy sponsors a "start where you are with what you have" approach to becoming an entrepreneur. So do you want to become a biomed *runway* entrepreneur that opens up an alternate choice to standard career paths, commendable as they may be? Ponder this as we proceed through this book.

Real World Lessons Learnt

General
1. Biomed is where the action is.
2. Biomed business opportunities will continue to abound.
3. You have to separate the hype from reality.

Specific
1. Academia has a role in biomed.
2. Regulatory issues are a key factor in biomed.
3. *Runway* biomed start-ups are for people with strong and determined character.

Quote for the Chapter

"It is not the critic who counts; not the man who points out how the strong man stumbles, or where the doer of deeds could have done better. The credit belongs to the man who is actually in the arena, whose face is marred by dust and sweat and blood; who strives valiantly; who errs, who comes short again and again, because there is no effort without error and shortcoming; but who knows the great enthusiasms, the great devotions; who spends himself in a worthy cause; who at the best knows in the end the triumph of high achievement, and who at the worst, if he fails, at least fails while daring greatly, so that his place shall never be with those cold and timid souls who neither know victory or defeat."

Theodore Roosevelt (1858–1919; 26th President of the United States of America)

References

[1] www.questconnect.org/ak_klondike.htm

[2] http://www.gene.com/gene/about/corporate/history/

[3] Vietor RHK, Thompson EJ. Singapore inc. *Harvard Business School Case* 703-040, February 2008 (Revised from original February 2003 version.)

[4] Van Epps HL. Singapore's multibillion dollar gamble. J Exp Med 2006;203:1139–42.

[5] Cyranoski D. China's biomedical research takes flight in new directions. Nature Med 2004;10:656.

[6] Cyranoski D. 'Independent' biology institute targets China's exiles. Nature 2002;420:257.

[7] There are detractors to this widely held viewpoint. An example of this alternative perspective Angell M. The truth about the drug companies. NY: Random House; 2004.

[8] Matinez B, Goldstein J. Big pharma faces grim prognosis. *Wall Street J* (online) 2007 December 6.

[9] Robbins-Roth C. From alchemy to IPO. Cambridge, MA: Perseus Publishing; 2000.

[10] Stipp D. Biotech's billion dollar breakthrough. A technology called RNAi has opened the door to major new drugs. Already it's revolutionizing gene research. Fortune 2003 May 26.

[11] Trout J, Rivkin S. Differentiate or die. NY: John Wiley & Sons; 2000. 61.

CHAPTER

2

The Academic–Business Conundrum

From Academia to Entrepreneur.
DOI: http://dx.doi.org/10.1016/B978-0-12-410516-4.00002-1

21

2.1 WHERE THE SCIENCE IS CREATED

The premise adopted in this book is that the scientific knowledge useful for starting-up *runway* biomed enterprises is created in academia. This is both a blessing and a predicament. A blessing because all the potential is there: creativity and innovation; individual drive and ambition; enthusiastic young minds to be inspired; and an infrastructure suited for simultaneous multi-level-, multi-directional-investigation that has already been paid for by someone else (the tax-payer, private sources and donors). A predicament since despite all the pluses, academia is an environment that does not lend easily to the entrepreneurial pursuit.

In general, academic institutions exist to teach and train successive generations in various disciplines such as the arts, business, dentistry, engineering, law, medicine, the pure sciences and social sciences. A customary co-objective is to perform *basic research*[i] in a myriad of fields primarily to establish academic excellence. Each institution defines its own vision and mission. The emphasis can either be teaching, research, or both, determined by criteria such as the goals, funding (amount and source of funds), and the size of the staff and student population. The research-inclined institutions are normally the better funded and more renowned.

Research-inclined institutions are more likely to perform basic research that will generate results suitable to be evaluated for a useful applied purpose. Research-inclined institutions are highly competitive within the institution, as well as between institutions. Individual staff jockey for research space, promotions and recognition, while institutions vie for prominence. Competition for funds is particularly aggressive due to its determinate nature despite the varied sources from government agencies, non-profit specific-interest organizations, industry and many others. Research funding is of paramount importance as it pays for

---

[i]Basic research emphasizes attempts to understand fundamentals of an issue, problem or question posed by the inquirer.

the materials for research, scientific instruments and equipment, travel, support research students and other expenses. Today, many research-inclined institutions also have a technology office that is a repository of the scientific and technical results that have potential for commercialization. These offices are tasked with some form of intellectual property evaluation and protection, are the intermediary in licensing the technology to industry, and in assisting those interested in starting-up enterprises, among its functions.

As an illustration, I obtained my PhD from a research-inclined institution, Virginia Polytechnic Institute & State University (better known as Virginia Tech) and was employed for 27 years by an institution that went from being somewhat teaching-based to fully research-inclined, the National University of Singapore (NUS). At the Chemistry Department of Virginia Tech in the late 1970s to the early 1980s, many of the academic staff with the better publishing profiles, such as my research supervisor, Professor Larry T. Taylor, were inevitably more effective in securing research funding compared to other academic staff in the Department. My PhD research scholarship was sponsored by a NASA (National Aerospace and Space Administration) research grant that supported basic research in heat resistant polymers.

When I commenced working at NUS in the mid-1980s, research funding was (in today's terms) modest. In the early 1990s the Singapore government began to sponsor R&D progressively as part of an initiative for future economic growth. By the time I retired, the Singapore government through its various agencies was actively funding R&D across the board with biomed research receiving special attention. NUS had transformed successfully into a globally notable research-inclined university.

To put research funding into perspective, as an academic staff in the Department of Chemistry, the entire research funding that I successfully received over a span of 27 years (that included an EU grant, i.e. a non-Singapore source of funds) is equivalent to about double the value of what many of my colleagues in my last couple of years at NUS were routinely requesting on their research proposals (disbursed over 3 years).[ii] For a targeted field of research, two or three times higher amounts than a routine proposal were being requested. In other words, the funding level today is much higher.

An average research-inclined university usually has between 150 and 250 staff in its science faculty, and similar numbers or more in engineering, medicine and dentistry. Combined with other academic disciplines and centers on campus that include biomed and scientific research in their R&D, you will have on average between 500 and 1000 or more research groups per institution that are rampant (since the higher the

[ii]Unfortunately, real figures are normally not disclosed publicly.

research funding level, the greater the expectation) in producing potentially pertinent research results. Singapore has two such types of universities and at the time of writing, had started another. Countries such as China, India, Japan, South Korea and Taiwan have more than three each,[iii] and a significantly larger industrial and population base. Factor in all the other countries in Asia and what you have is the full promise of Asian academia for generating potentially useful research results for applications in the twenty-first century.

Consider the situation where 10% of this research effort pertains to biomed research and entrepreneurship. Even if only a fraction of the results from this 10% are found worthy, envision all the companies, employment and wealth this can generate and perpetuate. But reality is far from expectations. Let's look at some of the probable causes for this discrepancy.

2.2 LIFE IN ACADEMIA

An academic scientist[iv] in a research-inclined university has three duties: teaching,[v] research and administration. Depending on the institution they are associated with and their personal agenda, the demands of each duty on their time varies. Most often, starting, growing and sustaining a comprehensive research program is priority number one.[vi]

The prevailing methodology for basic research continues to be practiced in much the same fashion as it has been for decades. The academic staff, known as the PI (principal investigator), is the initiator of research proposals, the recipient of research grants and dictates how the research is carried out.[vii] A typical PI usually manages a few research programs that can, but need not, be related simultaneously, as funds can come from various sources. The funding quantum define two crucial benchmarks for the PI, the amount of laboratory space they command and the number of graduate students they can recruit, where in both cases, more is

[iii] Double and triple digit in number depending on the country and counting method used.

[iv] This term is used generically to include engineers, medical and dental academics.

[v] A loose term used to describe conducting lectures, tutorials, laboratory classes and other practical work or fieldwork. Unlike schools where teachers have to do most things themselves, graduate student teaching assistants, laboratory technicians and others (especially the staff's own research group members) support these duties, including marking and grading.

[vi] The medical and dental academics may differ because developing clinical expertise is their priority.

[vii] In a sense, a PI running a research group can be viewed much like a small business operation. However, taking this parallel beyond a surface impression is perilous.

typically better as it is an indicator of their relative prowess and success. A proficient PI will manage between five and 15 graduate students and perhaps two or three post-doctoral fellows (post-docs). To this count are added undergraduates (usually supervised by the post-docs and senior graduate students), as well as technicians and other research and administrative staff as funds permit. Therefore, a PI can manage or at least be responsible for 20 or more members in a research group at any one time, and the amount of research performed and results produced would be stunning. Naturally, there usually would be in place a well-developed hierarchical structure for some form of sorting and condensing of information at the source (laboratory) level. Implicitly, the PI when senior enough, may never be intimate with the exact details of each experiment in their laboratory. They probably cope well at the knowledge level, but the skills (hands-on) level is more difficult to sustain. Combined with the reality that at least some of their time has to be spent on teaching[viii] and administrative duties, this is a very busy work life.

The academic research scientist is likely motivated to do research well, as the primary measure of their competence and standing among their peers is defined by their research output. Accumulatively, the amount of funds brought in, the number of publications they produce, the number of papers presented at conferences, seminars and workshops, appointments to editorial boards of scientific journals, the number of post-docs and graduate students they train are key performance indicators (KPIs).

Their ability to meet the KPIs determines whether a scientific career is made or terminated. It is normally expected that a new academic staff will attain a favorable level in their KPIs[ix] within 6 to 7 years of joining the institution and be granted tenure. Achieving tenure usually equates to an academic staff being settled for the rest of their academic career, as they can only be dismissed under exceptional circumstances. For tenured staff, switching institutions is normally a matter of accepting a bigger challenge or a more prestigious appointment. Factoring in the 3–5 years typically required as a post-doctoral fellow prior to their successfully securing a first academic appointment and you will have on average, an academic staff in their mid-thirties when they attain tenure.

Against this backdrop, why would an academic scientist who needs to excel at basic research that permits them to build and maintain their scientific careers entertain career-arresting or -ending components such as product development and commercialization? Why would they want to further exacerbate their already tenuous existence as academics? Simply put, it would probably be tough to find someone who would want to take on the challenge of entrepreneurship after having just lived through,

[viii] 5 hours of preparation for 1 hour of lecture is average.
[ix] And expected to maintain throughout their academic career.

normally, 10 to 15 very hard and stressful years and when life just got better, if not easier. This is one matter that is far from trivial and made even more arduous as the next section discusses.

2.3 EXACERBATIONS TO THE BIOMED RESEARCH-ENTERPRISE AGENDA

Today, academic research funding that promotes *in-vogue* directions such as biomed and environment is common. But the situation is not as straightforward as awarding research grants in select fields, awaiting results and exploiting them. While not exhaustive, the following are indicative of the many impediments ahead that can impact biomed research and the utilization of research results for entrepreneurial pursuits that have to be sorted through.

2.3.1 The Scientific Knowledge Explosion

There has been an exponential growth in scientific discoveries and knowledge in the past 60 to 70 years. In the earlier years after the end of World War II, a sizable share of funding was placed in R&D, partly in response to the rivalry between the NATO (North Atlantic Treaty Organization) and Communist (Iron curtain) countries. The early programs in engineering, materials and the physical sciences led to many new inventions such as the semiconductor, materials for the space program and plastics that later spawned a myriad of industries and products. As the twenty-first century approached, two inevitable shifts occurred. Scientific R&D has become global, and focused increasingly on newer pet areas such as the environment, life sciences, biotechnology and nanotechnology. Many countries in Asia, Latin America, Africa and the Middle East now strive with the nations of North America, Europe (that includes Russia and states of the former USSR), Japan and Australia/New Zealand on all these fronts.

The primary consequence is an information overload, a direct effect of so much research being performed. The number of new titles for scientific and engineering journals appearing in the past 20 years and the astronomical increases in volumes and issues for existing journals are testament to this deluge. An example is the journal *Biomaterials*. In 1980, the first year of publication, Volume 1 had four issues for the year (Figure 2.1). The number of issues increased to six in 1984 and steadily to 36 issues by 2005. A biomaterials scientist has a lot more to read and evaluate in the year 2012 compared to 32 years before!

To be up-to-date and comprehensive in one's research field requires keeping track of at least five to ten journals consistently. Granted the task

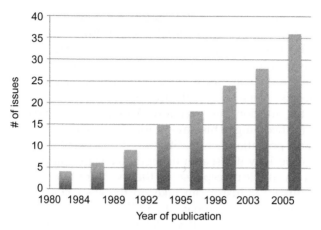

FIGURE 2.1   The number of issues per volume for the journal *Biomaterials*, 1980–2005.

is made easier these days by the advent of search engines, e-journals and associated technologies. But, the bottom line still remains that once the document is in hand (hardcopy and/or electronic), the scientist has to read the articles of interest and that takes time. Factor in the necessity to survey relevant patents applied and granted for applied research and product development, this exercise is quite overwhelming. The quandary is not only in understanding the science, but also in choosing correctly the right innovation directions to pursue. It is an astronomical challenge to sieve through the seemingly endless reports and claims that are being perpetuated daily.

2.3.2 A Crowded Environment

When I landed in Singapore on December 30, 1983 as a *wet behind the ears* PhD graduate, the percentage of the population with a Bachelor's degree, let alone a PhD, was comparatively small by today's count. When I retired in 2011, the number of persons with PhDs had increased dramatically. For example, my department of chemistry had about five graduate students when I first joined. Contrast this to about 200 graduate students (mainly PhD candidates) at any one time when I retired. Take this to the global level and what you have is an extremely crowded environment. Sidney Harris, the cartoonist for the Sigma Xi magazine *American Scientist* once noted that 90% of all scientists that ever lived are alive today. While this may translate as more research being performed at quantum speeds across the globe and the information overload (referred in the section above), an excess of PhD graduates brings about problems of its own.

The biggest issue a glut of PhD graduates pose is poor job prospects for the majority, since it will generally distill down to a case of *quantity versus quality*. A PhD graduate expects a higher starting salary based on the skills acquired during their studies. But there are only so many jobs requiring a PhD and, especially in academia, they usually go to the exceptional few. A tenured staff in an institution can stay for 30 to 40 years with the attrition rate very low. Additional new positions are not frequently forthcoming. This says a lot about staff turnover, academic vacancies and potential to hire. Starting a new institution is a big deal financially, especially if research of reputable significance is sought, and therefore is an atypical response to the oversupply of PhD graduates. And it is unlikely industry can take up the slack since the number of positions available is determinate. In addition, industry hiring is cyclical depending on the local as well as global economic and business needs. The implication of this *oversupply* of PhD graduates that cannot find jobs to contribute to the R&D fervor cannot be casually dismissed. This is because simple probability law dictates that the more PhD graduates working at R&D, the better the chances of striking a hit.

Finally, with the large number of PhD graduates around, it is very likely that one person's thoughts or ideas are similar to another's somewhere else in the world. Goodbye originality. This is a likely cause for the present fervor in research intensity and speed to be the first to publish. A corollary to the scientific explosion and crowded environment is that almost all known ideas that have the potential to be exploited are most likely to have some form of intellectual property protection. This makes proving the uniqueness of an invention gradually more difficult. And a licensing nightmare when progressing to the next step at the very least!

2.3.3 The Escalation of R&D Costs

Contemporary conduct of R&D is comparatively more sophisticated to when I was a chemistry graduate student. And that was in an era when large and expensive scientific instruments were generally shared among research groups, a less common practice now where the better-funded research groups have their own dedicated scientific instruments.

In biomed research, the needs are elaborate. For example, there is requirement for clean and controlled rooms, cold rooms, instrument rooms and general laboratories equipped with biohazard hoods and/or clean hoods. Multiple units of standard equipment such as autoclaves, centrifuges, fridges, freezers, shakers, etc. all of different capacities and temperature ranges, are basic necessities. Scientific instruments such as confocal, scanning electron and transmission electron microscopes, depending on their sophistication, can be costly but also necessary. Mandatory biohazard controls and disposal are another routine cost that has to be factored in. This is just a start of the compilation of what the average PI wants for her research group's exclusive use. Furthermore, scientific instruments are routinely updated, warranting periodical replacement.[x] And equipment, no matter how well made or rugged, has a finite useful lifespan beyond which repair is not economical. Factor in the amount of disposable supplies each research student needs and you begin to comprehend that the multi-million dollars request for a grant award sought by PIs is reasonable. Can this be sustained? That is a question for the funding agencies and other sponsors to digest.

More importantly, all these could translate into a preference to funding only those PIs that have a successful track record and powerhouse reputation, or a select few new entrants who show exceptional promise. This is the reality of a keenly competitive R&D environment. This makes it very difficult for less charismatic players or mediocre performers to participate. But since it is tricky to predict where results leading to innovation or potential products may occur, it is never wise to completely marginalize these perceived *peripheral* researchers. This is a tough call for administrators involved in determining the right balance in R&D funding apportionment and to whom the funds should be awarded. And it borders on fantasy to expect more frequent new fund allocations from sponsors.

2.3.4 The Demand for Affordable Healthcare

Traditionally, healthcare is big business. With each decade of the twentieth century, relevant scientific advancements were used by the biomed industry to turn out products that improved medical treatment, with corresponding good financial report cards for many of the companies involved. The appreciation that most patients are willing to pay the necessary to obtain the *best* treatment, based on the balance sheets of these companies, will not have been missed. This has been the appeal.

This state of affairs is changing. An indicator is that more governments are putting a cap on the amount of subsidies they are willing to pay per patient. Aggravated by the fact that an aging population is a given in most developed countries, this means more spending on healthcare. This equates as costs having to be controlled. The advent of the medical costs' squeeze has begun and can only get tighter. Private and public healthcare systems gravitating to lower cost alternatives such as curtailing excess testing for diagnosis, opting for generic instead of brand name pharmaceuticals and supplies, are examples of the responses to cost containment.

---

[x]For a PI that stays at an institution for 30 years, this denotes on average at least three cycles of equipment upgrade or renewal.

The impact of this new reality is that the financial bonanza anticipated that gives an impetus to start biomed enterprises (particularly from the viewpoint of recruiting potential fund sponsors), might be curtailed even before many entrepreneurs get going. Would this mean that this will eventually wither down to either the *big boys* or governments underwriting such programs? Hopefully not, because it is in the spirit of enterprise that surprises come from those who wish to break out of the mold that will make the difference in treatment, as well as in cost reductions. The would-be *runway* biomed entrepreneur would have to be more thorough and prudent in their undertaking, which is not a bad circumstance. Never underestimate the will of entrepreneurs to get the job done right, yet make profit at the same time.

2.3.5 Increasingly Litigious Environment

In Chapter 1, the regulatory imperative was introduced as a global phenomenon. The more mundane details of this topic will be covered in Chapter 8. Here we focus on the impact of this regulatory matter on aspiring entrepreneurs. Coupled with squeezing healthcare cost controls to get more for less, the other end of the spectrum is the emphasis that the manufacturer is responsible for the product. Justifiably so, but there are stories one can gather from the industry where the product was used outside the specifications or intended use that lead to, for example, the device malfunctioning or inadequate performance, adversely impacting the patient. The manufacturer is frequently the target of convenience to push the blame on in the name of patient safety. This trend, more noticeable in litigious countries, if projected across the globe in due course can be worrisome. This can become a disincentive for a start-up, as the cost in liability issues can be prohibitive, stifling entrepreneurship.

2.4 THE REAL WORLD'S VIEW OF "IVORY TOWER" TENANTS

Before concluding the snapshot of academia, it is informative to be aware of how the outside world views academics that are sometimes referred to as *Ivory Tower* tenants. Industry does value and respect academics, but are just a little bemused when interacting with them. Probably their number one wish is for the academic to see things from their perspective once in a while.

To the *real world*, academics have it made and live a *charmed* existence. When tenured, job security is rarely an issue. Furthermore, research funding once awarded has an average lifespan of 3 years and is infrequently withdrawn.[xi] In the *real world*, business is run on defined objectives, budgets and deadlines. In industry, you can be fired instantaneously; projects can be curtailed mid-stream because of budget cuts, shortfalls or re-allocation. Furthermore, the effect of client or customer complaints is felt more immediately and can be catastrophic. Changes in the business environment have immediate impact and responses must be prompt. Nothing is guaranteed.

While the goals of academia and industry are different, working together is possible and favored by many. Each brings respective strengths to the table. Academia can receive so much more benefit by interacting with industry appropriately.

2.5 BUSINESS-NIZING ACADEMIC RESEARCH

Many countries now look upon scientific research as one avenue where encouraging results with potential can be "harvested" commercially, thereby contributing to the economic prosperity of a nation. Decisions on funding academic research appear progressively more biased towards an emphasis on outcomes that have relevant moneymaking potential. For applicants who can articulate well, the possibility of a *return on investment* beyond scientific content, i.e. one that has potential for some form of financial returns that is not based on mere wishful thinking, will be preferred. This twist to the established practice of academic research certainly adds to the seemingly never-ending list of expectations imposed on an academic scientist. While the merits and limitations of this issue will be deliberated for some time to come, a principal question comes to mind. Can *basic research*, the lifeblood of academia, be carried out in a manner that becomes more translatable to downstream processes yet not compromise scientific content? If the answer is yes, how can academic researchers combine two seemingly contrary demands to profit both their academic aspirations and practical goals sought by research sponsors? This is the essence of what can be termed *business-nizing academic research*, the inclusion, co-existence or blending of prevailing academic research practices with manufacturing and business features.

To realize practical applications of basic research results is complex. Undoubtedly, scientific creativity and enthusiasm are necessary

---

[xi] Many suppliers of scientific wares have related to me why they prefer selling to academia. Despite the bureaucratic process and frequent delays in payment, they know they will **ultimately get paid**, a plus compared to selling to the private sector where collection of payment is never a foregone conclusion as companies folding is a common occurrence.

ingredients. Additionally in this instance, it is equally important to advocate that the academic scientific practitioner be aware of the interplay between research and product development from its beginnings, executing the research, developing the prototype, manufacturing, testing and bringing the product to market. This is because decisions made at the lab bench can influence the timely introduction of a good product, minimize the chasing of dead-ends, and maximize limited resources. How can the academic researcher embrace these aspects?

It may just be a simple matter of changing their mindset. The academic researcher can still retain their penchant to dictate research directions but realize that research can only go so far if the research methodology does not change to better accommodate the goals of industry. While implementation of this proposal may appear challenging as it is against academic instincts, from experience, only slight adjustments would be required in most instances. For example, in chemical synthesis, most often the research goal is to demonstrate that a conceived substance can be prepared. What is important to the PI is for the chemical to be prepared in suitable quantities (for chemical characterization), whatever the yield (amount of desired chemical produced) is recorded. Optimizing the yield and demonstrating reproducibility much desired from the industry perspective is a secondary goal that is pursued but rarely exhaustively. Another example, the practice of good laboratory notebook keeping, was already implemented university-wide at NUS in my final years there. All that was required was for the PI to be firm about follow-up in reviewing and verifying the entries (with the accompanying signatures and dates) on a consistent basis. This would facilitate the patent process if and when required. Of course, not only the PI has to buy in, but also students and administrators on a consistent basis. Therefore, the real question is how do you develop a more *business-nized* approach to academic research? To address this, let's look at how academic research is performed and how it can be modified to suit a more *transportable to industry* format.

2.6 PRODUCTS FROM BIOMEDICAL RESEARCH: SERENDIPITY OR PLANNED OUTCOME?

Basic research is the mainstay in academia. The PI may have stated the potential usefulness of the research in their grant proposals but that, in most instances, is the extent of their effort. Not out of willful insolence, rather more out of habit, of wanting to stay true to their training and independence. Applicable outcomes of basic research are most likely unintentional, not evident at the start, and where *serendipity* likely plays a catalytic role. For the few that achieve stellar significance (the *cherries* scenario of Chapter 1, Section 1.2), big money would also no doubt, at some stage, have identified, chased and contributed to the final status. For the majority of scientific results that do not encounter similar providence in results and backing, they fall into a category that can best be termed "scientific solutions chasing applications".

For example, in the early years of my biomaterials research with chitin, one aspect we focused on was in developing bone substitute materials, a pertinent topic much investigated by the chitin research community at the time. My students, collaborator[xii] and I understood the general goals and directions, and performed the study using customary basic research format. We derived calcium-containing chitin materials that were scientifically relevant, receiving acceptance by scientific peers. We published several scientific papers, presented conference papers and even applied for two patents.[xiii] This was satisfactory on the academic level and, perhaps for most researchers and institutions, adequate. While the potential usefulness of the results were evident, how to turn them into useful products was trickier, an issue that badgered me, as I could not take it further along the line that the goal had suggested.

This is what basic research is good at, generating interesting and/or promising results. But to subsequently search for an existing problem that could benefit from using the basic research results is ludicrous, as it does not make sense. There are also probably a myriad of alternative solutions to address the same problem that may be better. Even if the problem is appropriately identified, matching the solution to the application will be horrendous to prosecute, similar to fitting a *square peg into a round hole*. Either the problem, or the solution, or both have to be modified for a match, and that is before factoring the additional time, cost and effort required, an arduous exercise at best.

How then can one better the traditional way of performing basic research if the intent is to go beyond just publishing? This leads us into considering applied research. My version of applied biomed research presupposes that the goal is determined from the start and research is planned around and directed in support of, or developed to, a predefined stop point, i.e. *planned outcome*. In essence, this would take the form of a reverse of the *scientific solutions chasing applications* stated above to "the applications seeking a solution" method. This evolved into the "needs-driven clinician-centered" method, having as a necessity clinician involvement to define the need and subsequently to guide the applied research by periodical review, as well as at critical points in the progress to be discussed in Chapter 3. Here, it is useful to elaborate on the *needs-driven clinician-centered* concept in greater detail.

[xii] A well-known British scientist in this field with whom the EU grant was obtained.

[xiii] Both patent applications were granted.

2.7 TEAM EVENT

It would be rare that a single person possesses all the know-how to do everything necessary to perform applied biomed research that eventually leads to a biomed product. Even if they did, would they have the time to navigate the intricate maze from concept to the end? In other words, realizing a biomed product from applied research requires expertise from others in order for it to be complete and viable, i.e. it is a team event. What does the composition of the team look like?

For applied biomed research, a key person is a clinician who is usually the person that identifies a medical need that leads to an applied research opportunity.[xiv] Why? The bottom line is that most times you are going to deal with a disease, a mode of treatment or produce something directly or indirectly related to the medical field. No matter how remote, a clinical input is essential to understand how your product or process fits in the scheme of things. The clinician is also the preferred person to carry out the advanced work such as performance studies using *comparative sciences models*[xv] and may participate in the first clinical trials. If associated with the project from the start, they will be familiar with the product and can be the advocate for the product, provided conflict of interest issues are managed properly from day one.[xvi]

While the clinician may be the most likely team member to identify the need, it is typically the engineers and scientists who can translate that need into applied research and perform the work that ideally will lead to the development of a prototype.

Once the prototype is resolved, by necessity, the program has to migrate out of the academic sphere of influence.[xvii] Taking for granted setting up a *runway* start-up enterprise is the path taken, two new participants, manufacturing and financial sponsorship, join the team. The production of biomed products requires facilities and procedures that are guided by regulatory requirements. Whether in-house or outsourced, the manufacturing partner must be familiar with the regulations and work

---

[xiv] There are of course instances where a clinician is not necessary.

[xv] A term used as an alternate for animal models.

[xvi] It is best for the clinician to settle conflicts of interest issues if they are likely to participate as a shareholder, adviser or other significant role in a start-up. When money in any form is involved, it is pragmatic to be prudent.

[xvii] Academic bureaucratic and operational concerns may be impediments. The most important reason however is a practical issue; business decisions are best made in an independent structure that permits timely and decisive action to be taken.

to achieve the common goal of producing a medical product that meets all safety, performance and regulatory requirements.[xviii]

Depending on the project, fund providers are brought in at various stages to propel the product to completion and into the market. Authentic fund providers who focus on biomed start-ups are atypical investors. They are intimately knowledgeable about the biomed industry, science and technology, the regulatory environment and the process of getting a biomed product to market.[xix] They are therefore more likely to be patient about returns on investment than normal fund providers with window horizons generally (but not necessarily) wider than the prevailing standard limit of 3 years.

Finally, a somewhat unusual "partner", but a very objective one, is the regulator. It is no small feat to maneuver a new biomed product or a significantly improved *me-too* product through the regulatory hurdles. Depending on the product, regulatory contact is initiated at various stages of product development or production. For example, a series of tests may need to be designed that are very often product-specific with no prior reference available. Regulatory input can go a long way in establishing whether these tests are necessary, or should be improved or modified. Regulators are there to assist the manufacturer (within limits and guidelines) and are a plus, not a hindrance. The regulators I dealt with have been knowledgeable, helpful and professional.

Therein lies the distinctiveness of this approach to applied research specific in developing a biomed product. Where there is no need, there is no product, and there is no need for that applied research.

2.8 RELEVANCE TO THE RESEARCH AGENDA

It is illogical to expect that the academic community will abandon the basic research way of doing things, as basic research does have its merits, unanticipated results that favorably surprise and training students being two good motives. The example of my former workplace of adopting some of the practices of industry will, to a large extent, suffice for *serendipity-based* research when results show commercial promise.

[xviii]Through the years, I gained competence on regulatory matters and *when push comes to shove*, can do it. But I prefer to have others do such tasks for me. One reason is sufficient to explain: keeping abreast of regulatory updates and handling audits is a full time job!

[xix]I once pitched to a venture capital fund in the US. The evaluator had an intimate comprehension of chitin (my research field) beyond the fundamentals that I would not have expected. Don't be surprised; be prepared.

For those considering the *scientific discovery with a goal* way of doing things, i.e. *planned outcome* applied research, identifying the need is the first step. Only when this aspect is settled satisfactorily should you develop an applied research program. But how do you go about considering what downstream processes would benefit from some form of blending into activities that goes on at the laboratory bench? Three facets come to mind. Acceptance that incorporating downstream activities in your research are necessary; define what is appropriate for inclusion; and last, implementation.

2.8.1 Research Re-Orientation: Establishing a New Culture

The desire to do *planned outcome* applied research right is more than mere realization and ready embracement of the concept. Unless proper internalization is achieved, it is no more than paying lip service to a passing trend. For orientation to an applied research cum business mode to be effective, establishing an alternative research group culture is proposed. An appropriately staffed[xx] technology office, if available in the academic institution, is best positioned to assist this process.

Planned outcome research implies having a specific direction, and all aspects pertaining to work in that area have to be controlled. A good place to start is having everyone in your research group sign a confidentiality agreement with you (the PI). This sets the mood for your students and staff that you are serious about doing good research that when results indicate, you intend to advance to the next level of intellectual property (IP) evaluation and further. This also informs group members that information can be shared freely within the research group, but to be judicious when discussing with others outside the group. This could be awkward at first but with refinement of how this should be done and periodical review, is workable. Give your group boundaries for them to freely exchange ideas and information in other research areas. This hastens adoption and improves comfort levels. A regular review every 3 or 6 months to assess on-going results, directions and refining is also helpful.

Have speakers from industry and other relevant areas such as law firms, accounting firms and regulatory bodies give talks to your research group on the patent process, product development, manufacturing and regulatory matters. Discuss all these talking points with reference to your *planned outcome* research within your research group to further stimulate your students and staff to the culture you want to inculcate. With time, you will recognize the change in the way research is executed in your research group that will be positive not only for the *planned outcome* research projects, but also over your whole research program.

[xx] The staff has to be knowledgeable, experienced, willing and decisive in action (is not a bureaucratic pen pusher).

2.8.2 Harmonizing the Needs of Downstream Processes into Research

In conducting applied research, experiments are designed to solve or answer the problems posed. The science should not be neglected. In fact, it should be done carefully and thoroughly. The obvious question to ask is what are the needs of downstream processes that have to harmonize with what is carried on at the research laboratory bench? Some of the issues that immediately come to mind are intellectual property protection, licensing and product development matters, to name a few. These topics have essentially not been part of any formal graduate school training, nor are they required for conducting institutionalized research activities. This has been made less arduous in many progressive academic institutions with the creation of technology and enterprise offices.

Perhaps the most important activities to harmonize are good notebook (record) keeping and traceability of data. A reasonably sized research group of 15 to 20 members generates loads of information. Record of every experiment has to be consistently entered into laboratory notebooks. Very often, the objective and experimental details can be input readily. The recordings of the observations, results, discussion and conclusions, and variations to the experiment sections depend on the experiment duration (days to weeks). Discipline for all to record all these events in a timely manner is not as straightforward to implement, but it has to be accomplished. In addition, a mountain of data from various instruments and service laboratories in the course of an experiment has to be organized. All have to be kept and traceable.[xxi] If it is to be electronic, there are further necessary procedures to explore. And all has to be confirmed by the researcher, checked and verified by another member of the research group and dated.

Documentation is of paramount importance when it comes to IP, licensing and prototype development. The reasons in the case for IP and licensing are intuitively obvious. Prototype development is based on the raw data and results of what goes on at the bench. Proper records make it easy to commence verification and subsequently duplicate on a consistent basis the prototype process, whatever the intended product. Results can be checked against the data records to confirm all new experimental outcomes.

Reproducibility and yield have already been mentioned. The yield in every instance has to be optimized until consistent and reproducible results are obtained. This has to be made second nature for the lab researchers participating in the *planned outcome* work.

[xxi] The normal standard is to retain for 7 years from date of document creation. There is a review whether the data is to be kept longer, at year 7.

Furthermore, repeating experiments will at this stage still be a manual activity, and therefore subject to variation from batch to batch. Some sort of statistical guidance must be instituted for results to be meaningful. If it is a biological sample, the statistical size has to be valid.[xxii] A sample size of 3 is a minimum and may be acceptable for physical measurements. For biological samples, a higher sample size may be warranted that should consider the identity and the characteristics of the biological material, and the measurement type and method. There are now many statistical software programs readily available to facilitate the statistical process, but they require an understanding of statistics to select the right method.

2.8.3 Laboratory Organization and Operations

Traditional practices in academic laboratories have been a sacred cow. Introducing some industrial practices such as proper documentation is not easy. At NUS, because of workplace safety laws, students and research staff are familiar with such practices as they relate to the manner in which research laboratories operate, especially in laboratory safety. This could be a trend that may eventually permeate institutions worldwide.

One of the first processes to implement is the use of SOPs (Standard Operating Procedures). Such documents outline in detail specific steps to perform for a particular task; identify persons (job function) trained/authorized to carry out the tasks; and the safety rules applying to this task. It may be difficult to write for research tasks, but general lab rules, cleanup, housekeeping, waste disposal,[xxiii] orientation of new students/staff, are some examples where SOPs can be effective. With experience, general rules to follow for carrying out research should be workable.

Another important task is inventory control. What comes in, who uses it and the amount/quantity, the stock remaining, and outstanding orders to be fulfilled, are items that need to be tracked. Instrumentation and equipment down-time affects research productivity, and maintenance and repairs are another task that should be scheduled. The use of reference samples should be another practice for laboratory operations. All temperature monitoring devices, pressure devices, mass measurement

---

[xxii] An obvious point, but I have reviewed journal manuscript submissions that at times do not address this issue sufficiently, i.e. $n=3$ is usually not good enough.

[xxiii] For a laboratory, this is more than just throwing into a trash container. There are specific measures for disposal, e.g. biological and chemical waste materials, "sharps" and broken glass use their own type of special disposal containers. All these wastes are collected by specialized contract companies managing such wastes for proper disposal.

devices should be calibrated periodically (weekly or monthly) depending on their usage. Annually, an accredited external contractor utilizing appropriate references should perform calibration.

2.9 INCENTIVIZE TO BUSINESS-NIZE

Business as usual, i.e. basic research activities, will remain unless academia pro-actively directs research towards being more product development oriented. Encouraging those with a proclivity for applied research is not a contradiction for academia. Even if a small percentage of staff subscribes to this course of action, this would go a long way to showcase the institution's progressiveness.

While it is inconceivable that those who choose this alternative path will ever find equivalency to traditional academics, the institution can promote this option as well as not penalize those who do. For example, I was once asked whether it was realistic to equate a patent to five journal papers, since publication is the lifeblood of academics.

Publication of a research paper is very much in the hands of the PI who makes the decision on what and when to submit a manuscript to a relevant journal. Journal editors make their decision to accept manuscript submissions on the basis of scientific content. Competent PIs will state their case convincingly and effectively counter objections made by referees.

In contrast, patenting an invention in academia is laborious. The science has to be defined in the context of the invention's usefulness, i.e. double the difficulty of a manuscript submission. The decision to patent the invention is usually made by a committee based on the potential for commercialization or licensing, not scientific value. Additionally, because patenting is costly, the invention may be put on a priority list in competition with other inventions, i.e. patent filing is not guaranteed even if worthy. There usually is a predetermined amount of funds available for a budgeted period, and being bumped off because of a financial shortfall rather than merit reasons is a real possibility. And it can take several years to publish the patent if the committee decides to proceed. Although the PI can proceed to publish in scientific journals once the patent application is filed, this may not be astute since competitors may get a head start to counter the invention even before the would-be entrepreneur gets going.

The institution can also evaluate the applied research-oriented staff performance based on a separate criterion from the normal way. Ultimately, if you want to go down the product development–*runway* entrepreneur path, do so after careful consideration and because you have the passion for it. When the venture works out, you will find that the vindication for that choice and decision will be self-explanatory.

2.10 MYTHS AND MISCONCEPTIONS TO NOTE WHEN TRAVERSING FROM ACADEMIA TO BUSINESS

Before concluding this discussion on academic activities dovetailing into business opportunities, it is constructive to comment on five prevailing academic impressions for reflection by those who, when they find success in executing *planned outcomes* research, contemplate taking on the challenge of starting up an enterprise.

2.10.1 Research Expertise Corresponds to Industrial Expertise

Research is the forerunner of any discovery, invention or method that can be translated into a product or service. It must occur. Research requires curiosity and imagination. In research the final answer is never known at the start, and in actuality, there is no need for a final answer, only stops along the way until the funding runs out or another topic appears to divert the PI's interest into a new direction. The research practitioner tries one path, explores another, and so on, until they arrive at an answer that by logic can be reasoned and substantiated. Frequent changes are common and experimental thoroughness is rare. Even if you are executing planned outcome research well, it is still at an academic level. Therefore, as the research practitioner, you must also realize there are boundaries beyond which you become a novice, i.e. in an industry setting.

Developing a product or a service entails rigor. There is an end result – the specific product. It requires proper conception, design, specifications, prototyping and testing. At each stage, stringent acceptance criteria must be met to proceed to the next phase. When the product goes into mass manufacturing, a production schedule and inspection stations are mandatory. A similar regime applies to developing a service. These are just some of the challenges before you, and it is very different from academia. The product process necessitates a different mindset. The research expert can acquire it, but must be willing to pay the necessary *dues*.

2.10.2 Expertise in Science, Engineering and Medicine is Transportable into the Enterprise Stage

Most clinicians, engineers or scientists spend their time in a world that accords them certain privileges. One benefit they enjoy is the recognition that they are experts in their field with the accompanying stature. Some have also been exposed to industry as consultants. This assuredness can carry over when they plan to become entrepreneurs. That is to say, these same experts believe that expertise is easily transferred to business with a sure success outlook.

One of the first things that will become immediately obvious when one traverses the gulf from academia to business is that the game and rules are diverse in the two realms. While academia celebrates discovery and publications, business rewards financial success. When you take the plunge to become an entrepreneur, the *real world* no longer looks at you as an academic. The same business community who treated you as near royalty will view you in a different way when you hit the streets. At best, they will see you as a new kid on the block, but more often as a business rival. Your treatment and survival will be commensurate with how you strive in this environment with very little goodwill brought over from before.

2.10.3 Running a Business is a Lot Like Running a Research Group

Continuing on a slightly different consideration is the way an academic usually interacts with their staff and students. The pathway to coveted academic eminence is research and publications. The academic is the principal investigator (PI) of the funded research. The PI directs the research program, supervising post-docs, students and research staff under them to churn out research results. These *foot soldiers* usually toil long hours because they are working for that PhD; or to gain experience and the PI's recommendation for a better job prospect; or the extra insight that could set them on an academic career path of their own. Cordial the relationships may be, but the primary reason for them to be in the arrangement is very specific individual goals just stated within a predetermined time frame.

A company setting is different from an academic research group environment. Unlike founders, most staff in a company, including those there for the experience and the opportunity to work with or be associated with an expert is concerned about their personal financial wellbeing even at a start-up. And rare is the employee (they are not your partners or sponsors) who views stock options as an incentive (since a start-up has no track record as collateral) until the basics are taken care of, such as putting food on the table and gas in the car. Granted the organization does permit them a channel to utilize their background training and maybe pursue their interests. But the prevalent attitude is for cash in hand today because tomorrow the company may fold! Therefore, your staff will most likely not work the long hours that are required without the proper compensation.

2.10.4 All You have to Do is Tell Your Staff and Employees What to Do

When someone commences an academic career, he will usually slave long hours in the laboratory alongside his team to get the results needed for journal publications. Once some success is achieved, he will usually spend less time in the laboratory by necessity, and disburse instructions to post-docs, graduate students, technicians and general workers. If he sets up an enterprise and runs his business similar to the way he runs his research group, this same method of transmitting instructions is unlikely to work.

In a start-up business, you have to get involved and be on the ground. Giving instructions via the phone, e-mail or other means but never actually getting involved in the day-to-day, hour-by-hour activities may appear chic and authoritative but it seldom gets the job done. The entrepreneur who conceived the enterprise has to have a feel for the business situation when it is launched, and through each step of the way to success. They owe it to themselves. It is a lot like a platoon commander or sergeant at the front leading his men into combat. Contrast that with a commander who shouts commands through the airwaves from the safety of an artillery bombardment hardened bunker. No prizes for guessing who is more effective.

2.10.5 Plastics Expertise is Not Equivalent to Medical Plastics Expertise

This last point is specific to working with materials. In the boom years of the latter part of the twentieth century, many brand name companies from Europe, Japan and North America relocated to the newly industrializing countries, especially in South East and East Asia, the so-called four tigers: Hong Kong, Taiwan, South Korea and Singapore because of the lower labor costs. For example, many plastics component producers blossomed in Singapore as outsource suppliers to support computer and peripherals manufacturers and consumer goods producers. These outsource suppliers gained much expertise in plastics processing. When the cost of labor in Singapore rose in due course, the manufacturers and producers relocated to other lower cost Asian countries such as Thailand, Vietnam and China.

What were the outsource providers to do? They could follow the money and relocate with their principals. Or they could contemplate an alternative use for their capital investment in production equipment. For some, biomed immediately came to mind. After all, plastics components make up a considerable portion of the medical devices industry, as well as packaging in the pharmaceutical industry. Those that settled for the latter option soon realized that the ballgame was different when it came to biomed. They had to deal with the regulatory issues mentioned previously.

To be specific, in dealing with materials intended for medical use, the biocompatibility and safety issues of the plastics become a primary issue. In contrast, plastics intended for consumer goods have more lenient standards to meet. Many of the additives such as plasticizers, lubricants, colorants and the like, are reduced, removed or replaced with non-toxic alternatives for biomed. Costs in re-tooling and production in a cleaner environment has to be incurred. It can and has been done.

2.11 FROM ACADEMIA TO THE REAL WORLD

The preceding section provides a taste for those considering crossing the academia–business divide. It is not straightforward to become a start-up *runway* biomed entrepreneur. Bear in mind that most science will remain a collection of facts and opinions. It is only the rare event that makes it past the hallowed halls of academia into an industrial setting. You have to be realistic and assess your science objectively whether it is worthwhile pursuing it beyond the standard publications and presentations. How to go about this begins with the next chapter.

Real World Lessons Learnt

General
1. Academia is about research excellence.
2. Business is about making profit.
3. Crossing the academia–business divide is mainly a mindset matter.

Specific
1. Biomed is a team event.
2. Foundations of a biomed product can be conceived and started in academia.
3. Academics exploring entrepreneurship have to mentally shed time-honored attitudes and practices.

Quote for the Chapter

"Basic research is like shooting an arrow into the air and, where it lands, painting a target".
Homer Burton Adkins (1892–1949; American organic chemist)

3

Taking Academic Biomedical Research Beyond the Lab Bench

From Academia to Entrepreneur.
DOI: http://dx.doi.org/10.1016/B978-0-12-410516-4.00003-3

3.1 FROM THE PATIENT TO THE LAB BENCH

The issues to work through for an academic contemplating the entrepreneur route while in academia were introduced in the previous chapter. In order to expedite academic research results to become a *runway* enterprise reality, a lot of the preparative work can be completed while in academia. To illustrate how this can be carried out, this chapter utilizes some of my NUS research activities in biomaterials development and their deployment in medical devices, specifically implants.[1] The ensuing information can only serve as an example, and is not meant to encompass all facets of biomed research that is overwhelmingly diverse and varied in complexity. It is hoped that the reader can obtain a sense of the many, seldom-mentioned or formally taught topics conveyed here and assimilate into their arsenal of practices in carrying out their own undertakings.

A biomaterial according to the ESB (European Society for Biomaterials) Consensus Conference II[2] is defined as a: "Material intended to interface with biological systems to evaluate, treat, augment or replace any tissue, organ or function of the body". The journal *Biomaterials* defines a biomaterial "as a substance that has been engineered to take a form which, alone or as part of a complex system, is used to direct, by control of interactions with components of living systems, the course of any therapeutic or diagnostic procedure". Both definitions are acceptable since the "use purpose" is stated, i.e. a material/substance becomes a biomaterial when the use is defined.

The science of biomaterials has progressed steadily since the 1960s. When I first began my biomaterials research program in the late 1980s,[i] I settled on a material called *chitin*, isolated primarily from the shells of crabs and shrimps. I was fascinated that this material, being obtained from nature, should be more acceptable by biological entities such

---

[i]My first research grant was more along the lines of what I did for my PhD. It takes time to gain the knowledge and confidence to change to a new field.

as the human body. My first encounter with chitin was using a chemical variant, chitosan, to assist a botany colleague to develop an artificial seed coat.[3] When my attention turned to applying chitin as a biomaterial, I settled to investigating the use of chitin for several conceived medical device applications such as bone substitutes and wound healing that were popular in the 1980s among the chitin research community. Publications in the 1990s and early 2000s reflect this bias. Taking the research results into product development proved fruitless until, by a gradual refinement process, the *needs-driven clinician-centered* applied research evolved. For me, the **start point** in using this method to turn biomaterials into medical devices is not research excellence, but **the patient**.

The human body is a unique biological entity that is extremely complex, highly organized, efficient, self-sustaining and self-regulating, functioning within a well-defined and restricted tolerance range. For example, the average body temperature is 37°C at 1 atmosphere pressure. If this body temperature deviates beyond ±2°C[ii] of this median, problems set in. The extent of problems depends on the individual, since no two persons are identical. Thankfully for most humans, divergences from normal fall within known statistically accepted limits that permit standard responses to be developed to bring the body back to a healthy state. In other words, when the human body breaks down or is damaged, the body turns into a patient that requires medical intervention.

3.2 MEDICAL INTERVENTION: SCIENCE AND TECHNOLOGY'S ROLE

Medical intervention can be described as all manners of treatment, be they pharmaceuticals, invasive procedures, etc. to relieve illness and injury in attempts to bring the body back to its normal state. In the context of this chapter, the issue is how to go about participating in medical intervention from the perspective of an academic engineer or scientist in the *needs-driven clinician-centered* applied research manner once the medical need is identified. It has already been made clear that interacting with a clinician is a necessity (Chapter 2). Equipping oneself with the *lingua franca* of the medical world, and an overview knowledge of how the human body is organized and works, should precede this. This would better facilitate communication and understanding to be initiated and grow when you start working with the clinician. While you do not have to become an expert, basic comprehension of disciplines such as anatomy, biochemistry, immunology, pathology, physiology and structural

[ii]2°C is used, as there is normally no doubt that problems exist at this deviation.

biology, provide a vital background. Once you have a grasp of the funda-mentals, secondary factors such as patient age, ethnicity and size should slowly creep into your thoughts whenever you ponder conceived solu-tions for clinician-posed problems worthy of developing into medical devices. And remember, while physicians are the principal parties you will interact with, do not forget their nursing staff, EMT (emergency medical technician), and those involved directly with patient care who may offer you a different but related insight. A surgeon can show you how she does her surgery, but her surgical nurse in charge ensures every-thing else is in order in the OR/OT (operating room/theater) and can complete the picture for you.[iii] *Your role is thus defined; you are the link from medicine to science and engineering. You handle the job at the lab bench level.*

Consider the process of developing an implant device. The surgeon from experience identifies the limitations of existing devices, and has a *wish list* of preferences that she would like in a new design. Better still if she has an original design to solve a need she has but has not been satisfactorily addressed, you have a rare opportunity. Your role as the sci-ence and technology component is to provide a technological solution for the problem at hand, i.e. to satisfy the *wish list* as best you can. A gen-eral background in the medical topics listed above will assist you as you go about defining the applied research. Take for example that you want to develop an implant such as a sub-5-mm blood vessel for heart bypass surgery. You will have an idea of the size,[iv] the structure of the heart and its location in the body, normally referred to as *the target site*. This gives you an idea of the challenges confronting you, such as blood interac-tions with biomaterials that you select and similar matters. You will also take into account in your deliberations whether the implant is address-ing a critical and/or life-threatening situation, the accessibility of the tar-get site, the complexity of the replacement procedure, and affordability of the intended device. For the first three points, you will doubtless be guided by your surgeon, while the last point you will most likely have to figure out for yourself.

It may appear to many as being cold and calculating, insensitive, bordering on inhumane, wanting to address this affordability ques-tion. But if no one can, or is willing to pay for what you intend to cre-ate, it is unlikely to become a business. Let's take as an example that

---

[iii] Much like in the military where an officer (platoon commander) is more focused on command and the mission, while the platoon sergeant runs the platoon. Be forewarned, from personal observation, you underestimate the senior nurse's influence on your surgeon to your own peril.

[iv] In this instance, refers to the heart's size in proportion to the body, not the literal size of the heart in an infant, child or adult.

you can conceive a totally implantable artificial kidney that will work near perfectly to address kidney failure, an illness that afflicts millions of people globally. The cost to the patient per device is estimated to be US$100,000.00, an exaggerated sum for elucidatory purpose. Is it realistic that the average patient can pay for it? You know the answer without doing the math, which is of course very unlikely. The real purpose of taking note of affordability for you, the academic applied researcher, is to work on possible solutions that may better the artificial kidney (dialyzers presently in existence) and yet will not overwhelm the patient financially.[4] And when done right, this is where academia has so much to contribute for developing potential biomed products before it transcends the academia–business divide. Research, as the term implies, is for you to try out the options that provide choices from which the best compromise (and it will always be a compromise) can be selected to take into product development. Academia is more flexible in resource utilization towards such exploratory efforts compared to industry.

There is one important detail to note using the *needs-driven clinician-centered* method sponsored in this book. Science and engineering is secondary when the practical aspects of implant surgery come into play. The decision to use or not to use a particular implant is the surgeon's, and the surgeon will choose accordingly. The surgeon also performs the procedure and the success of the implant depends to a fair extent on the surgeon's skill and care in implant handling and placement, and post-surgery monitoring to ensure the favorable performance of the implant. The success of an implant (or any biomed product that is the outcome of this process) by default relies on the clinician. Therefore, while the scientist and engineer have equally important roles in this collaborative effort, realize that limits are reached for them at the medical realm.[v] The only avenue available to cross this chasm is going back to university and getting a medical degree. An MD/PhD combination together with the requisite specialist training provides the holder with the necessary credentials minus the capability limitations to carry out the *needs-driven clinician-centered* method.

3.2.1 Interacting with Clinical Staff

Working with a clinician is similar to interacting with any professional. Depending on their clinical specialty, the demand on their time differs. The cardiothoracic surgeon I worked with in my first applied project was frequently busy, called to perform many emergency procedures that resulted in my meetings with him either being delayed or

---

[v] And by extension, includes the manufacturer, entrepreneur, investors and regulator that commence beyond academia.

re-scheduled.[vi] This was more about the number of cardiothoracic surgeons available at the time having its consequences. I subsequently worked with an orthopedic surgeon and an eye surgeon, episodes that will be recounted later in this chapter. Again many meetings with both were delayed as clinics and surgery take priority. However, in these latter projects, more than 10 years had elapsed and experience enabled me to ensure work progressed at a steadier rate between progress meetings.

Choose your clinical contact carefully. I have worked with a senior world-recognized authority, established surgeons, and up and coming younger surgeons. I find that it does not matter what their positions or reputations are, but how well you get along with the clinician you work with.

By far my best association and from whom I learnt the most, was my pathologist colleague, who was always on time or made time for appointments.[vii] My first biomaterials project was on the tissue heart valve that required the use of a rat animal model. I sought the assistance of a pathologist in interpreting histology results and from then on, a good professional relationship developed that lasted more than 10 years. She was very patient, explaining everything including how best to retrieve tissue samples from the explant site, process the tissue and of course comprehending the histological results. She continued with my research group when we moved on to bone materials and wound healing. The other gem of a colleague was the university's vet who taught me how to handle and treat laboratory animals, perform procedures and investigative studies the proper way. The point I make here is that working with clinicians is more than interacting with the clinical specialty of interest; you should gain as much insight from as many varied perspectives as possible. An animal study or histology interpretation can impact the final understanding of a research study, and it should not be trivialized just because you don't get the *prestige* factor you expect since in yours eyes, it may be less glamorous. Naturally, an experienced pathologist sees things you do not see in a histology slide, and a vet can provide you with a different insight into animal model selection that may be better for your particular study.[viii]

[vi]Never cancelled. Secretaries or PAs (personal assistants) are your best buddies in achieving this, i.e. do not underestimate the authority of personnel without titles before, or alphabets after their name.

[vii]A hospital pathologist's role in the healthcare system should never be underrated.

[viii]There are many ways and many animal models you can select for a particular study.

3.3 FROM THE LAB BENCH BACK TO THE PATIENT

After understanding the needs of the clinician, the first step in heading back to the patient is to settle on an applied research project, plan and secure the necessary funding for it. This entails conceiving, for example, an implant medical device based on your proposed solution to the clinical need, utilizing biomaterials. The traditional biomaterials have been metals, ceramics and polymers. Let's take a closer look at biomaterials.

3.3.1 Biomaterials: Building Blocks for Medical Devices

Metals as biomaterials usually (but not exclusively) mean stainless steel and titanium. Their primary roles are in load-bearing situations or where rigidity is required such as the shaft of a hip implant, knee joint replacements and skull plates. For non-implant Class 2 devices, they are used as syringe needles and surgical instruments. The shape and contours of the body can limit metal implant design and, consequently, utilization. Magnetic beads are a more recent innovation in this class of materials gaining a presence in diagnostics applications.

Ceramics as biomaterials can be crystalline or amorphous, the most common being alumina. Similar to metals, alumina-based ceramics in various compositions are employed where load-bearing and rigidity are required, for example, the ball head of a hip replacement joint. There are other types of ceramics that are created to be surface reactive and bioresorbable, used as coatings on metal implants to promote better adhesion between the implant and bone. A constraint for ceramics is their brittleness.

Polymers span a wide range from flexible to rigid, and are the most versatile of materials used as biomaterials. They can be synthetic (made from petroleum) or natural (isolated or extracted from biological materials). Traditionally, polymers are prepared to perform in various non-degradable, usually non-load-bearing situations. Polymers useful as matrices for controlled delivery such as pharmaceuticals and biologics have been fabricated to degrade by dissolution in body fluids or by action of enzymes in the body. The main role of biomaterials for drug delivery and gene delivery is to maintain integrity of the pharmaceutical or biological agent as they are introduced and transit the circulatory system. Polymer choice depends on the type of delivery: oral, nasal, systemic; whether the drug is encapsulated or chemically bonded to the carrier matrix; the mechanism and ease of drug loading; the drug release mechanism; and, the kinetics and how the biomaterials are degraded by, and discharged from, the body. New medical device possibilities are in tissue engineering, components of micro-machines, forming 3-D cell-cultures and as hydrogels. Research in the use of polymers in these applications include developing scaffolds and other structures for cell colonization, growth, proliferation, micro-fabrication, as temporary or permanent biomaterials and as various gel types: thixotropic, self-assembly and responsive. Polymer design includes tailoring to suit the application sought. Finally, polymers are used extensively in packaging of medical devices and other medical products.

Therefore, there exist a wide variety of materials that can be selected for use as biomaterials. Most material's chemical, physical and engineering properties are known, including their advantages and disadvantages. Research on improving material attributes by manipulating characteristics such as chemistry, microstructure and processing methods are of course on-going. More often, it is the creativity in deriving a solution to a conceived application, rather than the material, that will be a constraint in their selection. Last, there is no need to strive towards getting the ultimate solution that does not exist. If you have a 95% fit you are already well ahead of the curve. Know that the body can compensate for minor imperfections.

3.3.2 Shortlisting a Biomaterial for Applied Research

In selecting a potential biomaterial for a given end use, it is useful to have a procedure such as the following.

1. Draw up a list of requirements based on the identified need, the previously mentioned clinician's *wish list*. You will likely have many predecessors (other devices for the intended application), and that is a good place to start because you have a reference. More often, incremental improvements are the rule of the day. It is more a matter of alleviating the existing shortcomings. Revolutionary innovations are harder to realize.

2. Evaluate required specifications to existing materials to solicit a properties match. There is such a flood of information in the scientific and technical literature about metals, ceramics and polymers available that you should be able to find a material that meets most of your requirements. *Try and use known biomaterials*, i.e. materials that have been used in other medical devices. The rest is about studying the fit to reach a good compromise.

3. Start the research and look where initial results take you. **ONLY** after exhaustive evaluation to rule out the selection of known materials should developing a **NEW** biomaterial be considered. The same goes for new medical devices.[5] It would be unfortunate to embark on developing a new material just because you have the resources to do so. In this era of ever increasing demands on regulatory compliance,

existing materials will face a more amenable regulatory scrutiny.
A new material will be subject to strict evaluation for approval,
an expensive and timely process. At times materials study can be
totally circumvented, as described in Section 3.6.3.2. In this instance
bypassing the materials study outlined next and proceeding to proof
of concept is pragmatic.

4. Finally, a reminder that your applied research must also maintain
   academic goals, i.e. the target should at least be one patent and several
   academic research publications. This is because you are still the recipient
   of research grant awards and those commitments have to be met. After
   all, there is no guarantee the applied research will definitely yield
   something useful and keeping your options open at this stage is astute.

3.3.3 Material Characteristics

The bulk properties of the biomaterial are manifested in their physical
and mechanical characteristics that relate to functional integrity and stability of the biomaterial. Using polymers as example, some of the material's physical and mechanical attributes that may be considered are the
ultimate strength, the fatigue strength, the yield elasticity, toughness,
hardness, wear resistance and time dependent deformations (e.g. creep).
Again there is so much information available for first performance
approximations to be made. Applied research to support and refine these
estimations may involve studying dimensional stability, load effects and
in-use stresses that may arise. Both computer modeling and measurements taken on the physical models will provide information as to the
suitability of the material for the intended use.

The chemical make-up of the biomaterial governs the potential chemical reactions and biological interactions the biomaterial may undergo
in the body. Primarily, this is through the surface (geometry also exerts
an influence) of the biomaterial. The body, probably the ultimate hostile
environment, does not like foreign material and will respond. The scientific knowledge of what occurs and how to arrive at harmony between
biomaterials and body tissues and fluids is prevalent. Again, tailored
research for the conceived application has to be performed. Studies using
simulated body fluids, cell culture and comparative sciences models are
popular ways of defining the biomaterial's choice.

In investigating the physical, engineering, chemical and biological
characteristics, what is being established at this stage is the suitability
of the selected material for the intended application. There is a lot more
to do once the project leaves academia, but the groundwork put in here
provides the confidence of materials choice for downstream processes
and the usefulness of the device to maintain functionality throughout the
period of use.

3.4 AT THE ACADEMIC LAB BENCH

As the applied research progresses, there comes a point where you will find difficulty in delineating where research stops and product development begins. The recommendation is always to do as much in academia, especially in answering most of the scientific questions. Two case studies will illustrate this involved process a little later. For now it is useful to discuss three factors that can be limitations for commercialization and are best dealt with early. These are refining the science, scalability and sterilization.

3.4.1 Refining the Science

Preliminary research results may be good and encouraging, but require further fine-tuning. You need to corroborate the science by first confirming that it really works and second, to make it robust for an industrial setting.

Confirming the scientific results is about ensuring there is no *operator prejudice*; but if present, it is removed. Ridiculous as it sounds, researchers:

a. Do take shortcuts.
b. Do think everyone else is on the same wavelength as themselves.
c. Do indifferently leave out important steps in their records.
d. Do take it for granted that others in their field know how to *fill in the blanks* based on a keyword that represents perhaps 10 steps in a procedure.
e. (And, in exceptional occasions that have received disproportionate media attention) Do distort results.

Disagree with these assertions? Try the following exercise. Pick out any published paper in any journal in your field. Go to the experimental section. Try repeating the experiment as per the description in the article. The probability you can duplicate the experiment successfully based on what is written in the few sentences is very low. As a journal referee, I paid attention to this section and even when a better description was provided after the manuscript was revised, I maintain it would be difficult for someone *skilled in the art* to replicate that experiment well. Therefore, confirming the work independently (by more than the person doing the work, and outside the research group if possible) is a necessity to remove any reservations about the results. Second, ensure repeatability on a constant basis, again by several individuals followed by groups. This will give you the confidence that practically anyone with the right background given the proper training and information can do what is required.

The other aspect of refining the science is to make the science robust. Research typically utilizes expensive and/or customized equipment to perform the experiments, with much of the data obtained using sophisticated expensive scientific instruments. You now have to duplicate this process with cheaper and less sophisticated equipment and instruments, but with the same or better reliability. This is because generally in industry, multi-million dollars' worth of equipment for routine use is a luxury. Industry's preference is to have cost-effective processes, easily calibrated and maintainable equipment and instruments to verify the science at specific points in the manufacturing process. Your present task is to break up the science into well-defined parts, ensure that each component is workable, verifiable and when re-assembled, the end result matches your original exploratory effort.

3.4.2 Scalability

Scalability is about authenticating that the science can transit to a product or service, since the problem-solving format of the academic research lab bench is not readily converted into an industrial configuration. Experiments conducted at the research lab level use microgram or gram quantities or are performed one at a time. These experiments seldom work well when the capacity increases to the kilogram and ton level, or have to be carried out repeatedly.

In small experiments the microenvironment can be controlled reasonably well by careful manipulation of the settings such as temperature, stirring speed, sequence of component additions, etc. arrived at most likely by trial and error, and by one operative patiently spending weeks or months at the task. When you scale-up to 1000 times the original amount of a substance, the environment is of course no longer micro, and factors such as diffusion rates of reactants, viscosity and heat dissipation effectiveness, influence the course of the experiment. For example, conducting experiments with 10 times the original quantities used and seeing if shifts in the product quality, or reaction efficiency as deduced from yield, can be small steps to guide you to sort out this issue.

Assays are subject to operator skill. Regardless of standardization and practice, some people may do a defined task differently compared to others. Time and further work will have to be expanded to determine how to remove such operator prejudices.

And while in the end this may be achievable experimentally, it may not be at a cost that is acceptable. This is because when you do a large quantity or volume, the process no longer utilizes the same approach as a single experiment. Tooling-up, automation and remote monitoring, for example, are all necessary on an industrial scale, issues that you do not deal with at the lab bench level. It is important therefore to be guardedly optimistic when results on a small-scale prove promising. Until the viability of scaling-up is confirmed (execution as well as costs), and this is usually addressed outside of academia, it is premature to declare you have a true winner. Therefore, confirm the scientific aspects as much as possible.

3.4.3 Sterilization

As a referee for scientific journals in my latter years at NUS, one topic that my attention was drawn to for manuscripts sent for my review containing cell culture and/or *comparative sciences* model studies, was the sterilization method of test samples. Admittedly, this predisposition came about as a consequence of my involvement in BRASS (refer to Chapter 4).[ix] There were occasions when the written procedures left me wondering if the authors realized the difference between sterilization and disinfection. Furthermore, regardless of the sterilization method, I found myself searching for the follow-up comments on how sterility was verified using specific sterility tests that were not included.

The ability for biomaterials and medical devices to be sterilized is important, and should not be casually treated during applied research. This is because many lab scale sterilization methods may have no bearing on whether medical devices made from these materials would survive unscathed when subjected to the more rigorous commercial setting. This normally means exposure to ethylene oxide (EtO) gas at elevated temperatures or gamma irradiation under very strict conditions that conform to known Standards ISO11135 and ISO11137 respectively.[x] Even placement in a particular spot in the sterilization chamber can affect whether a sample is sterilized. Today, H_2O_2-plasma sterilization that is gaining popularity for small volume sterilization may also warrant consideration.

The researcher should be aware of this sterilization factor need and ensure their materials and/or devices can endure and remain unchanged by the industrial processes. There is no sense in carrying out applied research that will never meet industry requirements. Devise a proper sterilization investigation program that explores the sterilization method fit for the material or device during development to cover all your bases.

[ix] Sterility is a complex subject. Although it is supposed to be either yes or no, it is not that straightforward. You are urged to know this topic thoroughly if you are going to do this as a biomed entrepreneur.

[x] There are other methods used for commercial sterilization. EtO and gamma are presently the most popular.

To complete Section 3.4, it is relevant to comment from the standpoint of a potential fund evaluator or sponsor. When a prospect proposes a start-up biomed business, ask to peruse her publications. If some of the elements listed in this section are reported in her publications, the indication is good that the prospect has thought about some of the aspects of commercialization. She may not have it all, but she will probably be able to work through issues that pop up along the way. This is another plus factor in the checklist on her to tick.

3.5 IP AND LICENSING

When the scientific results are original and promising enough, there is a need to legally safeguard this intellectual property (IP) in order for these research results to have value. This legal safeguard can be in the form of a patent, copyright or trademark.[xi] The patent is the most common. The legal protections accorded are:

1. The rights to exploit exclusively the results for a specified time period.
2. The IP ownership permits the licensing of rights for others to exploit.
3. The proof of ownership in the event of disputes.

Each institution has its own process of evaluating the IP to make decisions on whether to pursue legal protection or not. If the decision is to proceed, the PI is usually involved in drafting the patent and providing input during the patent examination process. If the institution's decision is to drop, you as the PI can pick it up and utilize with no restrictions or prejudice to the institution. There are plenty of sources available to enlighten you on the patent process. I also recommend that you engage legal counsel when you plan to patent your IP. What will be expanded here is how this impacts your potential enterprise.

First, you have to license the IP from the institution *exclusively* to your start-up business entity. If non-exclusive, you must define the territory or types of products that are covered in the license. This is always tough and not a favorable situation you should settle for, and I recommend you walk away from these types of deals. For exclusive license, the terms are pretty standard and there is not much to negotiate except the percentage of the royalty based on gross profit and the number of years in force. Most institutions also require the payment of an upfront fee to formalize the licensing agreement. Often an accommodation can be reached to defer this fee, but it is unlikely to extend until you make your first

---

[xi]You should seek legal counsel on this matter. All I can tell you is that you have to pay; not once, but on a continual basis, and it is not cheap.

profit. So delay as long as possible, because near your launch date, you probably would have raised the funds to pay for the initial fees for the license. You have to settle licensing since the patent is normally a standard requirement by potential investors, the so-called *value proposition*. Conversely, it is also your leveraging tool during funding negotiations. The license to you must be in force before you launch your product.

Second, you have to reasonably determine whether what you intend to do will encroach on existing patents and other IP. This is not straightforward, as conflicts are not obvious by looking at the titles of patents based on searches using keywords. What is written in the invention descriptions and claims are more relevant to determine infringement. Again, legal assistance is recommended to comprehend the *legalese* and this will be money well spent as it may prevent you from paying more for litigation down the road. In the circumstance when you are the aggrieved party, know that protecting your patent is only as good as your financial war chest, and stamina to prosecute in a jurisdiction that will permit a legal exchange to be conducted.[xii] Arbitration may be a more cost-effective way to handle disputes in territories where your patent is filed and the rule of law enforced fairly, but be aware it is not a cure all.

Third, know that a patent is not a guarantee of success. The hard work commences from here on, as you attempt to turn a promise into a technology and, eventually, a product.

3.6 PROOF OF CONCEPT

Encouraging research results indicate a potential that has been demonstrated workable only at the lab scale, the preliminary promise. There are technical questions to be answered. Refining the science, scalability and sterilization have already been discussed. The corresponding scientific questions regarding the physical, engineering, chemical and biological characteristics of the selected material have also been answered and should be favorable. But again, regardless of the sophistication of scientific investigations, they only provide a measure of confidence. There is a need now to answer all these questions from a commercial perspective. You have to do a *prototype* of the proposed device to investigate whether the *prototype* device can perform the required device functions and be sterilized successfully by evaluating the materials' properties post-sterilization. This is the proof of concept phase. Again, where possible this should be within the confines of academia. In addition, everything

---

[xii] There are still places in this world where the barrel of a gun still rule, and others where corruption can negate or at least frustrate any legal discourse.

you do from here goes towards improving your own and, ultimately, investor confidence.[xiii]

3.6.1 Design

Design normally refers to the product, in this example a medical device. The drawing of the shape should be as exact as possible to the concept. You start with a virtual exercise, i.e. something you conjure up on your computer using software. There is now sophisticated software available for you to have 3-D representations, multi-layered sketches complete with accurate dimensions so that you can obtain a visual idea of how the device looks.[xiv] Some software permits the fixation of the device in pre-determined situations and calculates the potential for *in-situ* mechanical loading and/or stress points on the device using known materials engineering properties. Even the surgical feasibility can be animated with enough ingenuity. You want to define the specifications and tolerance of the model as much as possible here as well.

The design phase should follow a rudimentary traceability system if done in academia. Diagrams should be labeled, signed and dated and kept in a physical file as well as electronic folders. Each revision should be recorded accordingly. Elements of how to do these can be found in most Standards containing quality systems such as the ISO 9001. If the design phase is done as part of a business entity, the appropriate quality system should be in place and it is just a matter of following that system.

3.6.2 Articulating the Design into a Prototype

While much can and should be performed on the computer for mainly cost considerations, ultimately a physical model or prototype has to be built. This is essentially making a reproduction or doing a mock-up of the product you plan to develop. There is rapid prototyping equipment that can be used to make the model and this should be used where possible. The realization of the prototype follows the design specifications utilizing processes that follow as closely to full-scale production as is possible. Holding a model in hand is different from a computer visual as you get a feel of how the product should look and will work. This step

---

[xiii] Here, apart from those who provide you with funds, the term *investor* would apply to your partners, staff and backers.

[xiv] I work closely with a prototyping contractor in my present venture and testify that the visuals you can obtain from the software from a brief description are truly impressive. These types of software are priced upwards of US$10 K to purchase and most require an annual fee to maintain. Operator training may be an additional cost.

should be completed before you seek your first investor. Nothing is more impressive than being shown a model, demonstrating how it works and for your audience to handle it to assure themselves. Prototyping, although straightforward, should not be taken too lightly. Refinements and revisions are normally required and implemented as they occur. You may start with a final drawing from design, but you will find that you probably have to revise that drawing and model making several times until you get it right. And if the process takes less than 6 months, it would be impressive.

Once the prototype has been produced, it must be evaluated in as close to a *real world* situation(s) as possible. You will have to develop a protocol that includes what you intend to evaluate and what constitutes pass/fail. How data is to be recorded, what are the extreme conditions, etc. will need to be thought out. Be objective in this process. It is best to curtail the product here than to pursue further based on pride or pure stubbornness. Disappointment at this stage may be difficult to accept, but it is far better than going on and ending up having to halt later after expending more funds or effort that could have been channeled elsewhere more productively. When the device has passed the proof of concept, developing the device takes on a formal process. The design is "*locked in*" and progresses to manufacturing.

3.6.3 Case Study

Until now, a lot has been described on what and how to carry out *needs-driven clinician-centered* applied research. It is always useful to illustrate by example the process to provide a clearer picture. Following are two examples of how I executed this approach.

3.6.3.1 *Bone Cement*

Bone cement has been around for a long time and is used primarily as a filler to cement the implant to bone in hip, knee and other joint replacements. The principal bone cement in use for orthopedic surgery today is PMMA (poly-methyl-methacrylate), essentially perspex or plexiglass. Commercial bone cement is composed of two separate components; one is a powder that contains PMMA powder, radio-opacifier[xv] and a polymerization initiator; the other is a liquid made up of methyl-methacrylate (MMA) monomer, stabilizer and polymerization inhibitor.[xvi] When the two components are mixed, a chemical

---

[xv] To visualize the bone cement *in situ* by using a fluoroscope or X-ray.

[xvi] The function of a polymerization inhibitor is to keep the MMA stable during transport and storage, i.e. to prevent chemical reaction before the two components are mixed.

reaction termed *curing*[xvii] occurs, and in time solidifies into a hard material. PMMA-based bone cement has been a wonder for various orthopedic treatments but has drawbacks. First, incomplete curing of the starting material MMA when in the patient can lead to toxic side effects.[xviii] Second, curing temperatures can rise up to near boiling in the body, high enough for concern regarding damage to surrounding healthy tissue. Finally, the solidified PMMA bone cement's strength is much harder than bone that may result in local stresses leading to secondary fractures. Through the years, several replacement initiatives, most prominently utilizing calcium phosphate, have appeared. Most have only partially fulfilled the features that the incumbent PMMA-based bone cement possesses. Therefore PMMA remains the established bone cement despite its shortcomings.

My introduction into the world of bone cement came by way of an orthopedic surgeon's use of PMMA bone cement in spine surgery as a response to the effects of osteoporosis, a disease that is characterized by bone deterioration affecting primarily women over the age of 50, rendering them vulnerable to spinal fractures.[xix] The annual estimated number of clinically diagnosed spinal fractures due to osteoporosis in the USA is 700,000 and 550,000 in Europe. Furthermore, another 300,000 estimated spinal fractures are linked to various other diseases, as well as traumatic vertebral compression fractures. A "single-use only" bone cement package cost is affordable for the patient when placed in the surgeon's hand, the exact price depending on the manufacturer and country where it is sold. It does not take a math genius to work out that addressing this clinically relevant treatment is worthwhile for an entrepreneur.

In 2003, a scientific colleague whom I came to know when we were both serving as members on the Editorial Board of the journal *Biomaterials* was passing through Singapore. When I met up with my colleague, who introduced me to an up-and-coming orthopedic surgeon (OS) at one of Singapore's Government Hospitals, the OS had been attached to my colleague's research group at a renowned hospital in the Boston area, USA. In a subsequent discussion, the OS talked about some of his surgical challenges and we explored the possibility of joint research to overcome one of these challenges. Thus was borne an applied research project that was really exploratory product creation as it was targeted at addressing a specific clinical issue.

[xvii] Scientifically, it is polymerization. Curing is a more representative technical term.

[xviii] An entry in Wikipedia describes that MMA eventually degrades to carbon dioxide and water in the body. Harm may still occur in the interim.

[xix] For those who are interested to know more, the surgical procedures are vertebroplasty and kyphoplasty.

The applied research to be conducted in this case study was to develop a new bone cement that met all the performance requirements of PMMA revered by orthopedic surgeons, while eliminating or mitigating the handicaps described above. The first task was to derive the surgeon's wish list reproduced below:

New bone cement wish list
1. Retain surgeon's familiarity if possible, i.e. presentation format is to be a powder and a liquid that mixes together to form a paste.
2. Quick setting, preferably within 5 to 10minutes.
3. Delivery by injection of paste to target site.
4. Radio-opacity for clinical assessment by X-ray imaging post procedure.
5. Ease of use and longer duration as paste. Workability is paramount to the surgeon. The ideal bone cement properties sought were to maintain malleability during set-up and delivery, hardening only when implanted.
6. Reduced toxicity.
7. Lower maximum curing temperature.
8. Better compressive strength match.
9. Bio-friendly and biodegradable where possible.

In developing a response to the *wish list*, it is important to determine what needs to be retained, what is to be investigated for improvement, and if the whole exercise is worthwhile (i.e. will the undertaking have a good chance of providing something significant to justify the effort). This last point is not a simple question to answer but must be thought through. Sometimes the answer is favorable, other times not. You have to consider resource allocation (hands, facilities, lab supplies), effort and likelihood of payoff, scientifically and commercially. Publication definitely has to be factored in. Although you may not arrive at a solution worthy of commercialization, publishing your research may assist others in directions that lead somewhere. Your personal benefit may be limited, but ultimately doing humankind a service is still a meaningful undertaking.

In our preliminary assessment, the radio-opacifier could not be bettered, so we did not change that component. The other items we kept were items 1 to 3 of the *wishlist* that were characteristics of the existing bone cement. The powder and liquid two-component configuration was important for the potential replacement, as surgeon familiarity would make adoption easier. The rest of the *wish list* items were deemed as conceivable to attempt. As the orthopedic surgeon was from a non-associated hospital, collaboration contracts between NUS and the hospital had to be in place before we could commence. Again, I emphasize the importance of having agreements in place before you begin. Disputes usually arise only when results leading to financial or recognition gain become evident. If you delay agreements to that stage, you may have a nasty episode to deal with.[xx] I applied for and was granted research funding (from NUS), and recruited a PhD student to carry out this project.

This OS is a very good clinical collaborator who followed research progress, provided opinions on the various results, and performed the clinical (on cadavers) and animal model studies required to prove that the invention from the research was what he needed as the surgeon using the product. Many dead-ends were encountered but resolved over 4 years. After many, many revisions, we arrived at a formulation that remained a paste at room temperature for up to 60 minutes, was injectable, had a curing temperature maximum of 60°C, contained two components that were bio-friendly and potentially bio-degradable, had close compressive strength match to bone, and best of all only activated the chemical reaction at body temperature (approximately a 10 to 12°C rise depending on what your room temperature is). Another student verified the results. Cell culture studies indicated no toxicity aspects attributed to the formulation. The injectability was demonstrated in a spine model that also verified the radio-opacity of the formulation. From a large animal model study, the formulation was found to promote bone growth. You will appreciate that in the academic environment, with resources readily available and easily accessed especially by the student was convenient, and is preferred during such an exploratory stage.

What was achieved in academia
1. Formulation development over 4 years. This was a PhD student project supported by a research scholarship for the student.
2. The resources utilized included my (chemistry) and collaborator in the pharmacy department (cell culture) research laboratory facilities, Departmental scientific instrumentation access, and additional scientific instrumentation access in other departments. The instruments used in this project would cost upwards of US$10 million to acquire and more to maintain. The instrument time was on average more than 50 hours per instrument. Based on a per hour basis, this adds up costwise.
3. Chemical synthesis was carried out for one component of the formulation.
4. Animal facilities and pathology services at the collaborating hospital.
5. The decision to protect the invention by both institutions was positive and the patent was drafted, filed and published.

[xx]When money is involved, a person changing their tune is common and at times vehemently unpleasant.

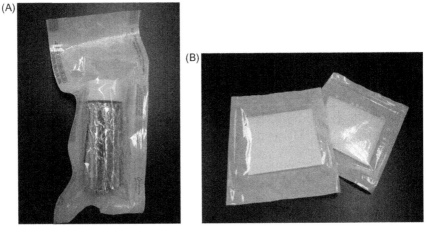

FIGURE 3.1   Prototype bone cement. (A) Liquid component. (B) Powder component.

The prototype consists of two separate packs as shown in Figure 3.1 that mimics commercial systems. Figure 3.1A shows a capped (internally Teflon® lined) clear glass vial wrapped in aluminum foil packaged in a plastic/paper format for EtO gas sterilization. The foil is to prevent light falling on the liquid inside that may initiate a chemical reaction.[xxi] Figure 3.1B shows powder packs in a sterile format for gamma irradiation sterilization. When combined, the liquid–powder mixture generated a paste that became bone cement when the temperature was raised above 35°C. This demonstrates that the sterilization procedures did not influence the materials' properties.[xxii] The prototype as shown is rather crude in terms of presentation aesthetics that will be improved in the final form, but it does the job in providing a visual and handling experience.

This work was taken beyond academia. Unfortunately, the project was eventually suspended, as explained in Chapter 4. The biomaterials reason was attributed to one component being an original biomaterial prepared in the laboratory. No cytotoxicty was detected for this biomaterial from cell culture studies and scalability was demonstrated to 20 times. However, the costs for further development work for this component to be produced under GMP[xxiii] that was necessary to navigate through the regulatory process were not met.[6]

[xxi] Despite the presence of an inhibitor. In production, the clear glass bottle and foil would be replacd by amber glass and a different sealing system.

[xxii] Sterilization was verified by a sterility assay.

[xxiii] Good Manufacturing Process.

3.6.3.2 *Glaucoma Drainage Device (GDD)*

I have an eye surgeon colleague whom I have known for many years. On one occasion, we discussed an issue that was suitable for the *needs-driven clinician-centered* method. This was the glaucoma drainage device (GDD).

Glaucoma is the leading cause of irreversible blindness worldwide.[7] Globally, more than 60 million people have been diagnosed as having glaucoma, with a further 105 million diagnosed as glaucoma suspects.[8] The number of people projected to have glaucoma in 2010 was 60.5 million which is expected to increase to 79.6 million in 2020. The prevalence of blindness due to glaucoma is estimated at more than 8 million people, accounting for 15% of all causes of blindness.[9] Glaucoma patients who do not respond adequately to intraocular pressure-lowering pharmaceutical-based therapy require surgical intervention. One surgery type uses an implant, the GDD. In all procedures, an alternative outflow pathway is created for aqueous fluid to leave the eye, bypassing the malfunctioning trabecular meshwork.

Contemporary GDD devices introduced since 1979 typically comprise a tube that is connected to a plate, as outlined diagrammatically in Figure 3.2. The tube end is placed in the anterior chamber of the eye while the plate is located under the conjunctiva. Excess fluid drains out from the anterior chamber via the tube where it is dissipated through the plate. This reduces excess intraocular pressure (IOP). The cost of a GDD is affordable for the patient, the price again is dependent on the manufacturer and country where it is sold. The clinical reports of the performance in patients of commercially available GDDs indicated a number of accompanying complications with these devices including poor fluid flow control, and progressive fibrous encapsulation. The functional lifespan of most GDD implants was also estimated as 5 years. Therefore, there is scope for prior experience with GDDs to be channeled into developing a new generation of GDDs that may surmount the limitations of the present generation GDDs. Based on the information presented above, the viability of a commercial undertaking is sound.

GDD wish list
1. Retain surgeon's familiarity if possible, i.e. presentation format is to be a tube leading into a base plate.
2. Better control of the IOP especially immediately after surgery.
3. Better control of fibrous growth on the base plate.
4. Better fit of the tube with the contour of the eye.

In my assessment, the success of a new GDD in this instance was dependent primarily on the design, since materials selection was

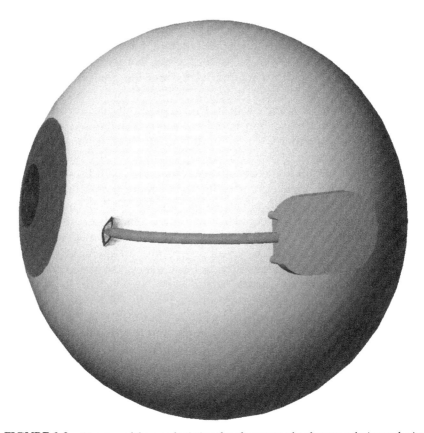

FIGURE 3.2   Diagram of the eye depicting the placement of a glaucoma drainage device and tube.

simply to utilize proven and regulatory acceptable materials used in existing GDDs, as there was no necessity to be inventive in this aspect. Manufacture of the device would also be straightforward in a certified facility.

I presented my design solution to my eye surgeon colleague. He was pleased with the proposed design features as they satisfied most of his criteria. I cannot elaborate further at this juncture as the design was subsequently reviewed and taken up by the hospital.[xxiv] Subsequently, a proof of concept grant was applied for and awarded.[xxv] Some months

[xxiv]Terms of employment contract. IP generated by the staff/employee in the course of their work belongs to the organization (the hospital's training arm is part of NUS).

[xxv]I was a named collaborator for the grant application. I opted out of continued participation when I retired.

later I was shown the prototype and was pleased to note how well the project was progressing.

What was achieved in academia

1. Defined the solution as design only. This took 6 months with repeated discussions between the eye surgeon and myself. A new GDD design that satisfied *wish list* items #1 & #2 were the result. Item #3 was reserved for later review, and item #4 was rejected. Another 6 months was taken up in going through the institutional invention disclosure and approval process that led to the take up of the inventive design by the hospital.
2. A "Proof of Concept" grants application submission and approval that was obtained. The prototype is being developed.
3. I presume some comparative sciences model studies would follow once the prototype device was acceptable and more prototype GDDs made.

In both case studies, a lot of effort was placed in defining what was to be done. Both clinicians were focused on addressing their surgical need. As the researcher you ensure that your proposed solution meets the need because you are the materials, science and engineering expert, as well as ensuring that the affordability was favorable before proceeding further. This is contrary to normal research where the PI evaluates the scientific problem and commences some exploratory laboratory work quite quickly. As is also noted in the GDD case, no real laboratory work was required. In applied research, you always only do what is necessary. This type of approach can be extended to developing new pharmaceuticals and biological assays, and should be adaptable to other situations. Finally to reiterate, using this approach to applied research may dismiss or overlook issues not contemplated that a basic research method might reveal, but makes this approach efficient. That is the trade-off.

3.7 INTO THE *REAL WORLD*

There will be a point where further effort in academia will be counterproductive. The mission of the institution and other bureaucratic restrictions will eventually impose limitations on your activities, regardless of how liberal or open-minded particular institutions may be.

It is imperative that you implement a hands-off relationship with the academic research lab for the project the moment you contemplate a *runway entrepreneur* possibility. Should you decide to remain in academia, the *one-foot in, one-foot out* existence, draw a firm boundary between your research laboratory and your company's activities. There is no advantage in leveraging the system from this stage forward because of your association and appointment with the institution. When there is a need to utilize university resources for that project, such as sophisticated instrumentation, your company staff should liaise with the relevant staff in academia (who are not part of your research group). The paperwork (invoicing) should always be direct between the academic service provider and your company. The service charges have to also appropriately reflect this interchange, as *real world* customers are typically charged the highest rate compared to intra-organizational and government/non-profit customers. Make a clear delineation and you can sleep easy at night.

To complete this chapter, I outline a few of the processes that will take place after you are satisfied with the prototype medical device all the way to the market. The details can be found in most quality systems and from requirements published by regulatory authorities. For now it is pertinent to provide an overview of what this entails.

3.7.1 Manufacturing

Manufacturing has to be done in approved facilities. It is costly to set up manufacturing, and costs even more to sustain them operationally. These days, there are contract-manufacturers with complete facilities that are viable alternatives to setting one up and they should be appraised.[xxvi] A good and experienced manufacturing sub-contractor will assist you to short cut the process, recommend steps you missed to include, or suggest alternative ways to do things and get you going.

Of course finding one in your neighborhood may be an issue, but even if you have to commute to one periodically (another city, province/state or nearby country), the cost savings may still justify this choice. The other factor is to ensure that they are credible. Pieces of certification and accreditation only tell you that when the relevant agency or approved certification contractor audited the organization, they met the requirements. What is done between audits is what you have to be aware of. This is not as outrageous as it may seem (more on this topic in Chapter 8). While most are reliable, you still have to do your own audit (continually) and be satisfied that their processes give you the quality of products you want. Finally, you also have to be sure they can do what you require. A good approach is to detail all this in an agreement, paying only when they have met the terms.

Matters you also have to handle on your own or with your sub-contract facility if that is how you plan to proceed are:

1. The sourcing for the biomaterial(s) you will use, confirming their availability in suitable purity and composition.

[xxvi] This is especially so for medical devices, less for pharmaceuticals and may not be that relevant for bio-based products.

2. You will have to work out the device specifications and tolerances with the appropriate accuracy and consistency that you need (if not done during prototyping).
3. Your products must tolerate safe and efficient industrial sterilization.
4. You will have to become competent with validation[xxvii] and verification,[xxviii] identifying what processes should be validated, the method, the statistical size and criteria for acceptance.
5. You will also have to define what constitutes non-conformance and when to reject a product.
6. You will have to define what constitutes a device produced according to the design, and the tests to be performed on the device to satisfy user needs and intended use.
7. Finally, you will also have to know what the base limit is when the project has to be abandoned.

Tooling-up for manufacturing will probably require the purchase of some capital equipment. For example, if your product utilizes polymers, paying for a mold is likely. You will have to work closely with your sub-contractor on most details. This is where trust comes in. You are a novice and have to be careful not to be taken for a ride. Document everything discussed and approve only when the paperwork is correct. But do not be overly paranoid. Most sub-contractors are reputable with long-term relationships and referrals from you uppermost on their mind. Therefore, their defaulting is rare.

Finally, mentioned in the prolog was the fact that biomed cannot be started from the comfort of your bedroom or garage. The preceding chapter and the earlier part of this chapter explained the process of developing the biomed product/service potential. Once you proceed to manufacturing using the sub-contractor model, you can in actuality work as a "virtual" business, since all the "facilities" requirements are satisfied through sub-contracting.[xxix] At this stage, the "work from home" scenario that you could not entertain previously, is now doable and is encouraged to cut down your costs.

3.7.2 Safety and Performance Testing

Safety studies are to ensure that the final product will not harm the patient. Performance tests provide confidence that the product will work

[xxvii] Defined as "Confirmation that the particular requirements for a specific intended use can be consistently fulfilled by examination and objective evidence".

[xxviii] Defined as "Confirmation by examination or direct measurement that specified requirements are met".

[xxix] That can include prototyping if done outside academia.

as intended. While you should think of all possibilities to remove as many doubts possible, realize the real answers can only be known when the product starts being used, especially for implants. Be aware that the product may perform well, but may not fulfill safety requirements. The following are some of the activities:

1. Function and performance. Engineering and performance studies to demonstrate that the device performs what it was designed for.
2. Safety and toxicity. These are the biocompatibility, cell culture and other relevant tests/studies to give you the confidence that the product, especially the materials used, are unlikely to be an inadvertent source of harm to the patient.
3. Shelf-life studies to ascertain how long the product will remain sterile and not change its properties while in storage before use.
4. Release tests. These are routine tests on sterile products to ascertain on a continual basis that the product is safe, especially its sterility and endotoxin levels.

Do not be overwhelmed. You can hire experienced staff who have done all this before. There are also reputable testing sub-contractors who can do the work for you (the author's company is highly recommended!). Kidding aside, the world is a small place today and you can have your products tested anywhere.

3.7.3 Regulatory Submission

This is an important step for your product. Approval gives you the legal right to market and sell your biomed product in that territory. This is country dependent, but usually if a product has been approved in a bigger market such as the USA or Europe, they meet easier hurdles in other countries. Most countries' health authorities have websites to inform you how to go about this process.

In general, creating a dossier of "evidence" to support your product's case for acceptance is necessary. Preliminaries include information such as the product name, what it does and who the manufacturer is. Most of the rest of the dossier is concerned about the manufacturing process and the tests and accompanying results that satisfy the requirements of the health authority. The size of the dossier and the amount of information are dependent on the type of product you are submitting.

Do not underestimate the complexity of the process. You will have to work with the regulator and/or as mentioned earlier, hire consultants to assist you through the process. Again these are straightforward as the procedures to do this are easily accessible. With experience, this aspect will be manageable.

3.7.4 Market Introduction

There are two aspects to market introduction. The first is a regulatory related matter. The manufacturer and/or supplier normally when approved and registered in the sales territory, has to maintain records of the goods, especially for implants and life-sustaining devices. Again, the procedures to guide you are published by most countries. There are legal and financial implications especially in developed countries, so do this carefully.

The second is more about how you plan to achieve sales that bring in revenue. Introducing a medical product is a drawn out process and adoption can be slow, so be patient. This is one reason why a clinician involvement is suggested as they can open doors for you. The most important point to remember is that you should begin the process concurrent with your manufacturing plans and execution. As a *runway* startup, you do not have the financial resources or brand recognition, so your job is much tougher. It is not necessary to have a big media blitz as you can be just as efficient gaining market share by methodically chipping away at the resistance to your new but awesome product. Persistence will get you there. This will become clearer in the following chapters.

3.7.5 Post-Market Surveillance

This is another regulatory requirement especially for critical care products. Monitoring of implants for significant adverse events is mandatory in many first world countries. Manufacturers, importers and user facilities of implants are required to report any deaths or serious injuries that may be directly related to the device, or any malfunctions that are likely to cause death or serious injury. Recurrences of these types of events may lead to withdrawal of the product from sale. There may also be a requirement for device tracking; a system for locating permanent implants and life-sustaining devices after the patient leaves the hospital. It is also prudent to have your own post-approval monitoring program of your products to gauge how they are performing (usage as well as sales) once in the market.

3.8 TIME TO MARKET

Typically, approved research programs in academia are funded for 3 years. Most prudent researchers would commence work 6 to 12 months prior to formal grant approval, making the time spent on research about 4 years. Proof of concept/prototyping can take 6 to 12 months to complete. Manufacturing can take another 12 months. Safety and performance testing will also take 6 to 12 months to complete. Regulatory approval takes 3 to 6 months on average. Therefore, in effect, more than 6 years will have elapsed from the day you plan something on the research platform until a product hits the street (provided everything progresses relatively smoothly). To some this is just too long to even attempt. For others, less demanding alternatives are more attractive. For the few who may find this strategy intriguing enough to try, time becomes another item to manage.

3.9 TURNING POINT

This chapter has provided a general idea of how you can carry out academic research that can position the results for commercialization. No matter how this is viewed, the easy part is still within the confines of academia. Even if the results do not encourage product development, the academic still can publish the results and continue unimpeded in their academic career path. It is when you choose to leave the shelter of academia to pursue entrepreneurship that you expose yourself to realities you have never had to contend with. And if you choose the *runway* approach, it would certainly make for an interesting journey.

Real World Lessons Learnt

General
1. It is a multi-step process.
2. Justification should be more rigorous for applied research.
3. Do as much as possible in academia.

Specific
1. Fulfill the *wish list* where possible.
2. Scalability and sterilization are deal breakers.
3. The real world does not matter if the work in academia is DOA (dead on arrival).

Quote for the Chapter
There are two key factors needed to start an enterprise, best summed up with two quotes from the same source. The first is presented below and the second in Chapter 4.

Before you begin, be sure this is what you want to do:

"Wheresoever you go, go with all your heart" *Attributed to one of China's most renowned sages: Confucius (551– 479 BC)*

References

[1] For convenience, the US FDA definitions for medical devices suffice. <http://www.fda.gov/medicaldevices/deviceregulationandguidance/overview/classifyyourdevice/ucm051512.htm>

[2] *The Williams dictionary of biomaterials*. Compiled by DF Williams, Liverpool University Press. 1999.

[3] Tay LF, Khoh LK, Loh CS, Khor E. Alginate-chitosan coacervation in production of artificial seeds. Biotechnol Bioeng 1993;42:449–54.

[4] Not as ridiculous as you may think. I believe that the totally implantable artificial kidney will be solved in the not too distant future. See for example: <http://www.washington.edu/news/2012/04/09/wearable-artificial-kidney-to-be-tested-for-safety-and-effectiveness-in-collaboration-with-fda/>

[5] Is new always better? I provide a reference for you to ponder: <http://drsvenkatesan.wordpress.com/2011/01/15/who-killed-starr-edwards-valve/>; Masilonyane-Jones T.V., Blackham R., Alvarez J. Swan Song for the Starr–Edwards valve. *Heart Lung Circ* 2010; **19**: 428–429.

[6] The explanation is discussed in: Khor E. *Chitin: fulfilling a biomaterials promise*. 2nd ed. Elsevier Science. Publication release date estimated as the latter half of 2014.

[7] Thylefors B, Negrel AD, Pararajasegaram R, et al. Global data on blindness. Bull World Health Org 1995;73:115–21.

[8] Quigley HA. Number of people with glaucoma worldwide. Br J Ophthalmol 1996;80:389–93.

[9] Quigley H.A., Broman A.T. The number of people with glaucoma worldwide in 2010 and 2020. Br J Ophthalmol 2006: **90**: 262–267.

To Become a *Runway* Entrepreneur from Academia

From Academia to Entrepreneur.
DOI: http://dx.doi.org/10.1016/B978-0-12-410516-4.00004-5

4.1 A PATH FEW CHOOSE

It is evident from the preceding two chapters that research can always be conceived in a for-profit direction, making the creation of new biomed businesses from academia realistic. The more difficult aspect is the enticement of academic staff to contemplate entrepreneurship as a viable alternate career direction. While a few may eventually make the attempt, unless they truly commit, their effort is likely to be fruitless. Fresh graduates can be acceptable entrepreneurship substitutes as they have the talent, would be expected to be less inhibited, and perhaps are more ambitious to be entrepreneurs. While they may lack maturity and experience (scientific credibility and depth), and may still be working their way up from the *tree* level to the *forest* perspective, they probably compensate for it by being more enthusiastic.

An academic environment is a limited training ground for many of the requirements necessary for entrepreneurs. A student may have obtained A+ grades in any number of entrepreneurial type modules and courses, but regardless of how realistic the classroom scenarios may be, these are never the same as what the *real world* throws at him. Traits such as situational awareness, adaptability and quick but prudent decision-making are rarely emphasized. Even when attached to a business concern, and having access to observing those in charge, he is not the decision-maker, and does not put anything at risk. When nothing is on the line at the personal level, you rarely experience the tension that makes an indelible and lasting impression. In the classroom, bad judgment leads to theoretical losses and at worst, a lower grade. In *the real world*, actual loss of revenue, people loosing their jobs, the company folding up and, in extreme cases, a few emotionally self-initiated life-form terminations can take place. And you have to live with these outcomes of your decisions. But the good news is, whether academic staff or student, if you have the desire, these shortcomings can be surmounted.

To provide a sense of what it entails, let me begin with an overview of why and how I started three companies, the results, and why they are in their present states, and my thoughts on how to make the decision on whether to be a *runway* entrepreneur.

As stated, I started my work life as an academic and remained as one for 27 years. Gradually, my inborn preference for research to have practical outcomes was harmonized with my academic responsibilities as a necessity to facilitate my entrepreneurial aspirations. The contributions my academic resources provided in the initial build-up stage were invaluable. Nevertheless, at some juncture, I had to move beyond the confines of academia and traverse into the *real world* of entrepreneurship. Let me start with BRASS.

4.2 THE BRASS STORY: BEGINNER'S PROVIDENCE

In 1991, I met Khoon Seng Goh, Operations Manager of Pacific Biomedical Enterprises (PBE) Private Limited, a Singapore company based in Science Park I. PBE had developed, manufactured and was selling a Class III medical device, the heart-valve implant. PBE produced two types of heart valves, the mechanical and the bioprosthetic. The bioprosthetic or tissue heart valve was derived from the aortic valve of pig heart retrieved at slaughter. Because of their natural shape, tissue heart valves permit better blood flow, thereby causing little or no blood damage. Patients implanted with tissue heart valves do not have to be on anticoagulation therapy (daily medication) to prevent their blood from clotting, an inconvenience with the mechanical heart valve. Tissue heart valves when implanted in elderly patients, usually 65 years or older, last the remainder of the natural life of the patient. When implanted in adolescent or young adults, the tissue heart valve begins to fail after a few years, attributed to the younger patients' higher metabolic rate. The slow deterioration of tissue heart valves in younger patients was believed to be caused by the chemical treatment to which the tissue was subjected, to make them usable in the human body. There was a desire to overcome this shortcoming in order for younger patients to benefit from the advantages of the tissue heart valve.

Khoon Seng had come to NUS (The National University of Singapore) to source a research scientist to assist PBE in studying bioprosthetic heart valve failure, and to look at ways of overcoming or at least deferring the onset of deterioration. Thus began my journey into the world of applied research and my relationship with Khoon Seng. With assistance from a Singapore government research grant, my team was successful in developing two patents and producing a number of decent scientific papers published in reputable biomaterials journals. More importantly from this book's perspective, the work was brought to a stage where planning for advanced *comparative sciences* studies[i] were completed and ready for implementation. In the interim, however, the company was sold to a larger Singaporean corporation and the name was changed to St Vincents Meditech (SVM) Private Limited. Around that time, the clinical founder of PBE/SVM, a renowned cardiothoracic surgeon based in Sydney, Australia, met his demise. The events led to SVM closing down not too long after, in 1995.

In the aftermath of SVM's closure, we went our separate ways, Khoon Seng to a new company and I to my growing research in biomaterials. But we had built up a good working relationship since 1991, and

[i]The animal model chosen was the pig.

wanted to continue our interests in the biomedical area built up over the previous 4 years. At one of our *shoot-the-breeze* sessions back in late 1995 to early 1996, it became evident to us that the medical device industry, of which SVM was a brief, yet shining example of a forerunner in Singapore, was an industry suited for Singapore. It was knowledge-based, high-value added and suited for a small but well-trained workforce in a confined piece of space such as Singapore. We kicked around a few ideas. The result was BRASS.

4.2.1 Background and Intellectual Assets of the Founders

In late 1995, Khoon Seng had been in the private sector related to biomed products for nearly 10 years. I had built up a biomaterials research program going on 7 years; I was and remained at the time, a pretty much hands-on scientist. Together, we had a combined knowledge of science and engineering pertaining to medical devices, the processes in product development, performance (not safety) testing as it pertained to heart valves, manufacturing and marketing. We had some clinical contacts that we maintained and extended, and began to form new relationships as a prelude for any future endeavors that may crop up one day. Two of the clinicians whom we met (a surgeon and a dentist) eventually became shareholders in BRASS.

Making the point about background of the founders is one of reinforcing the notion of credibility mentioned earlier. A biomedical-based start-up has science and/or technology (S&T) involved. The leader need not be a scientist and there are many competent business, law and even arts graduates that can do a fine job leading. But someone on the founder team has to know and direct the S&T development or make it available (the key words being *make available*) when required, i.e. there must be a Chief Technical Officer (CTO). Without this CTO factor present, a biomed start-up will not have credibility and will face a more challenging time going forward.

4.2.2 Pinpointing the Type of Business BRASS Should Be

When we decided to continue and grow our interests in the biomed area in late 1995 to early 1996, we knew we had to stay within our strengths, something related to medical devices. We immediately eliminated biotechnology, genetic engineering, cloning, AIDS cure, etc. areas that were very popular at that time and in biomed, but it was beyond our combined expertise.[ii] In late 1995, we had virgin territory, so the playing

---

[ii] Author's note: Today, Brass has gone into some of these areas as it continually adapts to the changing business environment by hiring appropriate staff trained in these fields.

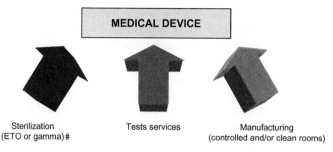

FIGURE 4.1 The possibilities of starting a medical device venture in Singapore circa 1996: components for the production of a medical device.

field was there for us to seize. Yes, there were a few manufacturers of medical devices in Singapore, but by and large, the ground was wide open. Eventually, we decided on a medical technology tests services cum R&D product development business concept as the best option, detailed as follows.

The most convenient starting point in shortlisting an activity in the medical device area was to settle on a possible medical device to manufacture. This is more in the domain of fortune telling,[iii] but there are some basic guidelines like determining the need and confirming by evaluating the market size as realistically as was possible. The more attractive medical devices usually are those that have some patient contact, i.e. for single use only, would require some design, prototyping, and the product supplied sterile.

The traditional model for creating medical device companies at that time was to raise the necessary funds, set up a manufacturing entity and proceed to produce. In mulling over the possibilities, we noted three features for such an endeavor to get off the ground in 1995/96 (Figure 4.1) in Singapore. The first element that would be needed was a production facility to manufacture the device. In general, a clean environment is required for medical devices. These range from controlled access areas to clean room type set-ups. In Singapore, the know-how to set-up clean room facilities in 1995 was a well-known and readily available technology (Figure 4.1, right green arrow). Based on our experience with PBE/SVM, we knew that it was a costly affair and we probably couldn't raise the capital to start, even if the cost was modest, which in real terms meant at least US$1 million in 1995. We quickly dismissed this course of action.

Second, after a single-use medical device had been produced and packaged, the product required sterilization. Typically, gamma

---

[iii] At that time, the idea for *need- driven clinician-centered* applied research was still incubating in my mind.

irradiation or ethylene oxide (EtO) gas sterilizations are the methods of choice (Figure 4.1, left blue arrow), dictated by the type of materials used in the device and costs. A commercial EtO facility was commissioned and made available in Singapore in 1996, while the demand for gamma sterilization was met across the causeway in Malaysia. Today, the volume of devices being sterilized may merit the establishment of a gamma facility in Singapore as a commercial service.[iv] For us in 1996, the set-up costs and the profitability again resolved for us that participation in sterilization ventures was improbable.

Finally, the third element necessary for developing and producing medical devices are safety and performance studies (Figure 4.1, center red arrow). The manufacturer is obligated to demonstrate that the medical device does not cause harm to the patient, and that the device performs well, i.e. functions as it was designed for.

Performance evaluations are device dependent, i.e. custom-designed tests are developed to show that a device will work for a specific application. It is near impossible to design generic performance tests since, for example, the function of a heart valve is very dissimilar from that of a hip-joint replacement. Each project that we agreed to undertake would require a steep learning curve on our part, and suitable customization that was costly to set up. In the 1990s projects of this type were infrequent where we were, and a business could not survive until the client pool became decent.

Safety tests, on the other hand, are a different ball game altogether. For example, the safety testing of medical devices include a series of chemical and biological evaluations centered on cell-culture and animal model studies encompassed presently as the ISO10993 Standards (or its AAMI[v] equivalent). These chemical and biological assays have been developed based on a consensus of international experts; they have been readily adopted by regulatory agencies of many countries and updated periodically. Safety tests were generic enough to be able to cover a wide variety of medical devices, both during the development as well as the production and release phases. The equipment and facilities required to set-up were within a realm of affordability and it was based on skills that we had, and could develop further.

When we looked and asked around, we found that no testing capability of this nature was available in Singapore in 1996. In fact some of the device manufacturers we knew told us that when they had to get

[iv] There was a gamma facility on the island, but was privately owned by a company to sterilize their own products and to the best of my knowledge, not available for contract sterilization to other parties.

[v] Association for the Advancement of Medical Instruments.

the necessary testing performed, they had to send their medical devices to North America or Europe. They described their experience as that of sending their samples into a *black hole* and waiting for a report that mysteriously appeared some time later. If the device passed, great, if the device failed, there was no clue as to why. They expressed dissatisfaction at not being able to know the status of their requests, and indicated that what they needed was someone to assist them not only in performing the tests, but also to consult on what was the best package of tests to execute. Here was a possible winner!

In our appraisal, we knew that we could do all three, but safety testing was the most obvious and attractive choice. The sizable financial outlay with producing a device or setting up a sterilization facility compared to testing is one facet. More appealing was the fact that no one present in Singapore at the time could or wanted to do testing, and that gave us our competitive edge in the first few years. When competition finally set in, even though testing is not a high barrier entry endeavor both in skills and know-how, there are features that we could exploit to differentiate us (that has been the mainstay of BRASS since the beginning to this day).[vi] Did we have a market? Maybe, but for all intents and purposes the market was small to non-existent in 1996. Was there a probability that the business could grow? Yes, but it was in the future and how fast and how much remained a guessing game. We also realized that we had to have more practice and fine-tune many of the things we wanted to do. So what did we do? Our solution was to incubate, convince someone to allow us to set-up, and consolidate our expertise within the NUS system as the best course of action. We did. Next step!

Some readers may still ponder why we didn't do a device. After all, not all medical devices are that prohibitive to develop and market. Correct, I knew that we had the ability to develop competent medical devices including implants. But the PBE/SVM episode taught me that the device's bells and whistles would play second fiddle to the device's country of origin credibility. The PBE/SVM heart valves were championed by a renowned Australian cardiothoracic surgeon, but still sold principally in third world countries in Asia and South America. The perception by would-be eventual customers of a start-up manufacturer of original medical devices emanating from a developing country was the reason that held me back. In the mid-1990s, many a person I met in first world countries would still ask me where in China was Singapore![vii]

[vi]How BRASS does it remains proprietary. In 2009 I created the tag line *Propelled by Science* that provides a clue.

[vii]I am pleased to note this perception of Asia no longer applies, steadily diminishing in the twenty-first century.

I opted to continue my academic research to come up with a potential product worthy of the undertaking.

Finally, to reiterate, the difference between a service and a device is the size of the *bet*. With a service company, a comparatively modest financial outlay will get you started and to the stage where you begin to generate revenue. With a medical device product company, you normally bet heavily that the device will be a winner and a lot of financial outlay is required upfront. A device's payoff comes only when you deliver the product. To be sure, the payoff is often significantly larger compared to a service company, but a product is a tougher bet to pull off, and therefore harder to obtain capital to start. Contrast an *outfitter* to a *stampeder*.

Our strategy was to get to the point where we could generate revenue and reinvest profits into R&D, and perhaps to pursue a device. A testing company would permit us to do just that. This approach, also known as *bootstrapping* (discussed in Chapter 7), has as a game plan the launch of a company with modest start-up capital while permitting the opportunity for an early generation of a revenue stream that is essential to keeping the company afloat without bleeding the founders or sponsors financially. It was our supposition that finding matching funds from Government agencies (through e.g. R&D grants), collaborators and partners would be easier once you demonstrated you knew what you were doing and that ultimately, when performance in revenue terms is realized, opportunities would abound. We also believed that we were creating an essential infrastructure for an industry that was suited and good for Singapore, and that eventually BRASS's success would vindicate our foresight.

4.2.3 BRASS: From Start-up to Profit

On April 1, 1999 BRASS (Biomedical Research And Support Services Private Limited) commenced as a start-up company in an entrepreneur incubator facility in the Singapore Science Park II. The University had given approval for BRASS to be launched and even provided some seed funding. BRASS's stated mission was to assist clinicians, engineers and scientists to bring any biomed idea for a medical device from concept to reality. It was envisioned that the major part of its focus was to perform the safety tests required for regulatory submission.

The 1999 formal launch of BRASS was preceded by approximately 2 years as an incubation unit in the Institute of Materials Research and Engineering (IMRE) under its biomaterials program. This was also where the first of a series of propitious events that were to be a critical factor for BRASS making it began. I highlight two events to alert you that you must be ready to capitalize on them when they happen, i.e. you must be hands-on. In late 1997, we were in the process of ordering endotoxin reagent to perform one of our tests. The usual supplier for some reason did not respond to our request for a quotation. Exasperated, the staff handling the matter went on the web and found an alternate supplier, Charles River Laboratories (CRL) that sold directly to end-users. She purchased what she needed from them and performed the tests. More remarkably, she recognized that an opportunity existed to represent this manufacturer as an agent for our region and brought this fact to our attention. Khoon Seng and I picked up on her suggestion, and as the saying goes *the rest is history*! This is a real world example of listening to your people on the ground, eventually leading to a revenue source that sustained BRASS financially through a prolonged start-up phase! This was our *bootstrap*. Today, this reagent is still used for tests in our laboratory services offering, and BRASS remains their local agent generating revenues from both tests services and product representation streams. In recent times, the relationship has expanded under the present management.

To have a testing laboratory suitable for the biomed industry requires certain credentials. For BRASS it meant obtaining the ISO17025 (ISO/IEC Guide 25 in 1999) laboratory accreditation. Obtaining ISO17025 informs your clients and regulatory agencies that the laboratory practices conform to an International Standard, and test reports from the facility are recognized and accepted. We also acquired ISO9001 certification, as we planned to participate in the design phase of medical devices. We applied and were successful in securing a government SME (Small and Medium Enterprise) assistance grant that permitted us to hire a consultant to assist us in obtaining both accreditation and certification. This launched our tests services business that has continued to grow.

A component part of medical devices safety testing involves the use of animal models. This required a sizable capital investment. On the path to figuring out how to add this capability to our offering, another unexpected event occurred. In December 2001, I was invited to give a presentation to a panel of industry experts brought in by the Industry Relations office of the NUS to review the concepts and performance of its portfolio of start-up companies, of which BRASS was one. One of the reviewers, a seasoned entrepreneur, asked whether I knew about NAMSA, to which I replied affirmatively. He made the point that BRASS was attempting to do similar things to NAMSA, to which I replied that we were. This reviewer stated he knew NAMSA's CEO and asked whether I would like to be put in touch with NAMSA and explore synergistic tie-ups. I replied positively. In July 2002, I received an e-mail from the NAMSA Vice President (VP) of International Business at the time. She informed me she was visiting Singapore and proposed a meeting. We had a 2-hour meeting at BRASS. At the end of the meeting, she offered and I accepted, after receiving the go-ahead from legal counsel for BRASS, to represent

NAMSA services in Asia. This was a big break. BRASS could offer its own test services, as well as provide its clients with an extended offering. Remember the *black hole* scenario experienced by device manufacturers mentioned earlier? With this tie-up, customers interfaced with BRASS for NAMSA services. As NAMSA representatives, BRASS staff (after the requisite training) explain the finer details to the satisfaction of the client, as well as provide updates of the status of their tests being done in the USA. This was a giant step forward in meeting client expectations for both organizations.

4.2.4 Introspection

I started out with a goal for BRASS to be an Asian type of NAMSA. That goal has been streamlined, as reality has a way of teaching you that although you can start out with grandiose notions, they will remain just that and can do you more harm than good if you do not learn from them, tame them and let them move you in a direction towards success. Today, BRASS (www.brass-asiapacific.com) revenue streams are from BRASS tests services performed in house, CRL Endotoxin reagent trading and NAMSA test services representation. The laboratory has continually been successful in annual reviews under ISO17025 and is expanding its offerings. I discontinued ISO 9001 as a business decision. We did one or two projects in developing medical devices, but dropped them as the business took off in the other areas.[viii] Costs savings no matter how nominal compared to our revenue is a factor that must be constantly reviewed and acted on. That's just good business practice: spend when you have to, save when you can.

Looking back, I was an amateur. I believed we were right to settle on BRASS, could do it and make it happen, and was only baffled by *why can't they see it will work* puzzlement. We put together a business plan (BP will be discussed in Chapter 6) that convinced us it could be done. I showed our draft business plan (Version 1.0) to a close friend who had run the Far East operations of a US Corporation for several years, he advocated caution.[ix] Let's just say I was not listening. Because sometimes after all that has been said and done, you just have to take the plunge and go for it despite the doomsayers. Trust your instincts and believe in your passion. Ultimately, only you can make the decision whether it is worth stepping off the edge of the world and believe you will not drop into the abyss.

[viii] Developing a new kidney dialyzer re-use equipment.

[ix] The more appropriate interpretation is probably closer to *"NUTS"*, a quote attributed to Brigadier General McAuliffe, US 101st Airborne Division, made during the *Battle of the Bulge*, December 1944.

If you asked me to start BRASS with what I now know, back then, would BRASS have remained a figment of my imagination? The answer is academic and I am glad I did not know too much back then, because what I did not know provided the compulsion to venture into the unknown. From today's perspective, I definitely would and could do it better and BRASS would likely be a different story. But it didn't turn out that bad. And of course, providence shone on us. 1996 was not 2000 when biomed exploded on the front pages of the local newspapers and TV channels! In other words, we got our feet wet before anyone thought of swimming in the pond and we had a lead-time. I am proud of what BRASS has achieved and that BRASS continues to be a leader (despite its size) in Singapore under the current board of directors and management.

In 2007, I disengaged from BRASS after guiding it to two continuous years of profit. I did return in mid-2009 at the beckoning of two major private shareholders, an episode that I will present in a later chapter.

4.3 INTEGRATED PLATFORM TECHNOLOGIES INC.: SETBACKS HAPPEN

By the year 2000, the university had patented four inventions from my research. As a staff of the university, it was my duty to assist the university in finding potential licensees for the IP developed from my research, or if so desired attempt to commercialize the IP through enterprise. Around that time, an e-mail was received from a company based in Atlantic Canada, regarding my research inventions. This company was exploring producing chitin from Atlantic shrimp shells. The big thing at the time was producing glucosamine from chitin. The CEO wanted to know if we had any other technologies related to chitin. I introduced him to my two patents on chitin and suggested some of the possible applications that the inventions could be applied to, as well as linking him with the industry relations office of the university. I subsequently received another e-mail from the CEO asking me to be a consultant to his company as he planned to license the chitin technology from NUS.

At our first meeting in Halifax, Nova Scotia, Canada, it became clear that a pay-as-you-go consultant was not what the Newfoundland Company needed. The IP in the patents had potential, but they required refinement to define useful products. The CEO was determined to have a go. I was interested to see how far the patents could progress along the development path, and decided to assist him by providing the scientific support sought. To make the matter tidy, a new company Integrated Platform Technologies Inc (IPT) was set up, and I accepted some shareholding in lieu of consulting fees.

The CEO expended a major effort on writing business plans, chasing down possible leads for partnership arrangements and giving presentations at various fund raising events. I went to Newfoundland a couple of times as scientific back-up to assist him in the big presentations. He managed to raise some capital and was in line for a large grant for product development that fell through in the end. The CEO continued to plod on, but after 2 years of chasing funding, I decided to terminate my participation, as a growing BRASS and a continuing research program required my full attention.

On reflection, the inventions were good but preliminary. They demonstrated general utility but lacked specific product distinction that one could articulate, the "*scientific solution chasing applications scenario*" discussed in Chapter 2. I went back to my research to refine the lessons I learnt from this episode, determined to find a formula that would turn research ideas into practical research that led to prototype development and product. Eventually, the bone cement project materialized and led to another point where decisions had to be made.

4.4 ANATOMIC REPLACEMENT MATERIALS PRIVATE LIMITED: REFINING THE FORMAT

The orthopedic surgeon (OS) in the bone cement project was keen to realize a product from the invention. Plan A was to come up with a prototype for the OS to interest one of the existing bone cement manufacturers. Of course we also had to have plan B, i.e. bring the product to market. This meant setting up an entity that would accommodate both plans. Both our institutions were informed of the intent to start a company and the licensing process was initiated. A product development plan and the groundwork for fund raising to develop the product via sub-contracts were devised. In late 2007, I took a year off from the university to pursue some personal matters, keeping in touch to assist the fund raising process where necessary. As the story goes, no funds were raised (a common occurrence) and the project was put on ice until my year away finished. During my absence, a company was also set up as Anatomic Replacement Materials Private Limited (ARM PL). Two clinicians[x] were registered as Directors.

Upon my return to Singapore, activities commenced. The prototype was developed with the assistance of one of BRASS' clients in his

[x]The other clinician was a US-based colleague with whom I had a research collaboration. He is very senior, well known and experienced with enterprises. He played the valuable role of sounding board for our ideas and plans.

manufacturing facilities that is ISO13485 qualified with no obligations. This channel was based on a relationship built over more than 10 years, and demonstrates the goodwill that sometimes exists among the small-time biomed manufacturing entrepreneur fraternity. There was also no conflict with his on-going business. A word of prudence, utilize goodwill sparingly. This prototyping was also made possible because NUS had given me formal permission to participate in ARM PL.

One other factor that had to be dealt with was the preparation of a biomaterial chemically.[xi] Through a PhD student's contacts in China, the initial chemistry work was settled. The crude material from China would be further processed in Singapore. I sought the assistance of my former Quality Assurance Manager at BRASS, who presently holds a teaching position at a technical college in Singapore. His bosses were supportive of the industry collaboration. The pilot study was performed successfully.

ARM PL was the best scenario to date, an invention co-developed by a clinician. In this instance the bone cement is a potential Class 3 implant medical device. Most of the details of the applied R&D have already been described in Chapter 3. The results supported moving forward. Suffice to state also that every patient safety and performance factor had satisfied our checklist pass criterion. In addition, 10 years had elapsed since the BRASS concept was born. I had learnt some know-how in manufacturing, and gained sensible confidence and experience to attempt product development. Interacting with a manufacturing facility and having additional resources in NAMSA to call on should the need arise (albeit that have to be paid) was reassuring.

Producing a prototype felt great and it proved the concept worked, and as bonus, it was done on an essentially zero budget platform. In order to proceed further, we had to raise funds. After 3 years of unsuccessful attempts at fund raising, we reluctantly discontinued the venture. You will note that in the prolog, it was alluded that one of the companies has a *to be continued* status. This referred to ARM PL. Why? One factor contributing to our *stop* decision was that the use of bone cement for the intended first clinical use, spinal surgery, was waning slightly in practice by orthopedic surgeons in 2011 following some clinical studies reports. The pendulum can easily change down the road if and when new clinical data surfaces to *overturn* the current thinking. The clinician in this project is also continuing the research in bone cement and may develop a better formulation or procedure. As only time will tell, it is premature to conclusively close this episode.

[xi]This was eventually to be the deal breaker.

4.5 VENTURING FORWARD

I tell the BRASS, IPT and ARM stories as I experienced them. I was filled constantly with self-doubt, discouraged more times than I care to count and was embarrassed often enough in my novice approach and manner of handling business. I relate my stories to impress on you that you do not have to know everything to try. You only have to have a desire and a tolerance level for uncertainty that most people are uncomfortable with, and a disregard for "saving face".

You may also have noted that through it all, I kept my daytime job. It was my choice. Personal concerns aside, the daytime job permitted a degree of financial fallback that was utilized periodically, especially in the first 5 years of BRASS. I was also the beneficiary of an NUS policy officially granting me the flexibility of taking one day a week off from my official duties to pursue the BRASS venture, as well as permission to be a non-executive director in the company.[xii]

In general the people I met on the streets were either politely dismissive or were very kind to give me a hand in going forward. Finally, there is one key lesson you learn in these endeavors that is seldom mentioned but ever present. Once you launch, to succeed you've got to hold on past the point of common sense, continue to bear the uncertainty each day brings, and know that beyond your final tolerance threshold, there is light that will lead you out of the proverbial tunnel. If you have support, great, but know that at the crunch times, you probably will have to face it alone.

One final note about IPT and ARM. I did not get anywhere with either venture, but the lessons learnt laid the foundation for my present undertaking, developing a Class 2 medical device using the sub-contract model described in later chapters. Only the future can tell how it will turn out.

So I have enlightened you on what to consider in performing applied academic research, and told you my experiences. Are you one of those scientists, engineers or clinicians who secretly feel that there is so much potential in your present environment that can be turned into products and services but you are stuck in a bureaucracy? Do you think this suits you? Want to give it a try? Ready to take the step to venture forward? Let's discuss what is in store and how to evaluate the center of attention in all this, you!

[xii] This was the policy at the time. Policies change from time to time and may not be the prevailing practice for a myriad of reasons.

4.6 THE IDEAL BIOMEDICAL PARTICIPANT PREREQUISITE

To begin, it is pertinent to address an obvious fact, why does this industry exist? The biomed industry is there because someone who is ill, injured, or otherwise medically compromised, requires attention. This is often construed as clinical intervention through suitable medical treatment. Making available the right medication, providing surgeons with the appropriate surgical tools, devices and associated hardware, having paramedics use the proper equipment, or giving the patients themselves the relevant home aids, are examples of how the biomed industry has responded. The preferred outcome is always *extending* the patient's life,[xiii] and more importantly, improving the patient's quality of life.

An entrepreneur in the biomed industry must have a desire to apply their talents to help clinically challenged individuals lead a more fulfilled life. Regardless of the nature of one's role, involvement in the healthcare, pharmaceutical and/or medical technology industries ideally is a noble undertaking. The first reward is the satisfaction that one's skill and knowledge has contributed to the betterment of a person's health that may otherwise have been further compromised and/or expire.

Know that in the end, your product is to be used on a patient who wants to survive, and has loved ones who want that patient to continue living. This fact must dominate your mind in every decision and action. You cannot shortchange the patient. This is the ideal essence of the biomed industry, doing what will benefit the patient.

Exoneration for the boldness in venturing on an undertaking, fame and financial rewards must always be secondary. Therefore, a choice to participate in the biomed endeavor even as a researcher should be approached with awareness that criterion number one is *for the patient's benefit and safety.* It is the author's contention that if you do not subscribe to this philosophy, you should not be involved in this industry, period.

Most participants that I have come across in this industry are honest about why they are involved in biomed. They have a sincere passion to solve medical challenges that can help patients. That a business entity is necessary to realize these good intentions is not contradictory. And there is nothing sinister or malicious in establishing a biomed enterprise to chase financial fortune. All that is necessary is that while chasing the financial gains, an entrepreneur's judgment should not be clouded, as the intent is always first and foremost about the patient's wellbeing.

[xiii] It is a personal preference not to use the term "save". From my perspective, all lifeforms will eventually terminate and "extending" is more appropriate.

Where do you begin? It starts with accepting responsibility for what you are about to embark on and letting conscience be your rudder as you maneuver the pathway to building your research program or start-up. Constantly emphasize to yourself to do what is right for the patient, do it well, each time, all the time. Embrace this philosophy and do not take short cuts or compromise on standards you set, especially when the going gets tough. And it will appear to cost, publication wise or financially at the start. However, if you have factored these costs in your research or business plan and are willing to endure the dictate of this unique criterion, the end result can be a financially viable enterprise with an added *feel good* factor. Certainly the industry has seen its share of failures and scandals in this regard, the substantive fines that have been imposed on a few big pharma companies in recent years come to mind, and imperfections linger. But like an unspoken code of conduct, this premise and acceptance of the accompanying responsibility that the patient's welfare must never be compromised, on the whole permeates throughout the biomedical industry.

You do not have to be a martyr above all else, relegating the priorities of good business and other attendant goals. Be sensible and when "push turns to shove", do what's right within the law, and act ethically and morally, responsibly. A case in point to encourage you to move in this direction is a story relating to Merck, a leading global biomed company.[1] Some years ago, the company was faced with a dilemma. Merck scientists had discovered a cure for a dreadful disease called onchocerciasis or river blindness. The predicament lay in the fact that the cost of development, manufacture and distribution of the drug was prohibitively high. And the intended recipients of the cure were predominantly the poor in Africa and parts of Central and South America who could not afford to pay for the drug. Merck had the choice to not produce the drug and let millions suffer their fate from the disease or produce it at a great financial loss. Ultimately, the company resorted to their founder's George W. Merck's principle, "We try never to forget that medicine is for the people. It is not for the profits. The profits follow, and if we have remembered that, they have never failed to appear". This medication has been produced under the trade name Mectizan® and donated to "wherever needed for as long as needed". This decision is an excellent illustration of how this industry responds.

The above example is not an exception. In February 2005, my US university colleague arranged a meeting with the CTO (Chief Technology Officer) of a medical device start-up in Redwood City, California. When we arrived and met the CTO, he did not start by introducing us to what the company did. He brought us to an area where files were kept. He started by stating that to be in the medical device business, you have to keep these files. This particular series was on design as stated in the

QSR (Quality Systems Regulations) put out by the US-FDA and is mandatory to comply for a medical device company selling in the USA.[2] He spent the first half hour of our meeting telling us about the responsibility of the industry. I was very impressed by how the CTO started, as well as the passion he had for his company's product for helping people. Another fine case in point of the attitude that is prevalent in the biomedical industry. Get the job done right and the money will come is not a philosophy to buy into easily. It appears to be one of the most unexpected paradoxes, but from what I experienced with BRASS; George Merck's words are true.

4.7 TO KNOW IF YOU SHOULD START

The first order of business here is to re-state that having a good idea is not a good enough reason to think about starting a business. You can be your own worst enemy because you live the idea constantly, yet you cannot convince anyone else it is a good idea. You and others must question your objectivity. Remember, a decision based more on emotions usually does not portend well. But you eventually have to make a choice to do something if the potential is to be realized because you believe in it. Let's begin the journey with considering your options when you have a biomed research opportunity that you want to carry out using the *needs-driven clinician-guided* method with the intent of starting-up a *runway biomed enterprise*.

4.7.1 The "Painless" Option

This option is about performing your research well and when results indicate, declaring your invention to your institution and having your institution patent the IP. Seeking a licensee and becoming a consultant to the licensee follow this. You will probably work with your institutional agents to license the IP, or may even be asked to find the licensee since you are the expert in the area of interest. More importantly, you will want to position yourself as the person to interact with the licensee on a longer-term basis as a consultant. Be aware that even when the IP is licensed, what at the start may appear promising can lead nowhere because the science can be surpassed before the product is launched, unforeseen issues especially associated with costs curtail the development, or the licensees themselves get sold or fold up, among many other reasons.

However, this is the best option for the majority in academia that I strongly advocate. This sounds contrary to what I champion in this book, but the cold hard facts are that for anyone, *runway* start-up biomed entrepreneurship 1101[xiv] is hard and should not be taken lightly. You have been duly notified.

4.7.2 The "Soft" Option

This option is about participating in a start-up, but having the luxury of an arms-length relationship. It may be a member of your academic team, usually a graduating or recently graduated student who plans to head the venture. Alternatively you hire someone that you direct. You maintain a relationship as the consultant or a member of the Board of Directors. This option works better the more senior you are in academia, as you have clout and contacts to assist the enterprise that may permit you leeway in defining the terms of your engagement to the venture. You will probably also have more available funds to handle the financial obligation. It also permits you to continue your research endeavors that may profit the venture down the road.

But you are unlikely to be fully immersed in the venture to the point you feel the *pulse and excitement* on a regular basis, likely missing out on the full *runway* entrepreneur experience. Still, this is a credible alternative and in the event it turns out well, you can savor the satisfaction of your contribution and of course, enjoy looking at your bank account monthly statements increasing positively, perhaps even exponentially. This is a very reasonable trade-off.

4.7.3 The "Tough" Option

This option is ultimately what this book is about. To be a *runway* entrepreneur is for you if you can meet the following conditions, and after navigating the next section, conclude if this is what you want.

The pre-conditions to meet for the would be biomed *runway entrepreneur* from academia are:

1. Must have developed the science over at least 5 to 10 years. This time span is arbitrary and is only a rough guide. This length of time is normal to turn out something useful, but your situation may be different. The idea is that you have built a scientific foundation post-PhD and what you worked on can be turned into a potential application as a viable business. Do not be impatient. The wave frequency in biomed is dissimilar to what is happening in the electronics consumer industry, where each new wave appears every

---

[xiv] This 4 digit code is a typical numerical representation assigned to the most basic entry level module/course for a subject in academia.

3 to 6 months, no more than 12 months. If you keep your eye on the goal, the time spent building up your foundation will pay off.

2. Know and accept what you put on the line:

   a. Your reputation at the start as well as at the end.

   b. Your money. Sweat equity has no value/credibility here (refer to Chapter 7).

   c. Your integrity. Your shareholders put their trust in you. This is a huge responsibility.

   d. You are the driver/leader. This is different from someone you hire to do the job. The bottom line is they can quit, you cannot.

These are what you bring to the table. The first is about your scientific credibility; the second is about your character. Ponder them over carefully.

So you are enlightened on the three courses of action before you. There's a saying I learnt from one of my Virginia Tech Chemistry professors who was originally from Brooklyn, NY, that is appropriate here: "You pays your moneys and makes your choice". To quote the knight in the movie *Indiana Jones: The Last Crusade* "Choose wisely".

4.8 "FINALS"

Once you can accept what you bring to the table, the final step is to work through the *1 H and 4 Ws*, i.e. *how, what, where, when and why* that are probably bearing down your thoughts. How? No one taught me how to get started. I had many people tell me various ways of how. But guess what? None of them ever started a business, let alone a biomed business. They stayed in their safe ports of continued well paying employment. I did, learnt, survived and thrived. But how, what, when and where can wait for the next few chapters. And they need not be attempted if you do not answer the crucial question, *why*.

Why is the only question you must answer completely and satisfactorily because you are the person who must be convinced! *Why* must be audacious enough to give you the courage to start; *why* must be clear enough to motivate you; *why* must be intense enough to sustain your passion and determination. *Why* must be fanatical enough, that to give up is so absurd that continuing is your only rational choice. And when the "stuff hits the fan", and there will be occasions when this will happen, the reason *why* will be what holds you together to endure.

Why must also answer how you motivate others, because you need partners, workers, investors and customers. Their motivation need not, and most likely will not, be the same as yours. They must be given a reason to *buy-in*.

So make a list of the *whys* you want to do this. *Why* typically has two interrelated components, purpose and motivation.

4.8.1 Purpose

Some of the reasons that would fall under this category are: *saint syndrome*; fortune, fame or both; and unfulfilled desire. There are many others but three are enough to enlighten *purpose*.

The *saint syndrome* refers to setting on a *bona fide* altruistic course. This to most people will sound improbable unless it is backed up by sustained genuine behavior commensurate with the purpose. Furthermore, if this is your true purpose, it will be hard to convince any party to give you funds. The credibility factors aside, the people who are looking for financial investment opportunities will definitely not appreciate you misrepresenting your purpose. It is far better to start a *bona fide* biomed enterprise, make all the money you can, and then pursue the *saint* causes you want with the money you make.

If your intent is to make a fortune or achieve fame, may I suggest activities such as spending time with the stock market or investing in real estate for the former, where if done right your chances are much better; or try being a celebrity by acting, singing, excelling in sports or embarking on a political career; or stay in academia and build your reputation, it is a more straightforward option. The reason is that you will rarely achieve the recognition or wealth sought unless what you have is a blockbuster and that is rather difficult to do, as indicated earlier, the cherries are very rare. Also, as stated previously, there is some nobleness in doing biomed that places fame and fortune as a consequence of success rather than the other way around.

Unfulfilled desire probably comes close to, in all probability, the best purpose for starting-up biomed. You may have stumbled onto something that is interesting, and if done right could lead to a medical or related solution. You have done your best in trying to ignite interest, but there are no takers. The only recourse open is to abandon or do it on your own. Your innate talent and reasoning works on your sub-conscious and grows to a point where you can no longer ignore the desire. You are ready.

4.8.2 Motivation

Some of the driving forces that set and sustain you in starting-up could be: *ticked-off* by someone or something; something in your life (past, present or future); something to prove to yourself. Again, here I highlight three issues knowing that motivation has countless origins.

Being *ticked-off* by someone or something in many instances is a strong motivation factor. Your *anti-fans* may learn about your entrepreneurial aspirations that can rock the boat of academia and collectively derive a way to restrain you; or the bureaucracy (more to do with people than system) just was not ready (or does not want to be ready) to operate in the twenty-first century. Channeling anger and frustration creatively is fine, but ensure that this is directed purposefully and sustained properly, otherwise the "demons" can sneak their way into your demeanor, tripping you up.

There are those who can be motivated by something in their life, past, present or future. Perhaps a tragic disease like cancer took a loved one, or an accident in the present is the initiator, or being told that a medical condition will worsen with time, can be a powerful motivator. There is nothing like a personal loss or crisis that can propel a person to direct their energies to right a perceived injustice, unfairness or handle a curve ball that life has placed in their path, when managed well.

Something to prove to oneself is the motivation I like. Athletes know that the most awesome competitors are themselves; and warriors know that the greatest enemy are themselves. To challenge oneself is the most fascinating goal to set. Do it well.

4.9 THREE STEPS FROM OBSCURITY TO NOTORIETY

Once you have identified the purpose and motivation to start a biomed enterprise, you must dare yourself to clarify that these are the fundamental reasons before you proceed further. Ask yourself if these are strong enough factors that will make you work maniacally to achieve; provide you with sustainable enthusiasm and inspire others to join you; and make you brave enough to *beg* for funds. Doing this right is essential.

Finally, you still have to make the decision. If your answer is no, that's fine. It is good to know what you do not want so you can pursue with passion what drives you. If you are uncomfortable, you can consider stopping here or defer your decision to a later date, or until more favorable circumstances occur. If you are sure this is for you, awesome. And sometimes, even if all the indicators state otherwise, you may choose to go for it. The best reason then is, *why not?*

Inevitably, when you have answered *why* and the overwhelming answer is to move forward, you set yourself on a course that takes you from academic obscurity to entrepreneurial notoriety (of the good type) in three steps. You do so because you can no longer contain what has been building up inside you.

STEP 1 IS TO *MAKE THE DECISION* BASED ON YOUR SCIENCE TO START

You have been entrusted with the talent to do special things. Discover, invent and explain has so far been what you are about. The decision to apply all these cumulative experiences to be an entrepreneur makes you unique. It does not matter if you blow it down the road. You immediately loose your obscurity because you are no longer one of the many. You now "live in a fish bowl". Many will ignore you, others condemn you and some will encourage you. But they cannot be like you.

STEP 2 IS TO *ACT ON THE DECISION* TO START-UP

This decision cannot have come easy. Winners don't dwell on what they cannot control or improve. They work on the issues that pave the way for success. So begin.

STEP 3 IS TO *STRIVE UNTIL YOU SUCCEED* HOWEVER YOU HAVE DEFINED SUCCESS TO BE

The world normally measures success in terms of financial achievement and recognition. For biomed, as you now know, it should be first about making a product that fulfills a medical need at an affordable price. This may not often be the case. So do it well and the world will be thankful (even though you may remain unknown to those you have helped).

4.10 WELCOME TO YOUR NEW JOB TITLE: THE SUPREME FIELD COMMANDER

You are now *runway entrepreneur in waiting*. You have also automatically set yourself up to be the only leader. You are going to be much like a general at the battlefront, the supreme field commander. You as the entrepreneur go into battle leading from the front.

Taking and handling responsibility is a personal thing. Some people have the natural ability to take on and handle seemingly large responsibilities with ease, while others cringe and avoid it as much as they can. Surround yourself with as many advisors, counselors and experts as you want or need. It is good to solicit as much information and advice as possible from those you trust to make decisions. But you have to make the tough and final decisions. You have to call the shots. This is what you have signed up for when you start an enterprise, to be the final decision maker. A phrase popularized by US President Harry S. Truman is appropriate, "the buck stops here" with you.

This completes the preparatory work. From the preceding chapters, it is clear:

1. Biomed offers ample business opportunities.
2. Academia offers a good starting platform.
3. Leveraging the strengths of academia while there is important.

4. Embarking on a *runway biomed enterprise* from academia is a personal choice.

This concludes what can be termed Part 1, *the background*. Next we proceed to look at starting-up a biomed *runway* enterprise, *the build-up*.

Real World Lessons Learnt

General

1. Biomed is not about you, what you want to do and achieve. It's about the patient you want to help live longer with a better quality of life that science, using the skills, talents and opportunities presented to you, can provide.
2. Service business brings in revenues fast.
3. Product business has a greater chance to stall.

Specific

1. You must know why you are doing this entrepreneur thing.
2. The first step to success is about overcoming your self-doubt and fears. You have to believe in yourself and have the courage.
3. There is only one driver. Guess who?

Quote for the Chapter

The second of two quotes from the same source on the two key factors needed to start an enterprise.

There arrives a moment when you have to get off the fence:

"A journey of a thousand miles begins with a single step" ***Attributed to one of China's most renowned sages: Confucius (551–479 BC)***

References

[1] <www.merck.com/about/cr/mectizan/home.html>.
[2] <http://www.fda.gov/MedicalDevices/DeviceRegulationandGuidance/ PostmarketRequirements/QualitySystemsRegulations/ucm2005736.htm>.

CHAPTER

5

What is the Business?

From Academia to Entrepreneur.
DOI: http://dx.doi.org/10.1016/B978-0-12-410516-4.00005-7

5.1 SO YOU'VE GOT AN IDEA FOR A BUSINESS!

Ideas are very dangerous; damned if you do, damned if you don't, a pain in the proverbial derrière! An idea left alone, shelved in memory is soon forgotten but can one day bring you immense regret because someone else may act on that same idea and achieve something with it. Perhaps, not as good as you would have done, but at that stage it does not matter. It's NOT your idea! If you act on the idea, it can also cause you endless grief and misery, especially if it leads nowhere after you have expended much time, effort and money. BUT the up side of acting on your idea is that you create the opening that may lead to the success you sought and deserve.

Regardless of how you feel about ideas, what must be said first about ideas is that they are not as unique as you would like or believe them to be. Think about it. As declared in Chapter 2, we are living in a time of human history where the human population is increasing rapidly. The parallel increase in the number of trained biomed-savvy individuals and the probability that many people can have the same thought about a particular piece of science as you is now higher was also discussed in Chapter 2. It is an exciting yet daunting time to be a clinician, an engineer, or a scientist. The pace of scientific advancement and change is fast, and it can only get faster. If you have an idea for a new product that you would like to realize through starting-up a biomed enterprise, your window of opportunity is probably small. So what will it be? Continue to dwell on the matter, looking for more data and input? Or take the bold step and begin? No decision can take forever to make. There will always be a degree of uncertainty in any endeavor. The only course of action open to you is to do all you can to mitigate the risks. Perhaps applying General Colin Powell's lesson #15 may help you out of your indecision.[1]

Once you have a good idea that you believe in and have made your decision to go for it, you really only have one option. You must act. Only if you act on the idea do you give yourself the chance to go beyond the starting line, testing the feasibility, building, shaping and improving the idea into a success story and not letting your idea be reduced to, or stay, a mere dream. And it is presumed you will do your best to the end. This is because the world is full of *initiative* but low on "finitiative" (completing the initiative). In other words, many people start things they do not sustain or complete. Think of the perennial New Year's resolutions made by many to lose weight after a month of feasting and drinking. How many enthusiastic determined January flab warriors slogging it out in the gym are present and accounted for once February comes around? It is important to start, make a commotion if you want and have the *lion dance* display as is typical in Asia. But making a good start is not a condition for success. Completing what you started is, *eventually*, only what counts. It does not matter how it turns out. If the end point is where you planned or better, congratulations. If not, determine a suitable place to wind up, learn the lessons and move on. You will never have to ask that question *"what if I had only* tried......*"*. So, have ideas. And once you decide to go forward, *act*. See it through the preset end point. And most of all enjoy the journey.

5.2 THE OPPORTUNITY OF A LIFETIME?

Let's digress to academia again. As previously covered, there are situations where the science is championed from the start and an enterprise is given full funding from the pertinent sponsor channels. This is great and it has happened when the *indicators for success were clearly evident* to its proponents who often have the clout and money to push the concept out. For example in Singapore, MerLion Pharmaceutical P. L.[2] and ES Cell International P.L.[3] are two such companies that came to life as an off-shoot of research performed in public-funded institutions.

In the case where the institution owns the intellectual property (IP) or technology, typically preference is to license the IP to suitable parties who are willing to pay the license fee, the negotiated royalty terms and other related costs. For the institution, this option has no apparent downside as cost recovery is upfront and the licensee bears the financial risks. These scenarios are out of context for further comment as we concentrate on individuals or groups of individuals starting up businesses where the presence of a *white knight* is non-existent.

When there are no takers for the IP, or where the IP or know-how does not meet institutional criteria for take-up after due-diligence, despite one or more of the inventors' strong assertions, the ground is left wide open and ripe for *runway* opportunists.

5.2.1 Why You?

There are three plausible reasons why unfavorable circumstances are suited to the *runway entrepreneur in waiting*. First, history is littered with examples of scientific breakthroughs turned into business ventures that have not fared well. These risky propositions are difficult to get right. Perhaps one of the better-known examples is Advanced Tissue Sciences' (ATS).[4] ATS was a favorite in the 1990s, an innovator in tissue-engineered wound healing materials that was making good headway, but the company ultimately went into bankruptcy. Reasons have been offered for ATS' demise (as well as for Organogenesis, referenced in the same article). The collapse of such companies has had a sobering effect on many biomed investors who have become more selective, i.e. it has become harder to recruit sponsors.

In addition, one thing I have noted for companies with good funding at the start is their normally more corporate-like structure from the outset. One of the possible occurrences in such a structure is that the management team is business focused, while the scientific team is science (not necessarily product) focused. Therefore, you have two different mindsets with their own way of doing things within in one entity, and this requires effort to gel. It takes a CEO with the maestro's touch to orchestrate the diverse groups into success. Matters are more straightforward when handled by the *runway* entrepreneur who will shuttle between the two extremes by necessity since both components reside in her. She can take a promising scientific advance into a *runway* enterprise that eventually succeeds.

Second, there are ventures that will never fetch the multi-billions sought, rather the modest millions that again do not attract the institutional investor, but are ideal for the biomed *runway* entrepreneur. The biomed *runway* entrepreneur who is not only about *value propositions* can tolerate better a longer time horizon to show returns, working on a modest budget for a purpose he believes in. There are many *orphan* causes that are vast opportunities waiting for someone to pick up. But most often, no one does. You may want to look here, as going where no one wants to go gives you a free shot and relatively competition-less ground until you achieve.

Third, in many instances *blockbusters* usually do not begin life as obvious superstars. There is normally a lag time between when a scientific discovery is made and when it turns into a business application with subsequent celebrity status. And yet it may never happen if a champion who is more often derided or marginalized at the start, does not surface.[5] There lies a potential start-up where the *runway* entrepreneur is the only thing standing between "never ran" and success.

5.2.2 Can You Make a Difference?

So how should an entrant wishing to stake a claim in the minefield of potential biomed entrepreneurship go about entering the fray? First, you must accept that there is a considerable business experience credibility gap and financial handicap compared to the big boys, much like the oft-told Bible story of David, the puny Bethlehemite teenager with a slingshot, a stone and no combat experience battling the giant Philistine seasoned warrior Goliath with his array of weapons and impenetrable armor.[6] David won, and so can you.

At this stage, contemplate what separates you from the pack, i.e. your one-upmanship edge that positions you to be the one to succeed where others will falter and fail. What can you use in your bag of scientific tricks to exploit and develop the situation at hand into a winning proposition? You must address all doubts posed by yourself, your close associates and others you are accountable to or responsible for. A special mention here about spouses. They should be on board otherwise you can find yourself in a quandary down the road. A spouse can support you emotionally and financially (they can take a job to lessen the financial burden). I do not advocate both to be in the venture because it can add to the stress to succeed, but that is a personal choice.

You should also ask the question why no one else wants it. Is it non-obvious, too difficult, or something else? You can have lots of ideas, but many can be just too costly to manufacture. Sometimes, the technology may not be available in the format you require and you will have to resolve the matter. Other times, the need has not manifested itself at the time you thought of the solution and you have to create the demand. Don't ask your drinking (or running, biking or whatever) buddies and well-wishers. Do a serious, objective and thorough evaluation.

Next, confirm how you are going to make money. A feasible science-based biomed business venture must have a clear foundation of what is to be done to obtain a PROFIT. The profit can come from a product or a service but cannot be *vapoirè chaud* or hot air. If it is a product, it must be realistic, a proper pathway mapped out to show proof of concept, achieve prototyping, pilot and scale-up manufacturing, and in the market within a reasonable timeframe. Remember, you perspire more with a product company compared to a service company. You are the last to get paid. The institution, lawyers, sub-contractors, and practically everyone else are paid first in order for your concept to finally end up as a product. And then you have to sell it. Do you have the mental, emotional and physical strength to endure until your payoff comes? I am not making this up. This is what you are going to face, so be very sure. There's a saying here that is appropriate: "Don't do the crime, if you can't do the time".[7] If it is a service, what is it that you are providing that would otherwise not be available, and why should parties choose you over other alternatives?

In both instances, if the profit is not real in the timeframe you have set, you don't have a business. A distinction is made between revenue and profit because you can generate great revenue and still be in the *red*. There is no other way to define profit. PROFIT is what you get to keep after deducting what is due to all your staff, other overheads, your creditors and the taxman, of course taking for granted that all your debtors, i.e. customers, have paid in full. And the profit quantum must be in the sphere where it makes the effort worthwhile. While your motivations for embarking on this venture may be varied, it is the potential profit that ultimately justifies the effort you will put in and is the main factor others will place a bet on you. Remember, it is not about you being a nice guy or gal, *it's business.*

In addition, your product or service should not be a *one-hit* wonder, i.e. you should have a stream of products or services that can ensure sustainable growth beyond the introduction of the first product or service. Realize that a product has a lifecycle and once you turn out the first product, you can go in many directions to sustain and grow the business such as new innovations, be bought out, acquire other businesses or products, etc. but you cannot rest on your one laurel and expect the world to continually beat a path to your door. Business and the business environment are dynamic. You must always be aware of what is going on and not shut yourself up in your own world enthusing about your next offering while the world and your competition pass you by.

Furthermore, creating and producing a product is one thing. Establishing the distribution channel to bring your product to the market is a whole new ball of wax that takes time. Rarely does a start-up have the marketing savvy or financial muscle to sustain a product launch until it is successful. You may have to form appropriate alliances or make deals to see you through. You will have to contemplate over how firm these deals are. Alliances and deals are only as good as the agreement, the clauses in them you sign and the extent of law compliance and, most importantly, enforcement in the country you do business in. Linking up with a partner that has a strong marketing arm and experience is something that should be considered, but always keep in mind that you have to protect your own interests. You must be aware of what you may have to give up to get on the fast track to market the service or product. You do not want to end up just being an original equipment manufacturer (OEM) supplying a product at a relatively modest markup while others take the lion's share of the profits. Last and most important, you should be aware that having another layer between your customers and you means that market intelligence and customer feedback may not be as effective, since you are not likely to have direct interaction with your end user and the initial launch period can be crucial for you to make the minor adjustments for product acceptance and proliferation.

5.2.3 It's More Than About You

Finally, while you are important for the venture to be born, business is about everyone else but you. The question to ask is: are there ready customers who will purchase your products or services? What do you promise? Can you really deliver on time, guarantee the quality and do it all at the right price? Of course, you cannot really answer many of these questions assuredly at this stage, but start asking them. Do not rely on a market survey, especially if done by someone else. A market survey can paint a tremendously beautiful picture, but ultimately someone must pay hard earned money at the premium you have set. We'll address how to convince customers about your product a little later in Section 5.6 Pricing. For now, how do you determine that you will have customers?

Look at what you plan to offer. If it is a product, are you a *me-too* or an improvement of an existing product, or truly a game changer? In all cases you are addressing an existing need and this is a good place to start. *Me-too* is mainly about *pricing* to convert, improvement is about *why* to convert and game changer is about *wow* to convert. All require effort but there are customers for all the categories, you only have to convert them.

Confirm you can beat the competition before you commit further time and money in development. Because you have S&T (science and technology), we shall disregard *me-too* client conversion and focus on *improvements* and *wow* products or services as what you should do to beat the competition. If a product, it was probably developed with a clinician's participation and there should be better confidence here that you have a *real improvement* or *wow* potential in hand. But still be prudent and do the verification by confirming independently the assertions. If it was developed without clinical assistance or a service, you have to work harder to determine that your improvements are significant enough. Find a few clinical experts and ask them about your intended product, conduct surveys of likely customers, or purchase market and product intelligence and evaluate them. Nothing is done in a vacuum these days and with effort, you will get enough information to verify whether your enterprise is worthwhile to start.

As has been discussed, the introduction and acceptance of a medical device can sometimes lie in the hands of a reputable clinician who may be resistant to using the better product despite the volumes of carefully documented data attesting to the product's safety and performance, and an approval from a regulatory agency. The reason is obvious, the clinician's reputation is on the line, and it takes time to convince and convert generally conservative clinicians to jump on the bandwagon of a new product. Why should they switch to a more revolutionary or updated product when conventional methods available are acceptable and economically more relevant? You must learn how to surmount these barriers to succeed.

5.3 GETTING TO THE STARTING LINE

Let's summarize what you have so far:

1. The clinical need (discussed in Chapters 2 and 3) or the demand for the biomed service is sound. You assess that your product/service is unique enough for a potential client base.

2. The business will be based on licensed or discarded biomed S&T developed principally by you in an academic institution (discussed in Chapter 3).

3. You take on a *runway entrepreneur* concept and will lead and do (discussed in Chapter 4).

4. Your first revenue goal is around $5 million with profits above 20% of revenue. You give yourself 5 years to achieve this. Your aspirations can be $100 million or more eventually. **Note:** You may not achieve the goal or the time horizon or both and that is fine. These are just preliminary targets to aim for.

5. First round funding is likely to be a trickle to modest sums. You have to put in cash as well (to be discussed in Chapter 7).

The first revenue goal of around $5 million may appear a very low sum, especially these days, but having a lower preliminary goal is sensible. Why? As presented in Chapter 1, a *runway* enterprise by concept is small. It is conceived to get you started, attain a level where you can gain entry into a larger endeavor, but also permits you to remain where you are if you prefer.

What can $5 million get you? $5 million can reasonably sustain a small business entity supporting more than 10 employees, pay for a facility monthly lease and most of your business functions. Therefore, if you were the more ambitious persona with a product that will definitely exceed the first revenue goal, it is still relevant. Because when you factor in that the first 2 years (and maybe the third as well) should be "revenue-less", the $5 million is not that easy to reach by year 5, and nothing to sneer at.

Whom you are serving is the purpose of the rest of this chapter.

5.4 DO YOU HAVE A VIABLE BUSINESS?

You are thoroughly convinced that you have got a winner. You are now also aware you have to rigorously think through the impact of regulatory matters on your potential business. You remain undeterred and are now eager to move forward to put a plan together. But as stated earlier in the chapter, a business is set up to make profit, a very simple principle. That you exploit the S&T you love is a plus. Therefore, while you may have a good product or service that can satisfy the regulatory issues at hand, can what you intend to build survive and later thrive as a business, i.e. *do you have a viable business*? What, you may ask, am I getting at since I covered the basics already? The answer is that there is still one more piece of the puzzle missing in the preliminaries that precede putting a business plan together.

Full marks if you realized no real numbers have been mentioned so far and you can't get very far if you don't have a clue about what constitutes profit in real dollar terms. The missing piece is about looking at the financial worthiness of the undertaking. How do you go about determining this? The following process illuminates what could be done.

1. Understand where you fit in the whole scheme of things in dollar terms (Section 5.5).
2. Next is about pricing that has two components, costs and margin (Section 5.6).
3. You add to pricing the estimated cost that you require to get to the point that you deliver your first product or service (Section 5.7).

In a nutshell, to get the business going, you need an idea of how much funds you have to obtain or set aside in start-up capital and the working capital.

5.5 REVENUE FUNDAMENTALS

Figure 5.1 depicts three contributing questions: Where is the $? How much $ is yours? How long to the $? as segments of a pie.

The question *Where is the $?* challenges you to consider the total market size for your product or service where your venture fits, i.e. the total pie. There are usually a few cherries on top of the pie, the *biggie* prizes that we have touched on previously and disregard here.

The question *How much $ is yours?* challenges you to consider your best guess as to your cut of the pie that you hope to get. Nobody will get the complete pie. If your final slice is 20% you're doing great; 50% excellent to fantastic; 80% or more implies most of the scientists and entrepreneurs who are your competitors are brain-dead or is it you!

The question *How long to the $?* is very important because if you are going to take forever, you won't achieve anything. Timing is everything, because the window of opportunity is your perpetual enemy. *Competitors never took a lesson in taking their turn*, and your innovation is one of very many innovations!

Why are these questions important?

Where is the $? Will become your enterprise's vision that you eventually develop into your ultimate goal (however you have conceived it).
How much $ is yours? Will become your company's mission from where your focus will evolve (path to your ultimate goal).
How long to the $? Will become your first market reach that will give rise to your business strategy to get there (first $5 million).

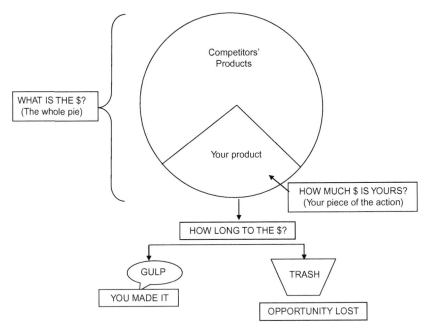

FIGURE 5.1 What is the business? Pie chart.

Ponder these questions carefully as we go through the details. It is challenging but not prohibitive to start a biomed-based business. *The bottom line is*: business is about making money. Good science does not equate to a good science-based business venture.

<h2 style="text-align:center">5.6 PRICING</h2>

Establishing the selling price of a product is an art, but there are basics that you have to satisfy.

First, you have to cover your costs. There are three main costs:

1. Development costs – this is a one-time cost for each product or service you offer.
2. Operating and overhead costs – this is a recurring cost.
3. Cost per unit of product or service – this is another recurring cost.

Second, you have to determine the margin (or mark-up).

At this stage, all that is required is a rough estimate of what your product price will be. The final exact pricing can only be confirmed when you have started operations and your real costs are known. However, your estimate should not be too far off. The following discussion uses a medical device as example.

5.6.1 Development Costs

This is a one-time cost per product. You are working to obtain a final product prototype for final approval. You can use a sub-contractor, lease or rent frugal space and carry out most of the work yourself. If you started in academia, the development can be shortened and costs reduced, but not obviated totally. Set an upper limit of what you intend to spend to limit your financial liabilities. This is because around one year will probably have elapsed when you complete the developmental work. Your prototype may fail at that stage with no cost effective alternative.

The associated cost included in development is the safety and performance testing on your final product. For these you can obtain quotes that should be quite accurate.

5.6.2 Operating Costs

When you progress into manufacturing, you can use a sub-contractor or set-up your own facility (details in Chapter 10). You can readily obtain estimates if you work with a sub-contractor facility. You should add some administrative costs, as you will interact with the sub-contractor regularly to produce your product. Starting your own facility is costly. Apart from the start-up costs, you should plan to incur running costs for at least 3 years, including staff salaries and other overheads. There is usually a considerable capital cost to outfit the facility to manufacture in the right environment (e.g. clean production facilities), as well as in equipment.

5.6.3 Cost Per Unit of Product or Service

The third cost is the per-unit manufacturing cost of your product. This costing includes the cost of raw materials and the turning of the raw materials into a product that includes labor, packaging, sterilization, routine lot release testing and shipping.

What you will have achieved by doing the preceding exercise is get a ballpark amount. You will have to do more fine tuning to get at a good figure and err on the side of being very conservative.

Alternatively, you may want to arrive at the cost by obtaining the price of a comparable product presently available. You next determine how your product or service measures up to the competitor, and if warranted set a higher (up to 25%) price. This will be your guesstimate sale price. Once you figure out your margin (discussed below), you can arrive at cost. The final part is to allocate the percentage contribution to development, operating and per-unit production costs, and assess whether the numbers add up for you to proceed. This shortcut bypasses the traditional procedure above and may be a reasonable way to derive a production cost figure. There are limitations. You will not be as thorough in your costing and this may haunt you later if you can't get the costs to tally. But it is a decent way to obtain a first estimate to see if your venture costs are doable.

Finally, all you have done are just preliminary projections, your most confident guess to what you require in terms of start-up funding for 36 months presuming your *best-case* scenario. Reality is that you will probably be off your mark, sometimes as much as 100%. This can be very discouraging and perplexing after all the time and passion you have put into your concept. But this sobering recognition of the situation is the incentive you need to plod on, since you will now realize it takes more than your *eagerness to do* to succeed, and you will revise your fervor accordingly.

5.6.4 Margin

The true value of a biomed product or service is in the mind of your prospective client. Your brainpower is valuable. People expect to pay some premium for a medical product or service. You have to consider a price for your product or service that matches the perceived value and reinforce that with great marketing. Work towards a percentage mark-up over your costs to arrive at a figure that will make you survive, and later thrive.

5.6.4.1 *Premium*

Setting a monetary value for your product or service is arbitrary. Everyone wants the highest price the product/service can command. Premium pricing is about exclusivity and how you position your product/service, how well you sell the idea, i.e. marketing, and your after sales support (if you have dialed a 1–800 number before to handle a problem with something you purchased that has a warranty you will understand that this is not trivial). There are a lot of examples in the business and consumer realm on these topics for you to survey and garner what you want. They work to an extent because biomed as we know sells differently. The more important task is to identify the need and from there, determine the pain level.

5.6.4.2 *Need Versus Pain*

You approach this by recalling the features for your product/service that match the need and how you are better than your existing and future (the more important) competitors. Ensure your product/service does what is required well, and hopefully better, than the equivalent already present. If you do have a truly original product or service concept, you have a head start. Fulfilling the need puts you on par with your competitors and you become a choice among others.

Next, you determine what the client's pain level is if she does not have your product or service. Needs and pain are different. Your customers may have a need but can still do without you. Only when you have identified the pain to them if they do not have what you offer will you move into the exclusive zone that you must aspire to.[i] This defines the price you can command, i.e. the premium your clients are willing to pay. Remember that your S&T differentiates your offering and your product/ service must command a premium.

5.6.5 Affordability

This is a very necessary exercise as it is about the patient's ability to afford the product that you make available. Obviously, if the majority of patients (that may include assistance from a health insurance plan, a government subsidy, etc.) cannot pay for the product, you are not going to have sufficient sales to support your venture.

Therefore, while your product should command a premium, there are finite boundaries that should not exceed affordability. For example, for a product such as an implant, a $10,000.00 sale price per unit may be the limit.[ii] Know what price the market you are in can sustain and attenuate accordingly. Again, if affordability cannot be resolved satisfactorily, you may have no choice but to stop here.

5.6.6 Profit

The profit per piece of product/service is normally your margin (mark-up) less your costs. The total profit you make takes into account several factors including:

1. The number of units sold per financial year (FY).
2. Many other miscellaneous expenses such as discards and rejects (products that do not meet inspection checks), samples for trial, etc.

The goal is to have item 1 as high as possible and item 2 as low as possible. Your finance team will guide you, and you will have to strike a balance with your R&D, sales and operations team who in all likelihood only want to spend (for valid reasons). Get on top of this from the start.

[i] The "pain" approach is a well-known sales method.
[ii] This dollar value may vary from country to country.

5.7 WHAT DOES THE BUSINESS COST TO SET UP?

From the preceding discussion on pricing, you already have your basic costs, i.e. development, operating and per-unit costs.

To complete, you include other costs at start-up such as costs of registering the company, some accounting fees, legal fees for licensing and other agreements and contracts, marketing, etc. You should set aside funds to cover all these, as well as unexpected and emergency expenses.

5.8 WHAT WILL THE BUSINESS BE WORTH?

In Section 5.3, the first revenue goal of $5 million with profits above 20% of revenue in 5 years was put forward as a target to aspire for. How do you go about this? You have already allocated 3 years to get your product to market. For a service, you probably start generating revenue earlier, but will probably still be making losses at year 3. That leaves you 2 years to achieve the target. If you achieve the target at the end of 5 years that's great, but it is not the true determinant of the business' worth. The real value is what you have built into the business. These take the form of physical entity, structure and operations, and platform for growth.

An established place of operations and business is a good indicator that you have arrived. For example, BRASS at year 5 was still making a net loss. However, in all its 5 years of existence, revenue growth was increased annually by at least 20% and in good years closer to 40%. BRASS had relocated from an incubator facility of 500 square feet with shared common lab equipment such as autoclave and clean water system to its own facility of 2000 square feet and its own fully equipped laboratory. Operationally, from the one accredited test in 2001, BRASS was accredited for around ten tests with a much more sophisticated quality system by 2004. This laid the platform for growth, and expansion to the present 10,000 square feet facility. In summary, at each stage, the value of BRASS was increased over the previous year.

Similarly, if you are a product company, you have to show growth by achieving or surpassing the defined milestones. And when you continue to grow, set your enterprise for consideration for exit.

5.9 HAVE YOU THOUGHT THROUGH YOUR EXIT PLAN?

Somewhere along the way when evidence (growth of market share, revenue, profits, etc.) suggests that success is imminent, the people involved in your venture, especially your fund sponsors, may begin to display restlessness. This is human nature as they sense their payoff is coming and it should be sooner rather than later. You cannot wait until that stage to handle the matter, it has to be in your plans at conception and while it can just be a line in your business plan, you should be thorough and know which of the following courses you want to pursue.

There are primarily three options that come to mind. First, building up the business to the point where an initial public offering or IPO on some stock exchange is realizable. Second, selling off the business at a sizable profit, often called M&A (mergers and acquisition), and finally, buying out some (or all) of your shareholders and running the business on a continued basis.

The IPO choice is usually what catches the eye of many investors. Different stock markets have different rules. A common requirement for listing is for your enterprise to have demonstrated survival for at least three consecutive years with revenue and profits growth, and other appropriate indicators. Listing is a big task requiring a contingent of financiers, lawyers and other experts. You may be the "figurehead" and you must prepare for this. Once you list, there are financial regulatory responsibilities that your business has to meet, since it will be in the public domain. Price per share in this instance is set by the market. There are usually clauses for you and some key members of your team that restrict you from cashing out for a fixed period after listing.

M&A or selling out requires you to have built a business attractive enough for a buyout. You generally would have demonstrated a consistent increase in revenue and profit, as well as business growth in terms of reach and client base. Business growth can be diversified or focused. The common three to five times profit offer basis to buy over businesses applies to small enterprises where the new owner carries on an existing business as in a trades (skill) business such as a plumbing or electrical service. Biomed businesses have S&T, patents, license agreements and therefore their value is much more than just simple profits suggests. There are also intangibles such as know-how and internal processes, long-term contracts, client goodwill, etc. that are invaluable. Know or assess your true value for negotiating and also know what you are willing to settle for.

Running the business on a long-term basis is also a possibility depending on your ambition and drive, but be forewarned that this is a path with the highest probability of leading to a burnout. You will have to value your company at some stage in order for those shareholders who want to exit to do so. My only advice here is that you do not take out a loan that you cannot cover to pay those who want to exit. There are many mechanisms and good accountants and lawyers who can advise you to come to an equitable solution.

Each exit option has different commitments, returns and rewards. To reach this stage, you must be clear even before you begin the business, what you want to achieve. You need to define the science, make the connection to your business, and show it has real promise and viability, through your strategy for entering the market and growing. If you are unsure, nobody will be motivated to put up the money to support your venture (Chapter 6). Finally, be clear it is not an ego trip!

Real World Lessons Learnt

General
1. You must be clear what your enterprise is to be and will become.
2. Is the enterprise feasible?
3. You must have a product or service that clients want.

Specific
1. The venture must be worthwhile.
2. Ensure your product or service is affordable.
3. There must be clear signs that you will generate profit on a sustained basis.

Quote for the Chapter

Every time I stepped on the field,
I believed my team was going to walk off the winner,
Somehow, some way.
Roger Staubach *Quarterback of the Dallas Cowboys (1971-1979)*

References

[1] Harari O. The leadership secrets of Colin Powell. : McGraw-Hill; 2002.
[2] History: "MerLion Pharmaceuticals Pte. Ltd was formed in 2002 through the privatization of the former Centre for Natural Product Research (CNPR), a unique unit of Singapore's Institute of Molecular and Cell Biology (IMCB). MerLion Pharma acquired all of CNPR's assets, including its unique collection of natural product samples. The company is now focused on developing its lead antibacterial candidate, finafloxacin". Extracted from: <www.merlionpharma.com>.
[3] Now a subsidiary of BioTime Inc: <www.biotimeinc.com>.
[4] Bouchie A. Nat Biotechnol 2002;20:1178–9.
[5] Look into the story behind how the 3M Post-it® product became a success.
[6] *The Bible*: 1 Samuel, Chapter 17, 32–50.
[7] Attributed to a line from the theme song for *Baretta*, a 1970s TV detective series.

CHAPTER

6

Business Plan

From Academia to Entrepreneur.
DOI: http://dx.doi.org/10.1016/B978-0-12-410516-4.00006-9

6.1 THE PERFECT BUSINESS PLAN

The next step in the process is to articulate your ideas, thoughts and directions into a document called the Business Plan (BP). This is where you assemble in a formal way all that has been discussed so far, the science, the products or services, the business opportunity and the financial viability. Many books you may have read and people you may have talked to, tell you that the BP is very important. I can only state categorically that it is obligatory for every start-up to have one.

THE BUSINESS PLAN SERVES TWO PRIMARY PURPOSES

First and more important, the process in drafting a BP compels you to think through your intentions and coerces you to organize every detail for your venture. Putting your thoughts on paper (or in an equivalent electronic form) taking shape in bullet points, flow charts, sketches and tables containing numbers will take the giddy euphoria out of you and replace it with cold stark reality. There is nothing more powerful and convincing than to see loosely held thoughts take physical form, giving structure to your undertaking. This exercise acts as your final check that you have been thorough and that you are not deceiving yourself.

Second, the BP will become your first marketing tool. Coupled with a Powerpoint® presentation (that is expected these days), the BP will be your main implement in raising funds. Temper your expectations in the value of the BP as a fundraising tool. True, no one will be prepared to give you an audience without first receiving a copy of your BP. What they do with the BP once they receive it is anyone's guess. The executive summary is likely to be perused but the rest of the BP may not be reviewed in its entirety before being filed away and never retrieved again. What you may also find interesting is frequently no one will sign an NDA (non-disclosure agreement) to obtain your BP. This is not arrogance on the part of the recipient. If you really do have that great an idea and plan, I believe that the NDA does not matter. Few if any can duplicate it and more likely, everyone will be beating a path to your door to buy-in. Of course this borders on fiction. So why should they commit themselves to a legal contract of no advantage to them? And the institutional investment community does have its own systems of practices, one of which is reputation, that makes it unlikely for information inside BPs to be exploited unprofessionally.

Reality is that you will have to knock on many doors, utilize every contact you know to refer or sponsor you. In my time, I have presented to *angels*, venture capitalists (including in North America) and government-related bodies, all to no avail. The reason is simple. Few propositions are really worthwhile and rare is the gem. And for a *runway* prospect, the difficulty increases since champions to get you through the door are fewer. There are also other contributing factors, such as the size of your proposal may be too small for the "big boys", your inexperience, and many, many more that lead to dead ends. Do not be discouraged. Many roads to success do not come with a precondition of sizable funds in the bank as a necessary requirement to commence. Last, a BP is seldom a good indicator of how well you will execute. And that in the end is what counts.

Let's take a closer look at the BP. Everyone has a right way to prepare the perfect business plan. There are books you can purchase that teach you about creating BPs and consultants you can hire to guide and assist you to do the necessary. What will be presented here are comments on the purpose of each component that I deem necessary. You may disagree with some or all of the headings since they reflect my subjective preferences. Include what you decide you believe relevant and figure out your best format.

The first order of business about a BP to inscribe in your mind is no one needs to be impressed by your sizable *curriculum vitae* of scientific achievements and awards. Potential funders are not agreeing to listen to your BP because you are a great person (except in rare instances where the status of the scientist commands respect), nor are they donating to a charity. They have a gut feel for this sort of thing. It is like betting on a racehorse, pedigree has bearing, *but current form and potential matter more*. In your case you are practically a start-up virgin of a *runway* venture and their reference point of you is zero. Impress you must, but with the right information and details and absolutely avoid regurgitation of your extensive résumé.

Second, prepare your BP well. It has to reflect your best effort. This document speaks more about your character, your aspirations and what you plan to do to achieve than on the enterprise you plan to start. If anyone cared to read your BP, the reader must conclude that you are serious with regard to this endeavor as well as being a worthwhile contender. And if you can come up with a document that no one wants to put down like reading a good book when a great looker walks past you on the subway car, or a movie that keeps the audience rooted to their seats, kudos to you. The only caution is that while you can entertain suggestions from your team, spouse and others around you, the final document must bear only your thought through effort. No matter how pressed for time or how well others have written sub-sections, redo it yourself. Avoid cut and paste, and joining the document together from several sources. Re-write until the flow of the text is completely only you.

Third, respect your reader. Never come across as condescending. You are the expert, but that does not mean your readers are clueless. Many have experience in science and biomed. If they require an additional opinion, they have a good network they can rely on to assist them. They can and will spot uncertainties, flaws and limitations in your BP. You venture into their territory and they have the advantage.

Last, realize that there is really no need to generate **a perfect business plan**. The reason is simple. Again using a military metaphor, the best battle plans are just that, plans. Once the battle begins, the situation becomes amorphous. The troops on the ground have to react to what they encounter. Thorough planning and practice is essential, but no one can predict the outcome once the operation is set in motion. The better the execution, the more probable a victory. The same is true of business plans. Good BPs matter. But implementation counts more. Reality will dictate how you will implement. Rarely does the execution pathway go smoothly according to what was planned. The end result is all that matters and you achieve the best by doing, being flexible and hands-on, adjusting on the fly. Put every effort into developing your BP, with the most important details not part of the BP but in a notebook (ensure it is written in permanent or ballpoint ink). In the notebook, you should jot down your *what ifs* scenarios and your thought through responses. These, you will eventually discover, are the most important aspects of developing a business plan. The probability that you will encounter up to 50% of these scenarios once you start is high. Having thought through responses will help you to keep calm and think carefully before you act when confronting anticipated situations and build your confidence to react and handle unplanned incidents. This notebook is invaluable and should be kept safe.

Now that we have a better idea of how you should, and others will, treat business plans, let's explore the details of what normally are components of a BP. Apart from the executive summary, you can organize the ensuing headings in this chapter according to your preference for the effect you desire. You can follow the traditional format (as I more or less adopt here). To impress or shock, a suggestion is to put the financials immediately after the executive summary. Whether you will catch your reader's attention by this order cannot be predicted, as I have no prior experience with this approach. Your reader could well be enticed to work through your financial table(s) and get interested enough to continue. Think through the impact you wish to make with the order of these headings, the decision is yours. Finally, be judicious what you put into a BP. Do not overkill by providing too much information.

6.2 EXECUTIVE SUMMARY (EXECSUM)

According to many knowledgeable experts, this is key. The Execsum is the page or two at the start of the BP that is supposed to *wow* everyone into believing you're the best thing that ever happened in their life, second perhaps to winning a million dollar lottery (or more since that amount doesn't take you very far these today). Ignoring the latter (as taking calculated risks and not chances is what you are about), know that the Execsum is best presented on one page where possible.

The importance of keeping to one page (and at most another half page) is simple. First, persons who appraise BPs for a living can sum up very well whether you have got it all together with just one page. Second, more than one page and inertia to reading further begins to set in. You find this hard to believe? Just ask yourself how often you have read a 50-page research proposal, report or any document from cover to cover some poor soul took hours but more likely days, even weeks to put together? Your concentration probably would have begun lapsing if your attention had not been caught by the second paragraph, because frequently these documents are bland. The reader may never admit it, but the sleep-aid (or nap-aid) effect of these documents is well known. Frequently as well, these documents will remain on a desk until *filed* away at best or end up in the day's trash collection without ever having been viewed by the intended pair of eyes. To put it bluntly, if the reader's interest is not aroused very early on, the reader will start to feel that the rest of the document is a waste of their precious time. So do yourself a favor, get into your intended reader's shoes and empathize with them, it is your business and in your best interest to do so. The essential rule of selling applies, you are not important, your client is, and in this instance, the people you wish to sell your business plan to are your clients.

Four short paragraphs should suffice. The first lays out the bleak situation in the field of interest confronting the world presently. The second introduces you as the hero to save the day.[i] The third outlines how you will do this. The last is the titillating factor of the time entailed to attain stated objective and the intended ROI (return on investment). Try to be precise and concise. Do not be overly witty or grandiloquent. While no details and specifics are necessary here, readers must surmise that paragraph four is authentic based on the preceding three paragraphs. Draft, edit, edit and edit until it is right, until the Execsum says what you want in a way that will catch the attention of the reader. Always take for granted that you only have one shot per person you are asking money or support from. *An opportunity missed is a prospect lost forever.*

6.3 VISION AND MISSION

Vision is where you expound what the company will stand for and become. It is your grand scheme of things, your aspiration, your dream. Vision should be imposing and distinctive to fascinate and entice. Your

---

[i]If you are really that good, you should make the case for being the *"only"* hero or *"chosen one"*.

vision should match your background and expertise (that can include your team's, but should be primarily yours). If you are way off base, you will face a credibility issue.

Visions are important. Nations fight wars, underdogs win sports championships, company turnarounds take place, all because they are inspired by a vision. A properly conceived vision defines the final destination that will get everyone you want on board going the same way because they know what they are aspiring to.

Mission is what the company must do for a living to arrive at your Vision. The activities that are put forward in the Mission must be consistent with the Vision. Mission should be precise, giving the confidence that it is readily executable and achievable.

Some practitioners have obviated this section from BPs for various reasons, but I am personally fond of vision and mission statements because if done well, they articulate in a couple of sentences your goals that can only be impressive! It is also something everyone involved in the venture can rally around to sustain morale, for comfort in tough times and for inspiration at all times.

6.4 INTRODUCTION AND BACKGROUND

Here, you start getting into the nitty-gritty. The purpose here is to provide comfort for the readers who go beyond the execsum. If their interest is stirred, you want to give them slightly more detail that will induce them to do their own research to verify your assertions.

You begin by describing generalities of the business sector and perhaps a brief history of the field that you are about to embark on. You may wish to reiterate your executive summary by describing in greater detail what needs to be improved in all that is wrong with the current technology. Highlight the present limitations tastefully; it is never good to talk down your competition or why no one else can solve the *dilemma*. Putting a BP in someone's hand means you cannot control where your information will end up. The last thing you want is to be blindsided by an ugly response that can be damaging to your venture.

Next, present your solutions that will resolve everything at a price that is absolutely a bargain for the client, but is an opportunity not to be missed for your investors. Be factual; list some statistics, reference one or two papers or quote a couple of thought leaders. If you are offering a new, better or *me-too* product there must be a clear distinction in advantage over all present competition or why you can sell more for less when others can't.

Last, you state your expert background and relevance to the issue at hand by informing your reader how you arrived at starting-up this biomed business, how your research tied in with your background to come up with the "solution". Be very specific. Two short paragraphs about your expertise should suffice.

6.5 BUSINESS OVERVIEW

The preceding section focused on history. In this section your emphasis of the BP is on the "meat" or substance, the deliverables and the execution plan "in waiting". State clearly the objectives of your business. You can number or use bullets but stick to no more than three or four points or bullets. More than four and you may lose credibility even though it is conceivable that you may achieve them. Store them away for the next round or as a back-up if quizzed at the presentation. This must reinforce the impression you ARE NOT a one hit wonder.

Outline briefly your strategies to achieve your objectives and prioritize key activities you will execute to achieve your objectives. Finally, declare clearly what is your *return on investment* (ROI) aim, e.g. value of a share at year X. Your reader can work out the math by working through the proposed share structure discussed next below. This should be significant for a product company or else it won't excite. You must always have in your mind that you will exceed that mark and communicate it very clearly as your intention during presentations and meetings.

6.5.1 Proposed Share Structure

Describe the share distribution you are proposing. This would depend on the funds you require, how you want to spread it out and your confidence in achieving milestones. It is probably unrealistic that you will get all the funds at the start. Therefore, your proposed share structure will need to take into account share dilution and the valuation after each round (that should increase proportionately with each round).

Your purpose for this section is to satisfy upfront those who want to put money in your venture, what they are in for. There will obviously be discussions on the percentage as well as the price, and be prepared that there probably will be conditions imposed on you and your team. Know what you are willing to compromise, settle and permit, but also areas where you cannot give up and stick to it during negotiations unless the requests are warranted and acceptable. Do not make immediate decisions. You should seek assistance financially and legally beforehand to understand this issue as well as when interest is expressed. Good legal counsel will protect your interests.

I recommend having the share structure being described in the BP, as it demonstrates you are clear about your stake in the venture.

6.5.2 IP Portfolio

List the primary IP (intellectual property) developed by you in academia and the terms of the license from your institution (that should be exclusive to your company), primarily the agreed royalties and any other fee payments.

If you have IP specific to and owned only by your company, that would be a good plus factor. List other intangibles and capabilities that the company has such as yours and your team's expertise and specific processes that were developed but not patented and are kept as trade secrets. These are your company's worth and your bargaining position when negotiating for investments.

Potential investors can size up the approximate value of the IP to your venture with the information you provide. Therefore, be factual, accurate and complete.

6.5.3 Products

In this section you describe what your first few products or services are. This must be thought out well because products and services make your enterprise credible.

6.5.3.1 Lead Product

This is the first product you develop, manufacture, test and bring to market. List and describe the uniqueness of your product compared to the competition. State if you have a prototype and remember to bring it along when giving a presentation for your audience to inspect. Provide a precise road map for development and manufacturing, including flowcharts. Evidence to demonstrate you are well on the way should not be held back.

6.5.3.2 Follow-on Product

You are obligated to have the next two or three products that you plan to introduce 25–50% in the works. These could be variations of design, formulation or packaging for a different market segment, for example a more transportable version for EMT (ambulance) use. Showing you have product #2 in prototyping, and product #3 in design speaks volumes about how you will run things.

6.5.3.3 R&D Plans

You should have R&D of future products in your plans. This is your guesstimate for what you bring on-line around or after year 5.

Note: You can work on conception and continue to keep abreast of changes and advances in your scientific field, i.e. literature searches, and making notes. Have a working file on R&D. Allocate a specific time per month for this. DO NOT start any kind of practical work on your R&D ideas and plans, not even if you can assign the task to another team member. Remember where you come from. You (and your scientific team members) are trained as research scientists and old habits die hard. If you begin any exploratory work, your attention may divert, and that can result in you neglecting your focus on the lead and follow-on products. *Products,* and *not R&D,* bring in the revenue and therefore should be where you must concentrate your efforts.[ii]

6.5.4 Business Model

There are many business models you can adopt.[1] The emphasis, however, should be to show how you plan to *generate revenue and make profit on a continual basis* regardless of the business model. Why? Let's zoom in on the incubation section of the standard time–revenue lifecycle for a biomed product, Figure 6.1.

The ordinate (y) axis represents negative revenue (spending) and the abscissa (x) axis represents time to produce and approve the product for sale. You will note that the line begins by tracking in the negative revenue region, i.e. you are spending. Even when the line tracks upwards, the revenue is still negative until it crosses the zero point on the abscissa. The goal in your execution plan is to reduce both arrows, i.e. control spending and complete the manufacture of your lead product in the shortest time possible. Once you cross into the positive revenue portion, your goal is to rack up sales to cover all prevailing and prior expenses.

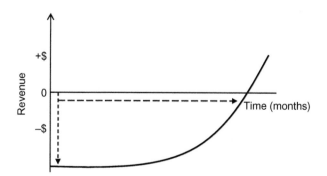

FIGURE 6.1 Time–revenue profile lifecycle of a product/service. Expanded view of the Induction period.

[ii] As an exercise, look up three companies you know that started-up 10 years ago but are no longer in existence. Five will get you ten that you find more information about their R&D efforts rather than their product development.

Not being on top of managing both arrows during the induction period can lead to disaster because you do not respect this plain yet essential point. Think through your strategy on spending and workflow and reflect this in your business model. This can only impress your reader.

You should also list some critical success factors, as these are crucial elements that are necessary in order for your business to succeed. First you must state the obvious; you are the KEY factor for the undertaking to succeed. If you are not, may I suggest you place your money with property, at least you will have a roof over your head. This is highly critical, if the enterprise does not hinge on you, something is wrong. Next you can mention a few (not too many) elements that are required such as attaining minimal funding to commence, licensing agreement of IP from your university/institute (since this may be on-going), specialized facilities and/or equipment, etc.

6.6 MARKET ANALYSIS

You are required to have done some market evaluation. You can obtain market size information of your product field from market research providers, or find one or two references that estimate these for you. The market size should be attractive.[iii] Estimate and explain how you arrived at your market share.

Competitor analysis is also obligatory. List as many competitors as you can, their market share (if possible) and each competitor's advantages and limitations. Recount briefly your product's features that can match or surpass existing products. You are reminded to be factual and respectful of your competitors.

If you have identified entry barriers that competitors and *me-too* followers will find difficult (never impossible) to overcome, state this without fanfare. What you identify as a weakness may be only yours.

Finally, you present a market strategy of how you will make sales (generate revenue). This need not be sophisticated but must be sensible. Marketing does not have to be expensive or/and extravagant.

6.7 SWOT

A risk analysis commonly termed SWOT (strength, weakness, opportunity, threats) assessment is customary.

For *strength*, you reiterate your credentials, your product's virtues, the favorable business climate, etc. that benefit your enterprise.

[iii] Most are usually in the $ billion range.

In *weaknesses*, be truthful in evaluating your shortcomings, but in a positive manner.

Opportunity is when you explain why seizing the opportunity now will result in a successful business venture that is both financially profitable and technologically satisfying within X years. Discuss the likely good impact your product(s) will have on the status quo.

Finally, with *threats*, discuss other non-obvious on-the-horizon technologies that may leapfrog your products (this is where your R&D plans can be used as a counter), slow adoption by users, and other trends, perhaps lifestyle or national health programs, that may supplant you unintentionally.

However you do SWOT, never downplay the impact of others – competitors (known and unknown) – and show that you are aware of present and future scientific progress. This will leave the impression that you continually keep your pulse on your *surroundings* to suggest being surprised is remote as well as your ability to cope in such eventuality. You conclude by stating your execution plan has a favorable probability for success.

6.8 ORGANIZATIONAL STRUCTURE

The requirement for this section is to inform who will run the show and who will play a supporting role in advising the team.

6.8.1 Key Management and Team

Identify the CEO or managing director (Commonwealth countries). By default, the CEO post is yours. Be practical not ceremonial, as the glamor runs out with the first crisis you have to handle. You should identify an able assistant and maybe one or two more scientists and/or engineers to complete your R&D team. A brief summary of each member's qualifications, experience and their role in the business suffices.

6.8.2 Board of Directors

When you incorporate a company, by law a company director is required to run the company and perform fiduciary duties. Most often, you the *runway* entrepreneur are the sole company director. Know what you are required to do under the laws of the country you operate in. If you operate in a country where you are not a citizen, a local may be required to be director in addition to you. In this instance, make it clear that you run the company and define the role of your co-director.

Frequently, a sizable investor would also request a directorship. When you permit this, bring in another director (ensure this person is on your side) for the board vote to balance in your favor. Be aware that directors are entitled to director's fees (that you can justify to minimize or suspend until revenue starts) and other reasonable expenses. Make each director perform a useful function that supports the business.

When you have three directors, it is best to re-title the grouping as a board of directors with you as the chairman. Ideally, the other directors permit you to run the show with only quarterly review meetings at most to provide oversight and suggestions. It is always wise to listen to others who are not involved daily. They can give you insights on matters you might have missed or not noticed.

6.8.3 Scientific Advisory Board (SAB)

This is definitely not something you need at the start, since it is hard to justify for a *runway* outfit. As your company grows, you may determine that an SAB should be established to support the scientific R&D. Define the specific areas required and ensure the candidate can provide the relevant expertise, contacts, prestige and personality fit (at least with you) to narrow the list of potential candidates. It is common practice to compensate SAB members' transport and other related expenses to attend company meetings and scientific conferences when they present research related to your company. Discuss with your board members regarding SAB member fees and stock options, keeping in mind the mention of a SAB appointment on the scientist's résumé has value.

6.9 SERVICES AND SUPPORT PLAN

This section is intended for a service company or for products that require maintenance. Drugs and implants already have regulatory controls that must be adhered to and are not discussed.

Supporting after sales service, especially for equipment and tests, is a marketing function. A satisfied client is not one for long if the goods sold or test report in hand cannot do what the client intended. If equipment requires servicing, how you respond in attitude, timeliness and solving the matter at hand will determine how your client in turn reacts. You are looking for a repeat customer, as well as someone who will refer you to others. Your community is small, and word about you, good or bad, gets around like wildfire.

As a service, BRASS' response whenever an issue with a client comes up is to try its best to resolve the problem to the customer's satisfaction. At times this was disruptive to on-going work and impacted our bottom line. But it is easier to forgo a little expenditure when these situations occur than to recover a disillusioned customer.

Build a service plan that is reasonable, responsive and cost effective from the onset. Convey this in your BP (and execute when you set up shop). These are the details that may further enhance your credibility among your readers.

6.10 FINANCIAL PLAN

A financial plan will typically contain two components, the revenue projection and the budget.

Revenue projection is a guesstimate at best that is, more often than not, inaccurate. Most readers will discount the numbers you provide, the extent based on the premises you present. Therefore, it is important to show here what your thought processes are and why the numbers you put forward are reasonable. Proceeding along this line of thought, you will realistically not generate revenue until year 4, since for a product, it will normally take that long to develop, manufacture, test and obtain regulatory approval. For a service, revenue normally starts when you obtain accreditation and/or certification, again usually at least one year down the road. If there are clients who are willing to audit and pass you to perform their work even without these credentials, state so.

If you plan to bootstrap (refer to Chapter 7) as part of your funding strategy, exclude what you receive from this channel to your revenue stream. Even if bootstrapping provides a stable income, the revenue generated should not count to your core business. Bootstrapping demonstrates more your resourcefulness rather than your entrepreneurial effort.

A 5-year projection is standard and should span from years 4 to 8. There is normally a gestation period of slow revenue growth leading into faster and even exponential growth. You must justify each year's projection with production and sales forecast, and explain why they are reasonable.

For budget, you will have to work out a plan to take into account the funds you will raise, how you will spend and the assumptions you make. A proposed budget that covers 3 to 5 years is adequate. Depending on the level of detail, this can get quite complicated. Identify who needs to be paid for the project to proceed until your product reaches market. Try to be accurate in your estimates by supporting with quotes from potential vendors and sub-contractors.

The general practice in deriving a budget is to include a buffer directly into each line's fund allotment. I recommend you refrain from this mindset for a BP budget. Evaluators usually know the market rates for salaries, utilities, etc. in a base of operations and you do not want to come across as "over-charging". It is better to provide as precise a budget as possible and indicate a 10–15% premium based on the fact that prices may increase at the time of purchase, which is 6 to 12 months from when you execute your business plan, or as a "contingency" line in your budget explaining possible uses and the anticipated amounts. If you under budget, explain why you can get away which spending less.

6.11 SOURCES AND APPLICATION OF FUND

Define clearly where, and how much funds/capital you intend to raise. The next chapter discusses funding sources such as from venture capital funds, banks as a secured/unsecured loans, "donations" from relatives and friends and of course, yourself. Work out the percentage mix.

You must have a clear utilization plan for the funds. What percentage goes towards equipment, human resource, facility rental, utilities, phones, fax, etc.? They should be clearly itemized. If you are projecting for up to 5 years, annual increases must match your expenditure need as you ramp up.

In conclusion, a BP is about transmitting your ideas, thoughts and plans with a realistic positive spin. Do it well.

Real World Lessons Learnt

General
1. A business plan is a sales job, not a snow job.
2. You must articulate your thoughts convincingly.
3. Your business plan must excite yet be believable.

Specific
1. The real beneficiary of a business plan is you.
2. The most important item on a business plan is the financial plan.
3. Notebook your courses of actions for recall in the execution phase.

Quote for the Chapter

"Success is what happens when 10,000 hours of preparation meet with one moment of opportunity".

Anonymous

Reference

[1] Read for example Lang J. The high-tech entrepreneur's handbook. A FT.com book.: Pearson Education Limited; 2002.

Raising Funds

7.1 THE BOTTOM LINE IS ABOUT MONEY

By this time, you should be quite satisfied that you have put in all the hard work of thinking through and developing your S&T into a potential enterprise with the best thought out business plan that will surely work. You show the right enthusiasm and are all charged up to get going. Still, a promising enterprise remains just that, until real hard cash is put out and applied to start-up the venture. Now begins the final crunch part before you launch your *runway enterprise*.

You need money to really get going. Reality is that the sums you need are not insignificant. Even for a *runway enterprise*, a pragmatic starting point is in the six to seven figures bracket. Unless you have cash-rich and willing supporters, you are going to find that this phase is nowhere near as easy as you've been led to believe by all the probably enthusiastic talk of how much funding channels are out there for biomed.

For most of us, we're in a tough spot even before we start when having our own funds to stake into something such as a *runway biomed enterprise* goes. Selling your car or home are not straightforward options. Few even have these assets fully paid up to make a dent in their *total net worth*! If a spouse is involved, it gets dicier. Factor in children and you probably have a non-starter in some form of self-funding. The best many of us can muster up after scrounging around is perhaps $10K? A trivial amount in the scheme of this type of venture! But $10K is far better than nothing, and you must at least put up this sum at the start because that is expected of you (to be explained a little later).

While selling or re-mortgaging your home may sound romantic, adventurous, and may have been what you've read or heard others have done and succeeded, I do not advocate you follow. I also do not suggest you take a loan. This may sound very contradictory to what I have been promoting in this book about taking risks, but as far as putting your personal finances and other essential assets in jeopardy, I am not a fan. I do not buy in to this popular entrepreneurial way, even though many have succeeded with it. Having a roof over your (and family's) head is too rudimentary to chance on something as uncertain as a business venture. You will discover that too much of your subconscious mind will be concerned about how to take care of your personal and your family's needs. This will distract you disproportionately, and places your venture at greater peril of imploding. So save yourself the anguish, if you can't see yourself succeeding at raising funds from sources other than yourself (except for the token sum), stop.

Consequently, this phase is exclusively about trying to acquire appropriate sums of money from people who have money, know about money and how to use it, and for some, their livelihood and reputation depends on their making the right call enough times to matter. The bottom line is that no funding source worthy of their reputation would readily part with their money easily. This is also the time you will find that you have few friends and that pool is about to get smaller; the banks are about lending to people who have money (since you are unlikely to have collateral and they usually lend up to only twice your monthly salary subject to you keeping your daytime job), and don't even think about VCs (venture capitalists) unless you have a megastar product or service and you are looking for big numbers. And as the number goes up, so does the resistance to part with their money and the effort required to procure it. But it is not impossible, and if I could do it, you should be able too. Let's leave the specifics to later in this chapter.

The other side of raising capital is that when you finally get it, you become encumbered. Expectations and obligations are placed on you, be they written, spoken, or implied. The folks who gave you the money may tell you to your face it is fine if you lose it all, as they know the risks. In truth, their position is probably very different from what they have asserted. Just place yourself in their shoes. You made such a good job convincing them that they really believe they had made a wise decision with their money. They believe (and hope) you will make it and that they will not only get their money back, but a good deal more. And if you took money from an institutional type source, all sorts of clauses and restrictions are placed on you so that at times you will wish you never took their money. So you wear this imaginary *metal*[i] *bracelet* around your neck and every decision you make is that much more critical. Do you really want this? Can you handle the mental and emotional demands this responsibility places on you? As informed, it gets harder the further you progress.

Last, you will have to rely on your ingenuity to harness every trick in your repertoire of survival skills to stretch every dollar you have, at times creatively use moneyless methods including barter trading to get things done, but never letting these inconveniences deter you.

For now, let me enlighten you on how I obtained the funds to start BRASS. My pre-existing conditions were pretty standard and nowhere near favorable. My financial situation was typical, the house I lived in was mortgaged, and I had a car payment with little excess funds. The only thing going for me was that I worked for an employer at a time in Singapore when start-ups from the university were just beginning to be fashionable. However, you still have to get *all your ducks in a straight line* for any request for funds to be approved. What do I mean?

I began as all academic scientists do, building my scientific credentials by doing the relevant research and publishing in my research field of biomaterials. I was blessed to learn my fieldcraft from a few good mentors (in biomaterials and chitin), and with time established my credibility. As I embarked on the road that would lead eventually to BRASS (at the time I did not realize this), my interests led me to seek exposure and gain experience in Standards and accreditation work, as well as in professional organizations, specifically as an ASTM (American Society for Testing and Materials) F04 Task Group member.

Finally, at an early stage, a trail of seemingly unrelated administrative appointments laid the groundwork in my being known to various

---

[i]Metal is heavy, cold and rigid (uncomfortable).

appointment holders within my university that were in the chain of the decision-making process for spin-off companies from the university. I also gained mentors from the NUS technology office who were supportive of my BRASS idea, helping me develop the BRASS endeavor into a sensible undertaking. This was not straightforward because while products-based spin-off companies were easily sized up, BRASS was to be the first *services* spin-off company for the university. In the end, approval was granted with the university providing *seed funding*, a bonus. This process of starting my research program to the approval for BRASS to start-up, took approximately 15 years to fulfill that I did not learn to fully appreciate until much later and after much reflection.

I was also able to persuade four colleagues (one each from medical, dental, pharmacy and business faculties) to participate in BRASS. Three of them had worked with me for many years and were comfortable with putting a modest amount of funds in the BRASS venture as long as I led. The business colleague and I had exchanged "battle stories" for several years during our "annual warrior" training as we served in the same reserve unit and also provided some "free" business counsel on top of funds. The business faculty colleague also pulled in a lawyer friend of his, who not only put in funds, but also became the lead Director for BRASS, offering legal services most times for free or at nominal fees to cover his costs. Khoon Seng also brought in another contact, buying in at a slight premium. The funds from the eight of us plus the NUS *seed funding* crossed the six-figure mark. This, together with our trading activities, enabled BRASS to start comfortably and survive financially until profit was achieved, interspersed with a few anguishing episodes that are recounted throughout this book.

I did do my rounds of presenting to potential funding leads, but a mix of unfamiliarity with what BRASS was about by my audience (this was the late 1990s) and my inexperience were probably the reasons why this process did not lead anywhere. BRASS was only able to secure a large investment after it made its first year of profit. In summary, it is not easy but you can do it. Lay the foundation by doing the necessary as apprised in previous chapters, and if you have prepared well it will show. All you really need is a single sponsor to take a chance on you and the rest will be history you can make. *The key is for your persistence to outlast the resistance to turn you down.*

7.2 HOW MUCH DO YOU REALLY NEED TO GET GOING?

You put in your business plan the funds you require to confidently start-up your company to the point where you generate revenue, normally up to 36 months, as explained in Chapters 5 and 6. This is the threshold amount that you want, as you probably will need all of it and more, eventually. In practice, you are not likely going to have that amount at the start regardless of how hard you try. Fortunately, to get going, only a fraction has to be available to start. So don't be overly concerned if you do not round up all the funds stated in your BP. As long as you have obtained sufficient for an initial fixed period, you should commence and focus activities on meeting the pre-set milestones. This is the normal way the next tranche of funds will be disbursed to you if you were able to get an investor.

Therefore, while you have a target amount to raise, you should determine your minimum sum you need as well. Do not be extravagant here. Definitely no European branded marque automobiles at this stage. Not even salaries except for one or two technical or lab staff. To use the prolog metaphor, *runway* equates to bare minimum; enough aviation fuel for your aircraft to takeoff and ascend without stalling once off the ground or needing to glide (when you run out of fuel) the last few kilometers to your destination.

To elucidate, let's take an example of funds requirements for a Class 2 medical device:

1. A start-up company plans to develop a Class 2 medical device and bring it to market. The medical device is based on in-house created technology that the company will patent and own.
2. The prototype will take 18 months to develop.
3. The Class 2 medical device will use sub-contracts to manufacture, test and submit for regulatory approval prior to sales.
4. The regulatory phase is expected to be straightforward.
5. The venture is estimated to require $100K for patenting, $150K for prototyping and $500K for manufacturing 10,000 units, testing and regulatory submission.
6. Marketing, sales, logistics (M, S & L) are estimated to be $100K.
7. Admin, travel, contingency (A, T & C) are estimated to be $100K.

The sum total works out to be close to $1 million. In actuality, the fund needs for the patent process is gradual, requiring only an initial outlay of $10K at the start. Incremental amounts are needed approximately every quarter, i.e. you have to make $10K available in 3-monthly intervals. Similarly, for prototyping, it is estimated that $25K is required quarterly in Year 1 and in Year 2, $50K every 6 months. This is summarized in Table 7.1, as well as the estimates for manufacturing and testing. You will also require funds for marketing, sales and logistics, and some set aside for admin and travel as well as contingency.

What Table 7.1 suggests is that you do not need all of the funds at once. As long as you have around $250K, you should get going. You more or less "select and pillage" from allocations to each item when the

TABLE 7.1 Cash requirements for 3 years for developing a Class 2 medical device

Time	Year 1				Year 2		Year 3	
	Q1	Q2	Q3	Q4	H1	H2	H1	H2
Patent	$10 K	$10 K	$10 K	$10 K	$20 K	$20 K		$20 K
Prototype	$25 K	$25 K	$25 K	$25 K	$25 K	$25 K		
Manufacturing					$20 K	$50 K	$150 K	$150 K
Testing							$100 K	
Regulatory submission								$30 K
M, S & L			$10 K	$10 K	$15 K	$15 K	$25 K	$25 K
A, T & C	$10 K	$10 K	$20 K	$10 K	$10 K	$20 K	$10 K	$10 K
Total	**$45 K**	**$45 K**	**$65 K**	**$55 K**	**$90 K**	**$130 K**	**$285 K**	**$235 K**

Q = quarter-year; H = half-year.

need arises as you progress, while working hard on finding more funds to meet future deadlines.

The purpose in using a Class 2 medical device example is that the scenario is realistic to achieve with the above proposed fund requirements compared to Class 3 medical devices such as the bone cement and glaucoma devices examples in Chapter 3. In those situations, comparatively more funds are required and you probably require a higher threshold (i.e. >$250 K) to get going. In this instance, going the route described in Chapter 3 (case study 2), specifically applying for a proof of concept grant, is a suitable option.

7.3 FUNDING FUNDAMENTALS

Let's return to our product/service lifecycle diagram again. You will recall the three time periods: the *induction*, the *growth* and the *cash-out point*. Die-hard fans, parents, siblings, spouse and really good friends are usually the ones who help you in the *induction* period represented by the dotted line at the bottom of Figure 7.1. Additionally, if you are successful in receiving one or two government industry-specific grants, you are truly blessed. This is really the *begging* phase when you start out with everything very hazy and the end is definitely uncertain. If your business is a product, this is probably the proof of concept or prototype phase (that should have been completed before leaving academia, but as explained in Chapter 3, sometimes it is better done outside academia). The funds required are modest. If you cannot even raise this amount,

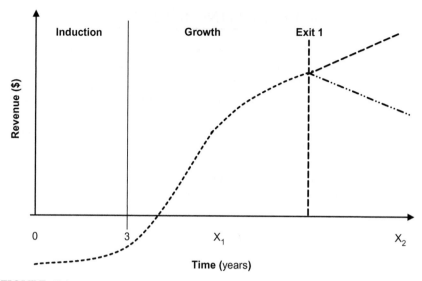

FIGURE 7.1 Product/service lifecycle diagram: exaggerated view of the negative funding period.

you have to seriously re-evaluate the premises for your biomed enterprise. If you conclude that your product to date still has sound potential, you will find the resolve to get funds.

When your product goes into manufacturing, you will require more serious funding. What you will have at this stage is a tangible working prototype that you can let your potential investors visualize, feel and gain the requisite understanding on what it does. For a service, demonstrate the experiment (by video) or invite them to tour your rudimentary facilities. Always remember that people are more willing to excuse appearances (your lab is probably barebones outfitted) when what you have to show excites. Do not undercut yourself at this stage. Stick to the amount of funds you need.

As you transit to the *growth phase*, this is typically where you need a larger fund pool for marketing, product penetration and R&D.

The *cash-out-point*, as implied, is where everyone who wants to exit will leave with a sizable monetary reward for their taking a chance on your venture. Again it is important to remember that you should build your business for continued grow, otherwise it will be more difficult to offload part or all of your enterprise to another party, list on a stock exchange, or buy out your shareholders.

Naturally, being able to obtain enough funds for the phases is all well and good, but it all depends on how effective you are in *recruiting investors*.

7.4 RECRUITING INVESTORS

"There are a lot of money available seeking good opportunities". This was a 1990s statement said to me by more than two friends who move about in the financial sector and a venture capitalist acquaintance who was introduced to me. I believe that statement is always true regardless of economic downturn or upturn, political upheaval and wars. To be *a good opportunity* was covered in Chapters 5 and 6. At least you have to get this right. You will now have to learn how to overcome the final resistance that is bound to be there. You have to read the signs, body language, and when all indications suggests, close the deal. Finally, until the money is in your company's bank account, you cannot relax. But how do you persuade potential fund sources to commit? You start by being the first to buy-in.

7.4.1 Put Your Money Where Your Mouth Is!

Capital investment is a funny game. The perception is that if the guy behind the enterprise isn't willing to place a bet, something must be wrong. Nobody wants to end up as a sucker for somebody else's dreams of grandeur. Professional investors are smart and shrewd, and are able to sense a dubious offer most of the time. The bank loan analogy here is appropriate. You've got to have collateral to be a good risk. Works the same in raising capital, only harder. Raising funds is very different from applying for research funding from some government agency, sponsor or benefactor. The term for this is "skin in the game";[ii] *ergo* you must be the first investor.

This perplexed me very often at the start of my exploits into business. I was willing to put the passion, hours, energy and effort into the venture. But my colleagues in the NUS Technology office kept asking me how much I was going to put into BRASS. Why did I also have to put in the cash? The reason is that others feel more comfortable when you are also risking your own cold hard cash. This is a simple fact. Don't try to understand it, just accept it. Start with that trivial but important amount of $10 K mentioned earlier. As your venture proceeds, you are likely to get drawn in to put more and more of your own funds in just to propel the venture along. Know your limit and watch your company's progress. Here I recommend that only the first $10 K be registered as shareholding. The subsequent amounts should be as loans (with interest) to the company with the option of converting that amount to shareholding at level 0 factoring (i.e. you don't pay a premium per share). This protects you on the one hand, as you can retrieve your money when revenue (not profit)

[ii] A term attributed to Warren Buffett.

begins to be generated, yet permits you the choice to own more equity in the company should you choose, when the company is "further down the road" after 2 or 3 years.[iii]

7.4.2 Don't Give it All Away!

When you ask for funds you have to give up something that is of value. In this case a cut of the payoff, i.e. a share of the company whose value is close to nothing at this stage of start-up. It is intuitively obvious that the more you give away up front, the less you have at the finish line. Remember, you, your idea and your forthcoming effort have an inherent value that is very precious. You should command as much equity as you can.

The flip side is that you have to give some of your potential value to get the funds you require to start. You will be very tempted to compromise your stake in the pie to get the funds to start operations. But beyond a specific limit of compromise the fund guys also know it won't be worth your while, so there is actually a target number to reach. Just know what that number is to you. Know also that as the venture progresses you will have to give up more, i.e. become diluted in your shareholding. Those that come in later have to pay a premium over what you paid.

Giving up is not just about the percentage of the shares. How you plan to execute the business is just as important. Sponsors may want you to give up some control of how you spend the funds they give you, have veto on key decisions, etc. My recommendation is that if you have to give up anything on these issues, it is best to forgo this potential sponsor, as this arrangement is unlikely to work. You can accept input and advice, but the final decisions must be yours to make. Novice and inexperienced you may be, but that goes with the territory of a *runway entrepreneur*. If your potential sponsors don't subscribe to this principle, move on. This will relieve you of the persistent "battles" you are likely to confront with these funding sources.

7.4.3 Other People's Money

The aim of raising funds is not only to reach a *numbers* goal, but also as far as possible, to use *other people's money (OPM)* to achieve that objective. The purpose of sourcing as much funds from others as possible to start a new enterprise is to spread the financial risk of the undertaking

---

[iii]Ensure all this has the proper board of directors resolutions and is documented by the company secretary. There are usually exercise periods to convert into shares – stretch this period as best you can.

over these investors. Each investor has a reason for investing, the level and amount of risk tolerance, and a target exit date and returns sought. Typically, investors can be assigned into groups based on their existing and soon-to-be-initiated relationships with you. Let's go through these different groups of investors and their risk appetite.

7.4.4 Shareholders from Heaven

This is a term used to denote people who give you money in exchange for shares in your company and generally leave you alone to do what you say you will do except for a once a year update. They are normally more tolerant, forgiving and your most sympathetic source. Your family, friends and some close colleagues fall into this category. They have an existing relationship with you and their reason for buying-in is more emotional than rational. They know what you are about and put few demands on you. They have already decided to lose what they put into the venture if necessary. Tap this crowd wisely. Understandably, money and family ties or friendship seldom mix well. Only if you show results are you likely to be received well the second time around. This is a good OPM source for you, as you have relative freedom in running your enterprise. Not having to frequently resolve disputes and negotiate how you spend funds saves time and is less stressful, leaving you to get on with the job. These are the people who invest when the venture has less than a 25% (most times a lot less) probability of succeeding.

I was blessed to have good shareholders in BRASS. NUS (*seed funding*) and my other shareholders for the most part left me to my own devices, but were there to provide counsel when needed. This may have been the trust my shareholders had in me as most knew me for more than 10 years. NUS Technology Holdings only required a once a year submission of BRASS's audited accounts.

Even BRASS's big investor who came on board in year 7 has not interfered with the running of the company and is always supportive of the Board and management. One of the reasons I returned to BRASS in 2009 was to repay his trust in me. Thankfully, I steered BRASS to ride the changing local biomed environment, increased profits, making shareholders smile after reading the annual (independent) auditor's report and collecting their dividends.

7.4.5 Shareholders from Hell

This is a term used to denote people who give you money in exchange for shares in your company and proceed to make your life miserable on almost a daily basis to make you regret ever taking their money. They are usually small-time novice investors who take their role as investors perhaps too seriously. They have no previous, or at most, very superficial history with you. They are not inherently mean or intentionally out to sabotage your venture; it is just in their nature to be more particular and detailed in their dealings about most matters, believing such an approach would better safeguard their investment.

The following story was recounted to me. A particular clinician[iv] and his wife put funds into a medical device start-up for 5% of the company. A condition of their investment was a board seat for the wife. The short version is that the company's affairs and decisions were questioned on a regular basis (a board member after all has fiduciary duties to the company), a real life occurrence of what was stated in the preceding paragraph.

I would avoid these types of investors from the start, even if they were willing to invest when the venture has less than 25% probability of succeeding. You can get a feel for this type of potential investor by the questions they ask and the attitudes they display during the "courting" stage. If your "alarm bells go berserk" you know you should avoid them. But it also really depends on your ability to cope working with these "charged-up" personalities with balancing your needs for funding. Be aware that these scenarios are real.

7.4.6 Participative Shareholders

This is a term used to denote people who give you money in exchange for shares in your company, as well as wanting a role in the company to assist you to arrive at your destination. The lawyer in BRASS who was my co-director is a good example. Lawyers, accountants, retired business veterans and retired colleagues fall into this category. These types of investors are usually street smart, knowledgeable and have money. Their interest in also wanting to be involved is not readily discernible. Find out especially, what they want in return and decide if the offer is on the level, something you require and can live with. They tend to invest when the venture has a 25–50% probability of succeeding, based on their own assessment.

Just be sure they put "skin in the game". You did, and they should as well. Don't buy in to the "service fees for equity" trade. Services rarely can be confined within a fixed scope, are usually not delivered on time or completely, and therefore are hard to quantify in dollar terms. You should also ensure you get along reasonably well and define the "rules of engagement" as the latter two "retiree" categories have time on their hands and may want to get involved more than is comfortable. For yourself, you must watch out for being a "hero worshipper" and/or relegating your decision-making solely to them or a consensus. Managed properly, these shareholders can assist you at tasks you are just learning

[iv]I was informed the clinician had a minor role in the product development.

and can benefit the organization. They should be non-salaried until the financial situation is favorable. Do pay for legal and accounting services and necessary expenses for all participative shareholders.

7.4.7 Institutional Shareholders

A start-up from an academic or research institution is likely to have a ready resource for a portion of the start-up funds, as today's institutional climate is pro-business. Make it work for you. The interactions and deliverables sought depend on the institution and the prevailing administrator. This is the best fund source available to you; try hard to get some of it. Your eventual success will be a source of credit to the institution and you can leverage this fact.

Next are the venture capital people who are much tougher but if you succeed, you know you have it made both in idea and resources to have a good chance of taking your enterprise to the envisioned destination and more. A variation on the venture capital people are the angel investor folks who are cash rich and looking for good prospects. These may be a bit more sympathetic depending on whether they are individuals or not. These two sources of funds are unlikely to participate in the first round of fund raising unless you come highly recommended.[v] If you are granted an audience, don't blow it. Prepare well with all the resources and assistance you can muster.[1] Mentally accept that most will be obligatory listeners whom you will not hear from again and there will be definitely no follow-up. Take it as a learning experience. Those that give you advice or tell you to come back when you are more down the road, thank them. Evaluate what they tell you. Don't go back unless you have made real progress, i.e. your product has been made, cleared all testing regimes, or cleared the regulatory hurdle.

It is unlikely that a *runway enterprise* would be attractive. However, if you survive the thorough scrutiny and are offered a proposition, accept that your venture is probably creditable but do not be overly elated. The forthcoming contract negotiation phase is likely to be loaded with extensive and binding clauses, as well as an equity position that may be unfavorable. You will have to negotiate well and this is where you may have to have legal and other support to get a worthwhile deal. And it is better to walk away from an unacceptable deal.

7.5 BEG, BORROW AND PRAY

Asking for money is not fun, is never easy and is a burden when you finally obtain it. This section attempts to ease your discomfort, to offer

[v] I leave to your imagination what "come highly recommended" implies.

some respite from the unpleasantness the exercise of finding money can do to your resolve. There are contributory ways to get things done other than with money. Not a cure-all, but this certainly can help you when the going gets tough. The operative catchphrase is *beg, borrow and pray* (a play on the phrase "beg, borrow or steal"). "Stealing" is a crime that is not a *runway* entrepreneur or honorable trait, and is substituted by "pray".

1. *You can ask (beg)* your suppliers to give you a break in meeting payment deadlines, or work out a partial payment plan. In the early days of BRASS, cash flow was tight and I did ask my suppliers to be flexible with payment. Some were compassionate; others were not. Those who were not were paid on time, you do not want to handle lawsuits or deal with collection agencies. But enough suppliers gave BRASS extended payment terms that we were able to survive. The other aspect was to call in payments due early, some clients will oblige if you are honest about your cash situation. Asking clients to pay before they received test reports from BRASS also assisted cash flow management. You can also consider leasing laboratory equipment instead of making full payment. While you pay interest on leases, the monthly sums due are smaller compared to a full payment that could be over $10,000.00. You get the picture. Stretch your dollar to survive before you thrive.

2. *You can borrow.* You work with a lot of different organizations that you can trade services with; they can extend you some facility or equipment on a short-term basis in return for something they need from you; perform all you require to do at your client's facilities using their resources. Be creative. You really can do a lot with little.

3. Finally, when all else has been exhausted, *you can pray.* At times when all you can do you have done, it is good to take time-out. You can meditate and have down time to recharge your *batteries.* Catch up with friends or business acquaintances and exchange *war* stories. You may get a suggestion or an inspiration may come. When you take your mind off a matter that has been hounding you 24/7, it may not go away after your break, but you probably will have regained fortitude to better handle the problem and that may be all you require to resume.

7.6 ADVOCATES, EVANGELISTS AND WELL-WISHERS

You will be surprised the following you accrue when you embark on a *runway* enterprise. Your anti-fans, may not wish you well for a myriad of reasons. But in your scientific career all the way to your start-up, you will have stirred a multitude of supporters to your dreams and causes.

This is the intangible that you can never predict with certainty, but you will have advocates and well-wishers in the background, most you will never realize or know. When the occasion occurs, they will do the little bit for you to help you along in many non-monetary ways, just for the sheer pleasure of doing a good deed. I have highlighted some of these instances in Chapter 4 and in Section 7.1 that confirms this is a true phenomenon. Some lead clients may also be impressed with your service or product that they will "evangelize" for you. If you encounter this, make every effort to do a better job than what you are currently doing in order to honor the evangelizers' enthusiasm for you. There are "good Samaritans" out there who never seek or want to be acknowledged. Be aware of this as you go about bringing your enterprise forward. For this crowd, your only response must be to continue to do your utmost, be courteous, and thankful to everyone.

7.7 ABOUT BANKS AND GOVERNMENT SCHEMES

In most instances, banks as a funding source are a non-starter. Banks require collateral, as unsecured loans are considered risky. Some governments have schemes to support small businesses and start-ups secure funds where some of the risks for default on repayment rests or is shared with the government. You will have to evaluate them carefully. Before you secure a loan, discuss with your finance resource person the interest rate and monthly repayment quantum.

BRASS did apply for one government-sponsored bank loan scheme that was approved. The purpose of the loan at the time was to improve *cash flow*. Revenue was increasing steadily and we knew BRASS could repay the loan. Khoon Seng and I still had to personally guarantee the loan. But you don't use your personal funds unless there was a default and therefore the loan made sense.

The situation may be different in another country. For instance in Canada, I am surprised at how ready bankers at local branches broach the subject of extending a company loan when a new company account is opened. Doubtless there are requirements to fulfill and maybe collateral is also required; but the situation appears more small enterprise focused. Perhaps it is the higher number of small self-employed businesses that abound.

Today, many governments are also known to be supporting biomed with various schemes; product development and related grants are common. You can evaluate and leverage some of these schemes if they appeal to you. Let me just highlight some common aspects of these schemes you should be aware of.

First, dealing with government bodies and their agencies is usually bureaucratic. There will be a lot of paper work (forms to fill) and maybe several rounds of presentations and/or discussions to satisfy decision-makers. Be prepared to work through a process that can change regularly. For example, a submission form format may change from the day you access it to the day you submit your application, and you will have to revise to the new format before your application is processed.

Second, your purpose usually needs to fit a pre-conceived definition, i.e. the "flavor of the month" areas of interests the government of the day view are important issues. There are normally government representatives or agents for the respective grant agencies that you can approach for guidance. Use this resource.

Third, grants for industry are different from research grants in academia. Academic research grants are fully funded. Industry grants funding is normally biased to human resource aspects (highest percentage up to 75%) and less on capital expenditure and other business costs.

Finally, the usual form of grant payout is on a reimbursement basis. This means you probably will not get funds upfront, but at least you can look forward to money if and when you complete the terms of the grant contract (some grants follow progressive payment based on completion of milestones). And that can only help your balance sheet.

7.8 BOOTSTRAPPING:
A DOUBLE-EDGED SWORD

"A type of business funding that seeks to avoid relying on outside investors" is one of the definitions provided by *business dictionary.com* for bootstrapping. In other words instead of seeking "donations" you make as much of your own money as possible to pay for the needs to bring your product or service to market.

There are two common ways to pull off the bootstrap lifeline. First, is in-house. You possess an expertise, scientific or engineering know-how you can peddle for consultancy jobs to bring in revenue. This depends on your local environment in terms of how many potential clients require your type of expertise and what they are willing to pay. If successful in securing these small jobs, apart from money coming in, your organization's credibility starts building a reputation, and you become more proficient of your business area.

Second, you can be an agent and represent your "principals" in services and/or products. In this instance, you gain revenue, knowledge of your industry with regard to the services and products, and a client pool, depending on the level of synergy between what you represent and your own products/services. Overall, in the initial period of up to 3 years, the advantages of receiving funds from bootstrapping normally outweigh any disadvantages.

BRASS did all three. We consulted before accreditation, and represented Charles River Laboratories (CRL) for their endotoxin reagents and NAMSA for their tests services. The revenue brought in permitted BRASS to build its testing arm, leading to market presence and eventually a premier service reputation. Because of the synergy with CRL's products and NAMSA's products and services, BRASS benefited from association with the industry and client pool.

The downside of taking on an agency is you can get "burned". Khoon Seng related a story of an acquaintance he knew who had taken on an agency for a medical device company. She developed the market for 2 years and the product was gaining acceptance towards the end of that period. Shortly after, the principal informed her they would enter the local market themselves and paid her token compensation.

Nevertheless, you should treat bootstrapping as supporting your main endeavor. Refrain from an over reliance on these relationships as sources of continued revenue, and when an appropriate occasion arises, untie your bootstraps amicably. Your overarching focus is to build up your own capabilities and pursue your true direction and goals to success.

7.9 IT WILL NEVER BE NEVER ENOUGH!

Biomed has the reputation as a capital-intensive game. It is triple and quadruple redundancy at its most maniacal extreme, all in the name of patient safety. You build processes in to check, check again and finally ensure that everything is checked. And when you submit for regulatory approval, the checking process begins all over again, only this time you have to convince a group of people who err on the side of caution. All this costs big bucks, in equipment, in personnel, in processes, in everything. This fact used to be constantly on my mind when I first started. You have gotten a glimpse in earlier chapters and more details are forthcoming in later chapters that I never let this matter deter me.

The simple truth is the "not enough money" predicament will be with you from day 1 until the day you completely are free of the enterprise. Your concern about money is not only in this start-up phase, but each day you are in business. How to pay your staff, the utilities, the rent and every invoice will be a regular issue. The best way to solve it is to grow your business to the point it is not a *daily* concern. That is what I did with BRASS with regards to money. You can too.

I reiterate: at the start, try and estimate as best your financial requirements and seek approximately 50% of what you require and get going.

And in the end learn to use what you have to cover everything. **Spend wisely.** This is literally all you can do. And if you do that, and adopt the pointers I dispense in Chapter 11, you will have a good chance of getting to the same position that money *will not be a daily concern.*

Real World Lessons Learnt

General
1. Biomed is expensive.
2. Don't be overly concerned about insufficient funding to start.
3. The first people wanting to part with their money for your cause are true supporters.

Specific
1. You start by putting your own money in first.
2. Choose your shareholders wisely. Better to walk away from someone difficult with lots of money than live in misery with that person after you take their money.
3. Use and stretch resources to extend the value of your funds in hand.

Quote for the Chapter

"A bank is a place that will lend you money if you can prove that you don't need it".

Bob Hope: (1903–2003; well-known American comedian and actor)

Reference

[1] For details on how to do this you are referred to Kawasaki G. The Art of the Start.: Portfolio/Penguin; 2004.

8

About Meeting Regulatory Requirements

8.1 IMPLIED, EXPECTED, DELIVERED

Imagine one evening you feel unwell and intuition suggests that it may be more than just the common flu. You get to a night clinic and after the requisite wait the physician in attendance assesses your situation as requiring immediate further treatment at the hospital. When the ambulance arrives, the paramedics place you on a gurney and load you into the ambulance for the trip to the hospital. In the tight cabin space you note all the medical equipment and supplies around you. The EMT (emergency medical technician) places an oxygen mask on you. She next dons gloves and rips open sterile packaging from which she removes a catheter to insert into your arm to start an IV line. She also wraps your

From Academia to Entrepreneur.
DOI: http://dx.doi.org/10.1016/B978-0-12-410516-4.00008-2
147

free upper arm with a cuff and takes your pulse and blood pressure, noting the readings.

Arriving at the hospital, you are received at the EMERGENCY area, examined by the medical staff and admitted as a patient. The nurse hooks you up to an electronic box that displays your vital signs continuously; the duty *vampire* (blood technologist) rips open a sterile package and inserts a sterile needle into a vein in your arm, collects your blood into color-coded vacutainers® and heads to the lab to assay the contents. This is followed by the duty nurse inserting a couple more needles into your arm, connecting the hub ends to tubes that lead into semi-translucent bags containing saline and pharmaceuticals all hung up above you, passing through pumps complete with various LED indicators and alarms, directing the amount of fluid and medication you receive per time period.

Lying in that hospital bed in emergency undergoing treatment, your thoughts wander through the events of the past few hours. Your life hung in the balance. Yet with the passage of time, you grew calmer. You became confident that barring the remote adverse event, you would pull through and recover. Your relief is probably founded on *three primary patient care perceptions* most people have acquired from experience, reinforced by your observations in the preceding episode. These are:

1. In most progressive countries, there is a rigorous selection criteria accompanied by a good training program, on-going upgrading of skills and periodical review by superiors and peers, resulting in a high level of competence and dedication for medical services staff. You are quite comfortable in accepting that these healthcare service providers from the clinic physician, the EMTs, and the doctors, nursing and support staff, will do their best for you, *the patient.*

2. You are confident that the pharmaceutical products used to treat you will contribute to your full recovery because they are clinically relevant and well manufactured. Your general knowledge assures your subconscious that these legal drugs have undergone a rigorous process of selection, evaluation, production and trials before they were ever used on the larger patient population.

3. a. The patient monitoring and assist equipment used on you are well thought out, properly manufactured and they perform robustly, with beeps and alarms going off when appropriate. If you were more perceptive, you probably had noticed sophistication in some units compared to others, a sign of constant upgrading by the manufacturers to match advancement in science and technology and the needs of the healthcare facility as much as budget can support.

b. Finally, the array of disposables such as gloves, catheters, needles, syringes, IV line tubing, vacutainers® and other supplies used for the benefit of the patient were properly packaged, with evidence of proper sterilization, production and expiry dates. Here again, you probably noted the varying designs and complexities of products that make their way into every aspect of clinical care.

In essence, for you, the implied and expected of the biomed industry has been delivered.[i] This favorable impression has come about because for more than 50 years, the regulatory agencies of many countries and the biomed industry have interacted with each other to successfully entrench this subliminal acuity in you. Let's explore this further.

8.2 GETTING TO KNOW REGULATORY REQUIREMENTS

The *implied* and *expected* alluded to above is that generally, patients and the public believe that medical products are properly made and of good quality, and have passed safety and use tests that meet health authority requirements, i.e. are *regulatory compliant*.[1] This perception is valid. The gains made in regulatory compliance for biomed products since the latter half of the twentieth century have been substantive, and continue to evolve.

To recap, selling a biomed product in a country requires you to meet the legal requirements administered by the pertinent authorities of that country as they pertain to manufacture, sale and use. The biomed product must be as safe as current understanding permits, and its benefits in use shown to outweigh (preferably substantially) potential risks in using the product. The intent is to protect their citizens from known or reasonably anticipated preventable harm with a medical product that works. Some of the regulatory agencies you probably will have to deal with are the Australian TGA, Health Canada, the Chinese CFDA, the EU member countries' Health Ministries, the Japan Ministry of Health, Labor & Welfare and the US-FDA.

There is a lot of information published on their websites, as well as most other countries' health authorities' websites, on how they accept biomed products for sale in their country. How to produce, and what and how to test biomed products, to provide the vital information required in a submission compilation to regulatory authorities in support of a biomed product for approval, follow a rigorous process. Once you know one system, you will be able to recognize similarities in another.

[i]Healthcare service providers (who are recruited and trained, not manufactured) are excluded.

Bringing a biomed product to market is a non-trivial exercise. Meeting regulatory requirements is more than ticking items off a checklist to satisfy in a legal manner that a product intended for sale in a territory has complied with the necessary rules. Do not be overwhelmed or intimidated by the deluge of information you have to master. All the complexity behind this regulatory enigma distills down to two straightforward facts:

1. The law of a country is what you have to comply with, as the manufacturer and/or supplier of biomed products.
2. Regulations are the mechanisms used by a country's health authority for you to comply with the law. The sponsoring organization (i.e. your company) must satisfy and reasonably prove by various processes imposed on the manufacture, and through tests and/or scientific studies on the finished goods, that the biomed product is well conceived, well made, works and is safe. Two insights on what this entails, quality systems and the use of science-based studies will be elaborated later in this chapter. The burden of proof is on the sponsor (you), not the regulatory agency. *Compliance is mandatory.*

Knowing, understanding and working through the extensive documentation that exists for compliance and related procedures, and keeping updated on changes, i.e. dealing with regulatory matters, as stated in an earlier chapter, is a fulltime job and someone other than you should do this. *Your objective* as a biomed *runway* entrepreneur is to be familiar enough with regulatory matters to:

1. Interact sensibly with a regulatory consultant or your own staff tasked with regulatory matters to get your product through the regulatory submission and approval process.
2. Make informed decisions in paying for regulatory-related matters as you control your company's purse strings.

Making a commitment to gain at least a working knowledge of regulatory matters will go a long way to establishing your credibility as an authentic player in the "biomed club". It is an important "license" to obtain and maintain, and I urge you not to compromise on this aspect for profit. To begin, let's narrow the information you have to cope with by answering three main questions.

(1) WHAT ARE YOU GETTING REGULATORY APPROVAL FOR?

The obvious answer is a medical product. This is further differentiated into:

a. Pharmaceutical or bio-pharmaceutical.
b. Medical device.
c. *In vitro* diagnostics (usually classified as a medical device).

d. Others (e.g. health supplements, cosmetics, depending on the classification method).

This is the part where you deal directly with health authorities. Each type of product has different requirements with regard to facility certification and mainly scientific evidence you have to provide to the regulatory agency/authority to demonstrate your product is safe and effective. For example, the FDA website posts comprehensive regulatory information on what is required for a medical device to meet compliance, such as "quality system (QS) regulation" and "labeling requirements". Working through the documents will help you find out what you need to do.

A biomed service, for example testing, is a component of this process in that the science-based testing results performed in these facilities provide the primary scientific information required by regulators to make a judgment on the product's overall safety and effectiveness. Practices normally conform to either GLP[ii] and/or ISO 17025[2] that dictate how facilities are to perform testing.

(2) WHAT ARE THE MANUFACTURING REQUIREMENTS?

The design, prototyping and manufacturing of medical devices were introduced in Chapter 3. To meet regulatory requirements, you carry out all these tasks, especially manufacturing in a certified facility, be it your own or a sub-contractor's. Some leeway can be exercised; for example the certified facility qualifies by audit the design component of a separate non-certified location. The certified facility takes on the responsibility that all work performed at the satellite non-certified location conforms to its certification. Before BRASS received accreditation in 2000, a pharma client qualified BRASS by audit to perform tests for them.

The type of certification depends on your target sales countries and the country of your operations. For example, a manufacturing facility for medical devices is required to be ISO13485 certified in Canada, while for the USA, the US-FDA QSR requirements must be met. ISO9001 certification normally suffices if you are producing raw materials and components.[iii] Many other countries adopt ISO13485 or have their own requirements that are normally variations or modifications of one or a combination of the above.

You will have to get your facility to the required level based on the Standard you are conforming to, and be audited and approved by a certification granting body such as a *Notified Body* for the EU member countries. The US-FDA does its own inspection. If you use a manufacturing

---

[ii]Good Laboratory Practice.

[iii]Be prudent and verify with your consultant. There are details in your processes or products that may require another choice.

sub-contractor, ensure that they have the necessary credentials that are *current*.

Pharmaceutical manufacturing follows a comparatively more stringent GMP[iv] process.

(3) WHAT ARE THE TESTING REQUIREMENTS?

For a medical device, testing normally applies to the end product that is in final fully assembled packaged form (some devices require assembly by the end user). The class of the device and the level and duration of contact with the body determines what safety tests are to be done. The ISO10993 provides a table that you can use to determine what types of biological tests have to be performed.[v] Biocompatibility studies are normally performed under GLP (Good Laboratory Practice – it is a regulation). Others include sterility assurance and endotoxin limits verification, bioburden and package integrity.

The testing regime for pharmaceuticals is more elaborate and stringent, as most drugs go inside the body. Furthermore, drugs have been regulated much longer than medical devices and more is known and applied. The chemistry has to be verified and how the drug behaves *in vivo* assessed. There are also requisite phases of clinical (human) trials.

Working through the three questions helps define and direct you to the necessary information you require for your matter at hand (that is already considerable), relieving you of having to handle the more routine and non-relevant (to you) aspects.

Understanding the information you require may be challenging for a novice since there is a lot to cover, but it is surmountable. For a *runway* start-up, your path to comprehension is more or less by trial and error. Alternatively, you hire a consultant from the get-go to guide you through the process. It is wise to do a combination of both. The simple stuff is obvious to do. You are familiar with the country you set up your enterprise in, and have settled on the intended countries of sale. You also know what you are going to make, a pharmaceutical, bio-pharmaceutical, medical device, etc. Therefore, you can obtain and familiarize yourself with the regulations of the countries of interest, including the specific requirements for your product type.

You follow this up by attending the many courses conducted by consulting companies and some regulatory agencies (some you may have to pay) on regulatory related topics. For example, the US-FDA has several free online courses that you can access. You will gain a general knowledge in these matters from these activities. The next step is when you

---

[iv] Good Manufacturing Practice.

[v] Ensure the regulatory authority you are submitting to accepts this.

consider bringing in a consultant. For a facility, a consultant will assist you to bring your operations to the required level to pass certification audit. For medical devices testing, I recommend where possible working with a regulatory consulting organization (known as CROs – contract research organizations) with testing capability or *vice versa*. This normally optimizes costs as well as workflow. The consultant on your project will be motivated to get on top of the testing component to move your regulatory paperwork along as they have access to their own tests experts. This is a reasonable and efficient approach.

8.2.1 Regulatory Affairs

The pharmaceutical industry is comparatively mature. For a pharma and/or bio-pharma start-up, the hiring of a Regulatory Affairs (RA) professional may be more appropriate due to the intense level of compliance required. Regulatory Affairs is a profession particular to biomed, specifically to pharmaceutical, biotech, medical devices and functional foods. "The RA professional in a company is the interface between the organization and its products and regulatory authorities. Their role is to ensure their company keeps up with changes in regulations and laws, and that their company complies in the markets they serve. Compliance is over all aspects, from development, manufacture, testing, marketing, registration and licensing of the company's regulated products". You may consider training an existing staff, or be on the lookout for a trained professional with the requisite experience.

Some smaller medical device outfits I know have a combined RA/QA (quality assurance – to be discussed later) position. Realize that the two functions are different, and preferably, the positions should be staffed separately.

Regulatory submission and compliance is a serious matter. A good RA professional that interacts well with the regulatory agency contacts and with personnel in their own organization tasked with duties in this area will facilitate a smooth progress before, during and after the approval process.

8.2.2 Industry Feedback

Before leaving this section, you should note that as new regulations or revisions to existing regulations are being prepared, industry is normally granted opportunities to review proposals and provide feedback. The manner in which this is conducted is again country dependent. This is an important practice as it provides industry a channel to share their opinions on impending regulations that affect a business's operations, finances and revenue. Consider participation where possible, as regulations impact your business and you should know what is forthcoming to incorporate into your work plan.

You should also think of being active in Standards work, either as a national representative or on a committee in a trades/technical group or association. For example, the ISO has technical committees on Standards for various aspects. You will obtain an insight into how representatives from government, agencies, industry and academia interact to derive or revise a Standard. Your scientific input could be another channel you can contribute to better biomed products.

Finally, realize Standards and Regulations are subject to interpretations that in practice rely on human beings who are reasonable people.

8.3 ABOUT QUALITY SYSTEMS

Manufacturing and testing (M&T) precedes regulatory submission. M&T are the two sources that provide much of the vital information you put in your submission that is reviewed by the health authorities. The manner these facilities have to operate to meet certification and/ or accreditation criteria, as well as other associated requirements stipulated by respective health authorities, are extensive and time consuming. Books, training courses and consultancies abound to address these important matters.

But at the center of all the activity common to manufacturing and testing facilities is a quality system (QS)[vi] which needs to be in place. A good QS can be inferred from the effort put in by the organization that can be garnered from its attitude, workflow processes, well thought out intra- and inter-organizational activities that produce a biomed product that is generally better rather than just meeting what is required. The organization must also continually strive to manufacture products that testify to its integrity throughout the products' lifecycle. What will be emphasized is that regardless of what system you adopt or follow, the three critical aspects for a robust quality system are:

1. The management being actively responsible for implementation and maintenance of the QS to the required level as the defining attribute for the organization.
2. Every single activity in the manufacturing or testing process comes under the QS. For example, how you purchase, install, qualify and use, service and maintain a piece of equipment must be specified. How you handle, check, store and bring raw materials to the production line; how you clean the facility, etc. are all activities covered by the QS. It does not take much imagination to conclude that this is a humongous task to initiate from scratch, fully implement in

---

[vi] An alternate term is QMS – Quality Management System.

a new facility, and maintain. Only by people performing the tasks as trained and responsibly can this be achieved, i.e. people matter.

3. A QS is dynamic and must be in constant review and update as well as adapt to changes when requirements are revised. Continuity is the only recourse.

Without these three factors being met well, whatever is implemented is just procedural. Even though the facility may obtain accreditation and/or certification, they may not reveal the true state of affairs in the facility. Consider the following excerpt from the medical devices sector.

"Medical devices that met standards have been recalled. Quality systems that were said by internal audits to be in compliance with FDA regulations or ISO quality standards received serious questions after external auditing. Devices meeting standards or produced by quality systems felt to be in compliance have put patients at risk by failing at critical moments. Something more than just meeting standards and regulations is needed to provide safe and effective medical devices".[3]

What does this imply? Despite knowing the requirements, and checks being in place, things are not so straightforward. How can it be improved? Let's look at these three factors in greater detail.

8.3.1 Is Management on Board?

All quality systems rely on the management taking the lead. This is realistic, as true compliance can only be achieved from the top down. Without management behind the QS to allocate the necessary human resources and funds, a quality system will not be properly developed and maintained. Paying for HR time to prepare documented procedures, controls and checks, and to properly outfit a facility to the level required is costly. Furthermore, the effort cannot stop or diminish in importance once the certification and accreditation has been obtained. Lapsing into paying transient attention to QS in order to pass subsequent mandated audit inspections can occur. Only management can provide sustained enthusiasm. Management's leadership must be earnest. Otherwise, staff will not take the QS seriously. This is the reason why all known quality systems have this management emphasis.

Ultimately, a good QS is an attitude to want to do things right, from management down to the staff on the production floor, in the lab doing the tests, right down to the persons clearing the trash and cleaning the lab. Clients and others interacting with your organization must get this "feel" that your company "walks the talk".

Your customers' audit teams are not going to be impressed by the number of document revisions you perform, necessary though they may be. They search for other subtle noticeable traces such as in the type of equipment you purchase (the GLP and GMP compliant types are good indicators of commitment), the frequency and how well you carry out your internal checks, calibrations, etc. that are all down in your procedures, recorded and available to be reviewed by your clients' auditors. Even your staff's work attitudes can be revealing. Former employees do talk about their training and how work was performed.

Auditors from accreditation and certification bodies are more likely to note how many times you sat in meetings on internal management reviews (minutes of these meetings that are reviewed during an audit would indicate your attendance). Even if you only just sat in for the meeting, you had to make time to attend, and that says much about your interest in your company's QS. The other notable role you can participate in is to be an internal auditor for some or most of the formal operational activities.[vii] This is particularly meaningful if you audit testing procedures where a scientific background is an advantage.[viii] Internal audit requires active involvement and will be noticed.

Word gets around and the prevailing attitude of your organization towards the QS will come out. You cannot hide. Build a QS you can be proud of. Nurture and permeate the culture throughout your organization.

8.3.2 People Matter

Regardless of what quality system you settle on, ultimately, people are the prevailing factors who determine the quality and performance of an operation in a facility to produce or test medical products. Personnel are involved from the onset of product development through to production, testing and product release. They must have the appropriate academic background and must be properly trained for the job in order to perform their assigned duties well. All training performance indicators should be clearly specified, and proper staff training procedures with records must be maintained. Staff attitude is the most important criteria for the good implementation of processes and procedures that quality systems rely on, i.e.:

Poor work attitude = Probability of poor product is high

Conversely:

Good work attitude = Probability of good product is high

Every employee has a responsibility to the company to ensure that his or her responsibilities are met, thus assuring a quality product is produced.

[vii] You have to train and be qualified as an internal auditor. I was the IQA (Internal Quality Auditor) for BRASS in its first 6 years of operations.

[viii] This presupposes you are competent scientifically in the areas being evaluated.

Who is responsible for compliance? Everyone. Quality is independent of job title and salary, and has no boundaries. Building quality into processes, systems, documentation and the employee's mindset makes sustainable compliance more achievable.[4]

The bottom line: hire good people and train them well. Motivate your staff to a mindset of doing the right thing. Emphasize to them self accountability and make the connection to *patient welfare*.

I relate here the BRASS indoctrination of new staff that I once practiced. I tell them the well-rehearsed hospital bed story, an abbreviated version of the opening scenario to this chapter. They are informed that as a staff of BRASS, they are part of that process that gives the patient assurance and comfort in the knowledge that their best interests are taken care of. Each task they do has impact on the biomed product or the manufacturing process that BRASS, as an outsource supplier to the biomed and healthcare industry, is involved in. They must do it perfectly, each time, every time. Why? The difference between a poor or good outcome may be in their hands. And what if one day that patient is the staff herself or her loved ones! It's a big responsibility. They are asked to own it and live it.

8.3.3 Maintaining the System

The QS must remain an on-going, dynamic activity. You cannot just start well, you also have to effectively maintain the QS well as long as you are in the business. This gets harder as time passes because:

QS IS A COST CENTER

Standards are updated periodically and new revisions have to be purchased.[ix] Check the ISO website and look at the prices for a Standard such as the ISO10725 or ISO10993. Or check the USP website for a subscription to the US pharmacopoeia that is updated annually. This is just a sample of a testing organization's such as BRASS requirements for documents that have to be kept current. You can spend several thousand dollars annually on documentation alone, a sizable sum for a *runway* enterprise.

Sending your staff for training courses in many related and increasingly new aspects of QS and regulatory related matters both locally and overseas; the constant updates of internal quality documents and their implementation, i.e. costs of staffing a QAU (see below); third party calibration of equipment, etc. and of course the recurrent audits and surveillance, all impact expenditure that can be substantial to your annual budget.

[ix]One of the reasons I reference the US-FDA frequently is because the information is freely available.

And this is where vigilance must be exercised, because in lean times when cost trimming is proposed, the QS is an easy victim. But the QS is an integral part of an organization's reputation where it is taken for granted that a high standard exists and is maintained. Find ways to continue supporting this aspect of your operations. Do not slack as your product's integrity can slide, and a person's health may be compromised for this lapse.

8.3.3.1 *About Quality Assurance and Internal Audit*

An important aspect of maintaining the QS is supporting the quality assurance unit (QAU). The QAU is normally an independent unit in your organization that reports directly to you as the CEO. The purpose of the QAU's independence is principally to provide unbiased assessment of all other units in your organization where activities pertain to QA matters. The QAU has an undeserved reputation as the "police force" of the organization because of its mandate to review, correct and recommend practices for all other units in the organization.

A key QAU function is to conduct internal quality audits (IQA) on a regular basis. An IQA, as the term suggests, is where units of the organization responsible for the manufacture and/or testing of a biomed product (typically operations) are "inspected" by the QAU, for example their documentation handling, record keeping and conduct of work, to see if they meet defined expectations. Traditionally this is where most of the disputes between the QAU and operations have arisen, as the focus was on "spotting" shortcomings for QA issues in operations. By training and nature of the job scope, QAU personnel are normally more rigorous and conservative in their interpretation of Standards and documented procedures. On the other hand, operations personnel are more focused on getting the job done. In most instances, it is a matter of the two parties' view of how work has to be performed. You have to manage this interaction between the QAU and the rest of your organization by stepping in and resolving through rationalization each particular matter that arises, another important reason for management involvement. QA is an important function and when performed appropriately, the entire organization benefits.

8.4 THE USE OF SCIENCE-BASED STUDIES

A well-implemented and sustained QS in the manufacturing component is the foundation of producing a good biomed product. When you advance to testing of your biomed products, science becomes a companion to providing good and reliable evidence for the product's safety and effectiveness. The ensuing discussion provides a snapshot of this topic utilizing medical devices as example.

The testing of medical devices for safety and performance can be extensive depending on the Class of device. Potential structural and mechanical failures of medical devices are more design and in-use related and is the purview of engineering studies that are outside this discussion's scope. Here we use safety as the platform to discuss the merits of science-based studies. A comprehensive presentation on this topic can be obtained from Gad, from which the following statement was obtained:[5]

"The assessment of safety to patients using the multitude of items produced by this industry is dependent on schemes and methods that are largely peculiar to these kinds of products, are not as rigorous as those employed for foods, drugs and pesticides, and are in a state of flux".

The above statement might at first reading give you cause for alarm. Be assured that the intention was merely to point out the "youthfulness" of the medical device industry. If the pharmaceutical industry is taken as an adult, then the medical device industry is more like an adolescent child. It is also a case of not knowing back then what we know now, i.e. there were unfortunate adverse events encountered with medical devices that have led to progressively better understanding of how materials interact with the human body. Lessons were learnt about materials' usage in medical devices that benefit today's activities in developing medical devices, as well as their regulatory approval process for use. Going forward, new science and better ways of carrying out existing processes can only improve understanding further, leading to even better and safer medical devices in the future.

Let's focus on the biological and chemical aspects in safety testing of medical devices. A key feature is biocompatibility studies. The biocompatibility of a material is specific to a particular end use. The reason is straightforward. A material in its raw form may, can and has been known, to undergo changes during manufacturing and processing (temperature and pressure are two common conditions that can change a material's characteristics) to convert that material into a medical device, and that process is device specific. Therefore, the biocompatibility of a biomaterial has to be evaluated each time a new application is devised for that biomaterial. The "ISO10993 Standard: Biological evaluation of medical devices" describes how to go about these studies.

The main features of such studies in trying to define the safety of medical devices are summarized as follows:

1. All tests are non-clinical (or pre-clinical), i.e. they do not use human subjects. These tests are intended to establish the extent biomaterials in their finished medical device form may present harm when in use. The detection of the presence of degradation (chemically and physically derived) products and leachable materials are two examples.
2. All tests are short-term (even if over several months), utilizing mainly a series of cell culture and small animal model studies. Results

coupled with experience can contribute to an understanding of possible effects that may be harmful.

3. By combining the results of individual studies, a broad profile can be obtained to make potential estimates on the device's safety prospects.

4. Therefore, these studies can be used as predictors of the product's safety. They should be treated as provisional, not confirmatory. The final position regarding safety can only be reasonably arrived at when the product is in use with patients, the longer without any issues, the better. This is the purpose for post-market surveillance in regulatory requirements.

5. Furthermore, much is now known about the contributory causes of materials-related safety issues and resolution, attributed to a large extent by the more than 50 years of experience with medical devices and biomaterials. This is why materials with a track record are favored and new materials are relatively difficult to approve.

6. The latest trend is risk assessments, the key motivators being the move away from reliance where possible on animal models, and reducing costs.

7. The appearance of Part 18 for ISO10993, a Standard on chemical characterization of materials, is an example in this direction. Part 18 was not a component of ISO10993 in a previous edition published only in 2005. By reviewing data derived according to this Standard via a risk assessment, much can be deduced regarding the potential safety of a material when used as a component in a medical device, thereby facilitating materials selection as well as reducing testing requirements on the final product.

8. Science is subjective and there is a lot of scope in interpretation. The better the understanding and the better the experimental design, the more confident the results should be with regard to safety.

The purpose of the preceding summary to a biomed *runway* entrepreneur is to make you aware of and appreciate that these science-based studies have come a long way and can be useful. You know the product you plan to make and the materials to be used. Performing mainly literature-based searches and evaluating the information gathered can help you reveal or pinpoint many potential issues, if any, at the concept stage. This essentially "experimental-less" exercise can be beneficial to your overall development and manufacturing program by:

1. Further improving your confidence that what you are producing will be safe and will pass the regulatory hurdle.

2. Forestalling and avoiding an unfavorable result during the testing stage because many potential issues would have been identified and dealt with in the development phase.

3. Reducing the probability that revision of your manufacturing process down the road in light of an unfavorable testing study result will occur.
4. Saving you precious time and money.

Of course, this cannot guarantee that you will catch all issues, but this is a method to remove as much uncertainty from a costly undertaking and assist you to be on schedule in your timelines to producing a safe and effective biomed product.

The bottom line is that while you were in academia, this field has not been a concern. But as a biomed *runway* entrepreneur, paying attention to regulatory matters is an important aspect of your overall responsibilities.

Real World Lessons Learnt

General
1. It is about doing what is right and good for the patient.
2. It is a very "Regulated" world today.
3. Know what you must. Leave the rest to the experts.

Specific
1. Good quality processes begin and end with you.
2. Maintaining good QS is a lifetime event for your company.
3. It is about attitude, not just *comply-titude*.

Quote for the Chapter

"Quality is not an act, it is a habit".
Aristotle (384–322 BC; Greek philosopher and scientist,
student of Plato and teacher of Alexander the Great)

References

[1] Sample references: *Compliance handbook for pharmaceuticals, medical devices, and biologics.* Carmen Medina, editors. Marcel Dekker, 2004. *FDA regulatory affairs: a guide for prescription drugs, medical devices and biologics.* Pisano DJ, Mantus DS, editors. Informa Healthcare USA Inc., 2008.
[2] International Standard ISO/IEC 17025: General requirements for the competence of testing and calibration laboratories.
[3] Levin M. More than standards and regulations are needed to provide safe and effective devices. Biomed Instrum Technol 2001;35:331–7.
[4] *Compliance handbook for pharmaceuticals, medical devices, and biologics.* Carmen Medina, editors. Marcel Dekker, 2004 [Chapter 12].
[5] Gad SC. Safety evaluation of medical devices, 2nd ed NY: Marcel Dekker; 2002.

9

About Consultants

9.1 ABOUT CONSULTING

Among the many duties of an academic staff, one task is providing a suitable response to students who seek your advice on a range of topics such as modules to take, the specializations in your discipline (mine

From Academia to Entrepreneur.
DOI: http://dx.doi.org/10.1016/B978-0-12-410516-4.00009-4

was chemistry) to choose, types of career prospects for various study programs, etc. Through the years I have noted one recurrent detail. No matter how well intentioned or relevant my suggestions may have been (albeit from my perspective), an overwhelming majority of recipients of my "learned" comments generally follow the path they had decided before they sought me out.[1] I have inferred (perhaps skeptically) that *advice* is seldom followed for the simple fact that since it is unpaid solicitation, the recipient probably concludes that the advice does not have much bearing on them.

On the other hand, I have anecdotally observed that many listen and act on what consultant(s) tell them. The attitude appears to be since they paid for the experts who have (presumably) thoroughly evaluated the situation, the consultant must be right.

While both an academic staff and consultant are experts in their own right, the two are distinct.

Advice is freely asked and given, more on a personal level, therefore its value is harder to measure, and there is no real expectation by both the providing and (especially) receiving parties. Just an alternative among many pieces of advice that is handy to gather but can be superfluously discarded.

Consulting is paid, as it is a professional and work related matter, and there is an implicit expectation placed on the consultant. Both the paying party and the consultant treat consulting seriously.

9.2 THEY ARE OUT THERE

When you are an employee, the institution or organization you work for handle matters such as human resource hiring, salaries disbursement and legal affairs. When you start up a business, you enter a world where as the entrepreneur, these varied matters become your responsibility. In the real world, these facets are more important; there are laws that you have to be aware of and comply with. This is your learning curve, some of the dues you usually pay to succeed. Let me assure you, you are not as helpless as you think, and in my experience you have a lot going for you if you permit your common sense to rule over your trepidation.

One of the advantages of starting-up in a country like Singapore is its thought-out infrastructure. I have found that the pro-business environment assists you in starting-up easily. As long as you follow the guidelines you are pretty much OK. Furthermore, if you don't know, just ask. Many of the government agencies have websites that tell you in detail

---

[1]Based on the students' comments when they first seek you and their decision feedback.

what to do, what is required, how to do it and how much it costs. It may take some time and many mouse clicks to assemble all the information you require, but it is there and not beyond you. You can also call up or visit their offices. I was frequently pleasantly amazed at the service I received on both fronts, calling and at the service centers.[ii] Even if your business is not located in Singapore, there are probably similar rules in your country; you just have to get to know how government bureaucracy, business and labor affairs in your country are organized. Regardless of where you are in today's world, it is easier now than it has ever been.

Inevitably, there will come a time when you will have done all that you can. You need not feel inadequate because of your inexperience and scientific or technical only background. Being a "know all" is never a job requirement for an entrepreneur. There will be functions you know nothing about or are best done by another party. At this juncture, you will have to consider hiring some expertise on a (preferably) short-term basis, to assist you in sorting out specific matters. This is when you may wish to contemplate finding a *consultant*.

A *consultant* in our context *is*:

a. A professional expert with a specific skill set and/or specialized knowledge (oftentimes with experience).
b. A contracted service provider for a specified period at an agreed fee.
c. The terms and proposed deliverables are normally specified in a contract prior to commencement of work.

A consultant *is not* (or should not be):

a. An employee, and should not be treated as one.
b. A substitute for you in the areas they are expert in.
c. A cure-all approach to solving problems in your organization.

There are many kinds of consultants for all kinds of purposes available, but generally are of two varieties.

Category 1 are those who assist you to sort out strategic matters or help you identify fundamental flaws in the way you do things in the consultant's specialization. Category 1 consultants usually are one-off hires to initiate "grander schemes" or handle "mini crises", and are what most people conceive when the term *consultant* is mentioned. These consultants are typically senior persons who have built up their expertise in big corporations, and left for a number of reasons such as early retirement, independence, searching for new challenges, etc.

Category 2 are those who have expertise that you require to take care of more routine tasks on a regular basis, much like a sub-contractor. They

---

[ii]I state for the record, this was my experience. Your reception may be different.

are normally companies or owner-operated entities specializing in a particular field such as finance and legal matters. I include them under the consultant umbrella because as a *runway* concern, this resource provides you a *value for money* channel to get things done while avoiding wearing out your welcome with relatives, friends and contacts that you have been approaching for advice in their field of expertise for your business.

Listed below are a few common types of experts that you may consider engaging at various stages in your company's growth. Some are predominantly Category 1, others belong more to Category 2, but no differentiation is made, as there can, at times, be crossover between the categories depending on your circumstances.

1. *Business consultants* typically assist you in organizational matters, while others may assist you in plotting out your business growth strategies.
2. *Regulatory compliance matters consultants* can guide you through developing a quality system, product testing, and if you are registering a biomed product, the product submission and approval process. BRASS is considered a provider in this category.
3. *Accounting* services can assist you to organize your accounting system. They can also provide monthly bookkeeping services, as well as annual audits of your company's accounts (to be proper, the two functions, bookkeeping and annual audits, should be done by separate accounting firms), and can act as company secretary. Accountants differ in function to *financial advisors* whose role is to help you plan the utilization of your funds more effectively, as well as guide you in building value for your company for M&A or IPO.
4. *Legal services* include drafting and filing of patents, trademark and copyright applications, and other IP processes and protection. They are also required for business contracts and agreements, disputes handling, and can act as company secretary.
5. *Sales and marketing consultants* can provide sales training for your staff; plan and organize marketing campaigns or develop marketing strategies.
6. *Operations experts* can review processes in your organization such as daily workflow, and provide recommendations for improvement.
7. *Technical experts* can train your staff in skills and knowledge in manufacturing processes, as well as specific projects for your business growth.
8. *Human resource consultants* can guide you in recruitment, payroll, developing staff handbook, staff performance review, etc. They are normally different from "*Headhunters*" who specialize in the recruitment of high value-add staff.

9. *Media consultants* can assist you to project your organization's image in print, audio, visual and Internet presence as well as for product launches. Developing your company logo may also be a task you want a specialist to handle.
10. *IT (Information Technology)* consultants can assist with establishing your organization's IT infrastructure, including servers and security, and Internet and e-mail services.

For Category 2 consultants, their main purpose may be to set-up tasks to be taken over by any in-house staff you had already identified as part of the plan. Alternatively, the intention for the consultant is short-term until work volumes grow to a level that justifies the hire of a full-time staff to perform the consultant's function. It is best at that stage to hire a suitable person and have the consultant train the new hire to do the work. Few consultants would want to revert to full-time employment or become an employee, and if they propose such an arrangement, consider carefully. Interacting with someone on a regular basis is not the same as daily engagement.

9.3 BEFORE YOU FIND A CONSULTANT

BRASS has used many types of consultants through the years. In many instances, consultants were a cost-effective manner to achieve a missing link in our processes, or brought BRASS through an issue at hand that we did not have the know-how to resolve.

You should not look on consultants as an easy way out or a shortcut to handling matters when patience and a little effort on your part will achieve the same result. Ensure the situations warrant a consultant before you bring one in. Conserve your *cash flow* for many other more important things.

You are not likely to need business, HR and media (who are generally Category 1) consultants in the early stages of your start-up, perhaps until your business is up and running and generating revenue for at least a year, with indications that the revenue will be growing for the next 2 years. Another indicator that you may need them is when your staff strength exceeds 10 and/or your revenue goes over a $1 million. As you grow you need to be more organized, and a structure such as reporting and workflow has to be built to maintain the company's momentum. Your staff will need to convert from *Jack & Jill of all trades* to specialists. A good business and/or HR consultant will assist you to achieve this.

The caution of the threshold is that bringing in consultants too early will disrupt the harmony and synergy in your five-or-less-person team who are reacting to "crises" at a "gut" level. A small team understanding at the start-up stage is crucial for survival, since whoever is available has been empowered to handle the matter at hand. When a person is entrusted with responsibility, the results are uncharacteristically amazing as individuals usually respond well under such circumstances. Compartmentalization or "pigeon-holing" duties and responsibilities too early stifle this activity because the common response is "I thought that was someone else's duty".

Used wisely and at strategic junctions of your enterprise progress, the payoff in hiring a consultant can be worthwhile.

Identifying the role and duration for the consultant must precede the sourcing of a consultant. If you identify that you require a consultant for more than 6 months, the expertise is probably a staff you should be hiring instead of searching for a consultant. You should also determine what you plan to (or can) spend on the consultant. Take some time with your team and get their *buy-in*.

9.3.1 What Do You Need?

A consultant does not know what you want or need. Only you do. A consultant's effectiveness is commensurate with what he is hired to do and achieve. If you bring a consultant in and ask them to identify what you want or need, you will probably use the consultant incorrectly, waste precious funds, and almost certainly will not accomplish what you hired the consultant for. There are exceptions, such as situations when you know there is a problem but cannot identify it. The consultant in this instance, being an outsider, may provide a fresh perspective, especially in spotting what you cannot see because of your close proximity to the matter.

Do an audit of what is lacking either in skills or functions in your organization, or what you want done that you don't know how to or can't do. Be specific in defining your need for the particular situation at hand and the outcome you want, even though you may have encountered the issue before. This is because the same need may require a different approach each time the matter surfaces, so do not treat this as a trivial exercise.

For example, if you were considering testing your medical device product, you already know the device class and where you are going to sell. If you plan to introduce your product in China, you would want a consultant familiar with the Chinese CFDA's approval process and medical product testing requirements. The language, culture and requirements are different from what you have been used to in Western countries. Alternatively, if you plan to sell in the USA, a different expert familiar with the US-FDA procedures may be a better choice. The same expert may be familiar with both, but you have to verify. On a preliminary basis, you can have a discussion with the candidate consultant to assess the work required and the timeframe to complete. The consultant should be able to provide you with an estimate for the cost of the work. Ask your consultant to also include contingency amounts, as these can affect your *cash flow*. Leverage when you can. For example, NAMSA, whom BRASS represents in testing services, has offices in Shanghai, China and a head office in the USA. Conceivably, one organization can handle both jobs described above, but you may have to deal with two separate offices (i.e. two separate consultants). You can request for one quote that covers both submissions, but be prepared to receive separate quotes on the submission component, as there may be two billing practices for the two countries. In contrast, the testing is likely to be done in the USA; therefore you would probably receive only one quote for testing. As far as is possible, stick to an agreed program and insist on referral back to you for deviations in the work scope.

9.3.2 What Can You Afford?

Consultants span a whole gamut of prices. Big reputable consulting firms that are normally the one-off hires usually do not come cheap. Neither do one-person operations that project their expertise and experience as commanding a premium. Other times, it is just the nature of the job that requires a sizable fee. For example, depending on the scale and impact sought, some marketing or media events can be pricey. Settling for small consulting outfits usually appears to be a bargain but they may not deliver to the extent sought.

Furthermore, you can never predict the outcome of a consultancy proposal with finite certainty. What may appear sensible when presented to you in a conference room can exceed your expectations when launched, i.e. a good outcome, or can be very disappointing when the intended audience miss the point, i.e. you didn't get the effect you wanted despite you and your consultant believing it would. How do you figure out the balance in paying for what you think you will get? It will again be a cost-to-benefit ratio game, a compromise of the following two questions:

9.3.2.1 What do You Consider as Getting Value for What You Pay?

Value, as in beauty, is "in the eye of the beholder". The objective approach to handling this situation is to ensure that the achievable objectives can be fulfilled at a price that will not affect your *cash flow*. In this way, if the bolder objectives are achieved, that's great and you end up with a bonus. If not achieved, it was on budget!

9.3.2.2 How Much Can You Really Pay?

The proposal before you may be great, but out of your price range. Do not be tempted or persuaded unless you are very sure and others on your team support it.

Before you decide, you have in your control your company's financial and *cash flow* positions.

Once you hire the consultant, i.e. *after you decide*, part of that control is eroded because you have to meet the consultant's payment schedule, otherwise the consultant has the right to stop (usually stated in their contract) in mid-project if he is not paid (fees are normally paid progressively according to a time or task completion schedule). At that stage you are left with an incomplete project that may have to be abandoned after expending time and money with nothing to show for the outlays.

Therefore, you should settle for a fee within your *cash flow* capabilities (pay within your means), as this does not add to your stress. Your company may be financially sound and can access additional fund resources in emergencies, but this option should be used only in extreme (survival) cases. Paying for Category 1 consultants on balance are typically about improvements, not about vital functions, therefore they are not an emergency. You can forgo this expenditure until more favorable financial conditions appear.

Category 2 consultants are essentially regular service providers that if you have negotiated reasonably well, are another debtor line in your monthly payment list that has been accommodated in your *cash flow* forecast.

The bottom line: Put a dollar number down and stick to it. Deviate at your own peril.

9.3.3 What Should You Settle for?

High-priced does not necessarily equate to good, nor does it determine the quality of the consultant. This was the purpose for you to define what you need (plan to accomplish) and what you can afford discussed in the previous section, before you begin searching for a consultant. This will prevent you from being inundated by a convincing sales job that may not result in solving the matter at hand, or settling for a consultant you can ill afford. Even if you have the funds, you should refrain from the compulsion to hire a *brand name* for the "image" the consultant can project about your choice. Recall, you are a *runway* entrepreneur whose pride and ego went out the door eons ago.

Neither should you let the lowest bid win the job if the proposal is "not up to scratch". Cheap does not automatically mean bad, but you should question why the bid is low. For example, is the purpose for the low bid to get the job that the consultant can do well or just to get the job?

The bottom line: Do your homework.

9.4 SELECTING YOUR CONSULTANT

First, disregard consultants from academia in most instances, because that is where you originate. You are the expert in your science and engineering. If you require expertise from other academics, try the "in-house" approach first, by requesting some pointers and assistance as a colleague. This is normally a courtesy extended within academia.

You therefore settle for consultants from the commercial setting, because that is most likely what you require. Two pertinent aspects have to be addressed, first is whether they have the necessary credentials to do the job. This is about their background and experience. Second, can they do the job you require? This is about deliverables.

9.4.1 What is the Consultant's Relevant Background and Experience?

For Category 1 consultants, many have high profile credentials. An expert in this category normally would have been working in a relevant field for more than 10 years, usually 20 to 25 years is standard. Scrutinize their résumés (they should provide one; if not, ask). You should look for job appointments commensurate with their promotions and regularity of advancement. Did they change employer frequently, stuck with one their entire work history, or move at strategic points in their career? In your evaluation, it is not so much about one path of advancement being preferred to another, but whether she had made the right impact along the way. Relevant appointments and moves at specific junctures of a work history are indicators of competency, decisiveness, shrewdness and a well thought out personal agenda. These will provide clues about the consultant's potential fit to your requirements and ability to do the job you want done.

Whether the consultant under evaluation was a former corporate bigwig or in mid-level management also matters. The former corporate bigwig's expertise may be more appropriate for a big corporation rather than a *runway* enterprise. There are practices that can be implemented and work well with an organization that employs over a few hundred people, but do not work at all in a 10 to 20 persons outfit, i.e. check if they have experience (and success) working with smaller companies.

The mid-level management expert may be appropriate for the present task at hand, but may not have the broad overview of a top corporate executive for further expansion of the organization. This can be crucial in the overall plan that may stifle your organization down the road. These are just some of the issues you have to consider with regard to the consultants' background and experience. You have to be comfortable with what you eventually decide.

Category 2 consultants are easier to define with regard to work scope and pricing, and therefore easier to resolve. For example, setting up a bookkeeping and general accounting system that is followed by a monthly maintenance contract can be sourced out to a provider for a reasonable cost. Have a 3-month trial followed by a 1-year contract that is subject to renewal. This way you can change the provider or move the operation in-house without too much inconvenience.

In the first few years, BRASS sub-contracted its bookkeeping to a service provider. The bookkeeper that was assigned to BRASS discussed with me how to organize financial data in a fixed format to be sent to her each month for recording. She would have monthly accounts statements ready for collection within 3 days of submission. Agreeing to this format may appear trivial, but for a start-up this was vital. The statements contained the AR (accounts receivables), the information on who owes you money that impacts *cash flow*, are the lifeblood of a company. We were satisfied with this provider and stuck with them until we moved the process in-house many years later.

Others require more thought. For example, patent attorneys can be costlier than patent agents who are just as qualified.[iii] A patent attorney knows the law better. A patent agent would presumably know the science and engineering better. Should you go with the patent agent whose fees are likely to be the lower? Flip a coin? But a patent is not so simple. First, you have to determine whether the provider is familiar with biomed. Second, how specialized in biomed are they? Third, is the price commensurate with the task at hand? Most times a quick discussion would provide you with the feel to make a decision on the right consultant. Listen to what they say and don't say. If they are comfortable with the S&T or the field of the work (that usually gives confidence that your patent claims will be done well) it will show. If they don't mention specifics about the S&T, ask a few more questions. Sometimes they really don't know, other times they may just have left it out. The other aspect is how well they know and keep up with changes in patent related laws in major countries. Have a couple of questions along these lines and listen to the responses.

It is also important to remember that the same type of consultant can have differing background and experience. Using another regulatory example, an expert from the pharmaceutical industry may not be as familiar when dealing with a medical device submission to the same

---

[iii] The difference between the two is a law degree. An attorney has one; an agent does not.

regulatory authority they are familiar with, just because of the product type. They may have experience doing both that only further clarification can determine.

Finally, always be discerning in your assessment and once you settle on a particular expert, do not permit a substitution by the consulting organization or change to another provider barring exceptional circumstances. Seek the recommendations of friends, colleagues and associates and look at their track record. Speak to their previous or on-going clients if you know them or are introduced by the candidate consultant. Most of these service providers (both categories) that I have used came by way of referrals and recommendations. Cold calls require effort to sort out, so do your due diligence.

The bottom line: Do your homework (again). You can do a comparison table format:

1. In column 1, list the consultants.
2. In column 2, their plus points.
3. In column 3, your reservations.
4. Assign a grading number from 1 to 5 (or 1 to 10) for columns 2 and 3.
5. In column 4, tally up the grading assignment and identify the top three as your shortlist.

Talk to each prospect on the shortlist, get a feel for each and make your choice. Consulting is mainly about the relationship between the expert and you.[1] Your interactions will be regular (usually weekly) and you gain more if your relationship with your consultant is good, as that makes it easier to accept information, suggestions, and at times, challenges thrown at you by your consultant. Find one you can get along with and in time probably respect.

9.4.2 What Can the Consultant Do for You and Agree to Deliver?

There are two types of deliverables, tangible and intangible.

Tangibles are obvious, such as bookkeeping, filing patents, contracts, payroll, training, etc. For example, in training, there will be a training program, note binders with accompanying information for each staff attending the training, feedback and practice after the training that you can watch and assess the effectiveness of.

Always walk through the deliverables and agree on what you want prior to the consultant doing the actual work. It requires effort on your part, but this is no time to slack off. Assign to another person to handle only when absolutely necessary and even when you do that, you should keep in the loop. At an early stage in the enterprise when it is still permissible time wise, you must want to learn as well.

Intangible deliverables are harder to define and hold the consultant accountable for. You confront these, for example, with a business consultant you want to bring in to help you grow your enterprise. You can set clear goals, but the manner in arriving at the goals is diverse. No one can guarantee that the goal can be achieved because it will depend on execution, changes in the business environment that can be unforeseen, delays in production, processes going awry and require unraveling, etc. Despite these uncertainties, the consultant should have a work plan and you must go over this to decide what you want to get out of this. The tangible goal may not be achieved, but going through the process will gain you experience that though intangible, is beneficial.

9.5 EXPECTATIONS OF YOUR CONSULTANT

A good consultant is hired to help you focus or clear the mess you got into. They are best considered as trainers or coaches (mainly of your mind and attitude), and resource centers. They are not there to do the work for you on a daily basis. Neither are they there to hold your hand through a crisis, only to guide and assist you. Consultants are only as good as how you choose to deploy them. You already know what you want them to do. This has to be followed up by your own plan to maximize their time with you.

Depending on the terms, for example they show up once or twice a week for one or two hours, that time is best spent going over the work agreed on the agenda or the previous session, Q&A and discussion on on-going issues. You can listen and think through what has been proposed by the consultant to you, but you must come to a decision that makes sense for you and your organization, not your consultant. You know the overall picture, they don't.

Tell the consultant the issues confronting you openly, since every discussion is under confidential agreement. Listen to their responses and suggestions. Consulting is interactive. Question, listen to the answers and think them through. And come back for more the next session. Do not be only an information gatherer and accept the solutions provided to you. There may be some further customization to meet your specific situations, even if the proposed solution was dead on. And remind yourself constantly that consultancy is not a cure-all, but to help you work through specific issues to come out better.

9.6 MANAGING YOUR CONSULTANT

Consultants, especially Category 1 types that you bring into your organization, have a résumé behind them that can come with an accompanying attitude. They can be disruptive if they are not handled well.

You are still the boss. Be clear and always remember that. You should make all final decisions that affect your company, and you must lead the consultant, not *vice versa*. You, and not the consultant, should execute whatever the both of you agree on.

9.6.1 Protect Thy People

The consultant has a cordial interaction with you because he knows you are in charge and sign the checks that pay his invoices. This may not be the way they will interact with your team and/or staff, sometimes asserting their authority beyond what is proper. Conflict between your people and the consultant can arise. Therefore, do not let your consultant loose on your people without first setting proper guidelines, supervise the interaction and be ready to step in when you sense things going awry. This leads us into the next point.

9.6.2 Define Your Consultant's Boundaries

Damage control is a messy process at best. To deter inadvertent consequences, it is best to prevent unwarranted contact of the consultant with your staff, directors and clients from the start. You achieve this by defining your consultant's boundaries. Remove your staff from the obligation of interacting with the consultant as far as possible, except as suggested above. Boundaries for your director(s) can be less restrictive since all of you should be on the same page and they most likely had a hand in the hire decision. Your clients should be off limits to the consultant unless absolutely necessary.

In summary, consultants abound. They have their usefulness in various stages of your company's progression upward. It is a challenge to find, select and manage a consultant. But the right consultant at the right time (and at the right price) is a bargain if you manage them correctly to perform a defined (by you) task for a specific period. Disregard the jokes about consultants. They deserve your respect because many are independent entrepreneurs like you.

This concludes Part 2, *the build-up*. Next we proceed to initiating your *runway biomed enterprise, beyond the go-decision*, Chapters 10 and 11.

Real World Lessons Learnt

General
1. Advice is free. Consulting is paid.
2. Consultants know their expertise, not your business.
3. Consultant(s) are only as effective as you direct.

Specific
1. Know what you want to achieve before hiring a consultant.
2. Hire the consultant you can afford.
3. Manage your consultant.

Quotes for the Chapter

"An Expert is someone who knows some of the worst mistakes that can be made in his subject and who manages to avoid them". *Werner Heisenberg (1901–1976; German physicist, renowned for the "Heisenberg Uncertainty Principle")*

Reference

[1] Beckwith H. Selling the Invisible: a Field Guide to Modern Marketing. New York, NY: Warner Books; 1997. 42.

10.1 CHECKPOINT #1: PREPARE

The concept phase is over. You are clear about the product you want to make. As you continue to source for start-up funds, your next step is putting the nuts and bolts of the company together.

The questions that immediately come to mind are:

1. Where do you set-up?
2. How do you make your product?
3. When do you get going?

These are valid questions and the corresponding answers are:

1. Do you need an address?
2. To sub-contract or do it yourself? (This question should actually have more or less been settled by your BP phase.)
3. What's the rush?

But the more *appropriate question* for you to ask and answer is, how do you get from $0.00 to $5,000,000.00 in 5 years. This, as presented in Chapter 5, is your goal. Why is answering this question the more appropriate? Until now, the exercise has still been theoretical. You can back off any time with little or no consequences. All you will have wasted is some time and effort. Once money from a source other than you is in your hands, you are committed and/or obligated.

It can be an intimidating task to get going; it can overwhelm you considering all the big and small stuff that has to be done. If you take the "how do I start approach" you can easily get over your head in a hurry, become anxious and that can lead to discouragement bordering on despair. The reason is that *uncertainty* becomes a constant companion in going forward, and it is something you will have to grapple with. The objective of answering the more *appropriate question* is to set your attitude to continually focus on finding solutions to the goals you set for each milestone in the action plan you will develop, not on facing and becoming stuck on the problems you will confront. Put another way:

> You are not starting a company
>
> You are not even starting a biomed company
>
> You are growing a biomed company

You are now ready to move into developing an *action plan* to help you through the start-up phase that prevents you from getting lost and exhausted.

How do you go about putting an *action plan* together? What comes before, what follows, and after that, what else? Some experts at this juncture will tell you to break the whole goal into small chunks and complete each challenge one at a time, while others talk about parallel execution, and the list goes on. Different businesses require different components, and therefore the final *action plan* must be customized to suit your own specific needs. However, there are two considerations in formulating an *action plan* that are universal. The first is the physical plan to bring to fruition an operational facility that becomes the place of business and/or to realize a product. The second is the financial outlay necessary to support the completion of the physical plan. Both are intimately connected *but* the financial plan dictates how the physical plan unfolds.

The financial plan is the more important because your funds are finite and you will have to make available funds last and, more importantly, work for you. In business, debtors (when you have them) are perennially slow in payment, while creditors (you start accumulating these immediately) usually demand settlement on or ahead of time. These factors impact your *cash flow* and combined with your finite funds position, will bleed you dry if you do not have a financial component to your *action plan*.

The physical plan depends on the funds you allocate. If you have settled for a sub-contractor to do most of the manufacturing, you have an easier task. The decision in this instance is deciding whether you want to set up a physical office for appearances, or be a "virtual" entity for as long as you can. If you require a facility for manufacturing or conducting laboratory operations or both, your plan should be thorough, as your available funds will have to last longer because set-up takes time. Therefore allocating funds to each milestone has to be as precise as possible.

Finally, from this point on, get someone else to do the S&T. You should no longer do it except in emergencies. You lead, direct and provide solutions when problems occur, but you are no longer hands-on for the S&T component. This appears contradictory to what I have been promoting in the earlier chapters. But recall your job title is now Supreme Field Commander. You are in the battle and at times in the thick of it, as in a real battle, your position can be overrun or bombarded by the enemy. But your role now is more about putting things together, and ensuring that all else is taken care of so that your troops, i.e. staff, can do their job. So participate in meetings and discussions on the S&T (that has to be on-going), watch and supervise as it is being done, and interject where necessary. But your main focus is now on the business end that will consume all your available attention.

10.2 PLAN TO ACHIEVE 100% – ESTABLISHING MILESTONES

To plan, you need goals. Your goal is for your first product to obtain regulatory approval in order to commence sales, or have your service operational to generate revenue. You must plan to achieve this goal up to 100% completion. A straightforward method is to first list down the important tasks that need to be completed to reach the goal. Next, identify the sequence these tasks have to be completed. Figure 10.1 shows a sample order of events flowchart to reach the point where revenue can be generated for either a product or service.

10.2.1 Sub-contract Manufacturing (Class 2 Medical Device Example)

With reference to Figure 10.1A (the left flowchart), your action plan should more or less have the following six major milestones:

1. *Complete prototype:* Find a prototype sub-contractor that preferably has a quality system or accreditation to ISO9001. You should have a contractual agreement. Define as much as you can the price: consulting and labor should be in dollars per hour (or if you can, a fixed sum for the whole duration), and materials should be at cost. Realize that this process normally takes up to 12 months and estimate your costs. **Note:** Takes for granted that you have opted to do this phase outside academia.

2. *Prototype approval:* If you are working with a clinician, you will have to develop the documents for conduct, evaluation, and criteria for acceptance, of the prototype. Estimate your associated costs for this process (this could be purchase of supporting materials, rental of facilities to conduct the evaluation, lab analyses and tests, animal models, etc.). If you also use an additional independent assessor, you will have to factor in this additional cost.

3. *Sub-contractor selection:* Select and settle on a manufacturing sub-contractor (who may also be your prototype sub-contractor) that has certification for at least one jurisdiction's requirements such as the ISO13485. There are many details that you have to work through to get the pilot lot of product. You negotiate with the manufacturing sub-contractor and arrive at a contractual agreement.

4. *Manufacturing:* There is normally a consultancy fee to understand your requirements and set-up for manufacturing. Manufacturing cost is per unit of product for a minimum quantity. (Also refer to Chapter 3.)

5. *Testing:* The testing of the product. Here you can either work through your manufacturer or handle it yourself by going direct to a testing and regulatory sub-contractor. Tests requirements for your product have to be confirmed and conducted.

6. *Regulatory submission:* This is device dependent in the country you are submitting to. It is best to obtain quotes and decide. Your regulatory consultant will assist you in this process.

(A)   (B)

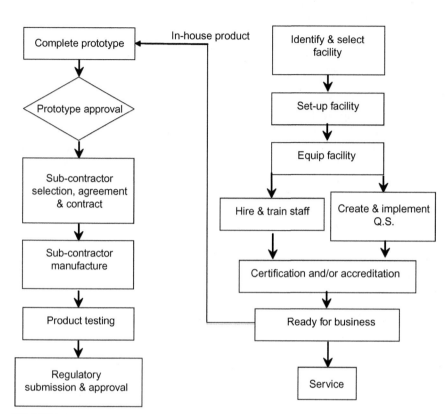

FIGURE 10.1   Flowchart of workflow. (A) Sub-contract product route. (B) Own facility product/service route.

7. *Marketing:* This can also be a sub-contracted function, and if you do sub-contract, factor in this cost as well.

For each major milestone, you could set sub-milestones that you define for yourself. The last detail to incorporate is estimating timelines for each milestone so you can have a reasonable schedule to follow. Remember that this *action plan* is your first cut or edition. The plan changes when you start implementing and requires updating on a regular basis.

Bear in mind the above sequence is one example of this exercise and you should customize it to your needs. With this approach your main function is *project coordination* as well as being involved in the process (many discussions require your input – sub-contractors ultimately require your decision and your *sign-off* before they proceed with the actual work) without the hassle of facility management. You can be the sole person in your enterprise managing all work by yourself. Alternatively, you may want to hire one or two staff to assist you, and that is an additional cost.

10.2.2 Setting Up a Manufacturing Facility

This is the more intensive approach, both in effort as well as in funds. Illustrated in Figure 10.1B (the right flowchart), is the sequence listed as your milestones. Again this is an example for illustrative purposes only. Note that in this example the hiring and training of staff is conducted simultaneously with developing the quality system (with a consultant). You can rearrange each sequence to fit your specific requirements.

At the ready-for-business juncture, the product and services follow separate paths. The product route at this stage adopts most of the sub-contractor route (Figure 10.1A: left flowchart), but without the negotiations and contractual agreements with the sub-contractor, as this is done in-house. A service is ready to take on and perform jobs to start generating revenue. Again, you can shortcut this or many of the other steps by various means such as partial sub-contracting. This is left to your ingenuity and creativity to resolve.

Taking this track for a product or service leads you to consider the following:

1. A place to do your business.
2. Outfit that place with equipment, furniture and people.

These matters will be elaborated in later sections. Finally, ward off the temptation to assemble everything at once. This is a common observation I notice in many new entrepreneurs who in their excitement and enthusiasm believe themselves capable of executing several tasks simultaneously and completing them in a hurry. There are multiple facets to setting up your own facility including some that are sequential, and taking care of the details in an orderly manner is what will get you there rather than rushing. To reiterate, think through and develop the most thorough *action plan* you can and stick to it.

10.3 EXECUTE TO ACHIEVE AT LEAST 50% – FINANCIAL PLAN

Your *action plan* can only be fully completed to 100% if you have all the funds you require. This may not be the situation. Therefore you require a companion *financial plan* to your *action plan*, allocating funds to meet the expenditure for each milestone, starting with the first milestone.

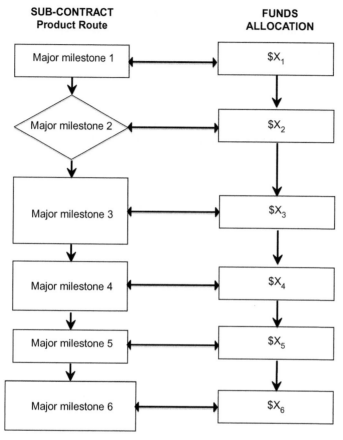

FIGURE 10.2 Flowchart of major milestones with corresponding fund allocations.

You do this by putting a corresponding dollar figure beside each milestone, as shown in Figure 10.2, to your *action plan*. Total the fund allocations for each major milestone and compare with the funds you have in hand. Funds promised and/or pending (not in your bank account) should not be included. If you have sufficient or excess funds, congratulations. Your excess funds should be designated as your contingency fund, hold on to it.

What do you do if you are short of funds? First ascertain your funds position. The probability that you will have the funds to implement up to 50% of your *action plan* is high. To help you decide whether to continue, consider for example having an associate (or two) handle the science (remember to keep your finger on the S&T pulse) and other day-to-day matters. This frees you to continue pursuing fund procurement and activities such as those listed below, reassembled from earlier chapters.

1. Beg, borrow and pray.
2. Leverage government schemes.
3. Bootstrapping.

Recall that as you achieve a milestone, you are more likely to break-through in securing more funding. Are you confident that you will bring in more funds by the time 40% to near 50% of your execution is achieved? The final decision is yours.

10.4 STAFFING

Getting the right people for the job is an important activity and has to be done properly. There are two types of hires you want in a company:

1. Category 1 staff help you drive the company. They are your start-up staff and hired first. They require minimal instructions and training, and are relatively independent. You can rely on them to assist you to deliver on what you set out to achieve.
2. Category 2 staff does the important routine work such as the laboratory assays, the manufacturing, sales and administration. This category of staff is hired when your organization becomes more settled, and you require more people.

You must determine how many staff you need to hire, what are their job appointments, job scope and have an idea of their total cost.

10.4.1 About Hiring

Hiring is always a 50:50 proposition. You have an equal chance of getting a great or a poor staff. Be prepared no matter how perfect the résumé, how supportive the recommendations, how well the candidate performs at the interview, that hire still may not work out.

Don't trust résumés too much for the simple fact that the candidate put it together. There are many websites, and other sources such as placement offices that assist candidates create *killer* résumés. The only purpose for you in looking over a résumé is to ensure the candidate has the proper academic background, i.e. they *know* (*not necessarily understand*) some scientific terms. From experience, good grades and letters of recommendations from their supervisors are only a small facet of the makeup of an applicant.

For Category 1 candidates, some tell-tale signs can be gleaned from the activities they participate in and the type of jobs they have accepted previously. The résumés of these applicants tend to evoke that they are "different".

For Category 2 candidates, look for consistency in their background. The types of courses/modules they took, and where and how long they worked. With practice you should be able to distinguish suitable applicants.

It is harder to determine the suitability of fresh graduates. All you can do is look at the total résumé while screening out the obvious self-promotion bits and get a "feel". If the résumé is appealing, you will get a sense of it.

You will probably get many applications that do not meet your minimum requirements, and you need to sort them out. Finally, if a potential hire comes to you via referrals, ensure that the résumé fits the profile for what you are hiring. Do not let obligations sway your decision process. Be objective. You cannot afford luxuries of having poor or mismatched performers since you are not a welfare organization.

Once you have shortlisted the candidates, ensure (check and verify) that they are legal, i.e. they can be hired. Citizens and permanent residents of the country are straightforward hires. If you want a foreign hire that requires additional documentation, realize that in most instances, you have to justify this on a case-by-case basis. Every country has its own rules on how to qualify a non-resident candidate, and you have to do the necessary.

For BRASS, I started out with fresh graduates from the Singapore Polytechnic (referrals from the teaching staff of their biotechnology program whom I knew) and NUS who were Singapore citizens. The first manager I hired was a trainer I met during one of my reservist ("annual-warrior") call-ups. I continued with this policy of hiring only locals for the simple reason that the paperwork would have been too tedious for a small operation to cope with. In my second stint at BRASS, the new manager I brought in required legal documentation for her hire, as she was a foreign national. But BRASS had grown, she had the right talent and fit, and I was prepared to do the necessary.

10.4.2 About Interviews

If a candidate has been shortlisted for an interview, you have to prepare well for the interview. Again, there are extensive resources available for you to develop your own style of handling this. I can only recommend that you prepare by carefully reading the candidate's résumé and forming some insightful questions. Most of the candidate interviews you participate in are for positions such as managers, scientists, finance and sales, i.e. the critical jobs that must deliver results. They are the people you will work with. Qualifications and experience aside, you have to intuitively assess whether you can work with them. If the "fit" is not right, it is better not to hire. Although they may do the job well, they may end up being a disruptive force in the company. Delegate all other hires to your general manager and team members who have to work with them. Try and limit your input in this instance to be about the salary and other employment terms.

My record in hires is average. In the early years, apart from my manager (we did not have a real interview); there was little necessity to sit in on interviews. As stated the manager was someone I was familiar with (you get to know people quite well in 3 to 4 weeks in the military where you work in close proximity), had a microbiology degree, worked for a research organization in the right field, and turned out to be business savvy. There have also been hires that did not fit in a small business-oriented environment even though they had good academic and industry credentials.

10.4.3 Working for a Start-up/SME Phobia

Being a start-up or an SME (Small and Medium Enterprise) can be an unattractive feature when it comes to hiring. Job insecurity, limited opportunities such as for travel and overseas attachment at corporate training sites, not being as competitive in perks such as medical and leave allowance, are real disadvantages compared to large and fund-capable employers.

Do not shortchange your start-up's allure by thinking that it will be near impossible to find good staff to join you. A start-up company has a work environment that is out of the ordinary and challenging, counter to the traditional job that can be mundane, hierarchical and bureaucratic. Take some time to think what attributes you would like a staff to have, what they are expected to do and what performance criteria would fit the job profile. Your company's appeal is to give a person the opportunity to gain an experience they may never ever again encounter in their lifetime. Those with an adventurous spirit will probably be the best fit.

Avoid applicants who just want a job, but do give fresh, wet-behind-the-ears graduates a chance at an interview. I once did give a "cold call" e-mail applicant a chance. She was in her final semester of studies. We interviewed her and found her suitable and hired her. She joined us after completing her studies, started as a laboratory technologist and eventually rose to be our laboratory manager. After 4 years of great service, BRASS sadly lost her when she got married and joined her husband on his overseas posting.

In today's techno-driven friendly climate, many may give your website's job postings a pass, but you only require a few. And there are always those economic downturns that make any job attractive. I had a few come on board during such times when in a better job market they might have been loathe even to apply. They found the job and environment good and stayed several years even after the economy picked up. And that is the reality. You have to constantly refresh the work environment to keep and recruit better staff. It gets easier once your cash reserves permit you to do this. Persevere.

10.4.4 About Compensation

Your job offer(s) must be within the realm of acceptable or close to market rate. Also, there are labor laws that you have to comply with and you should know your rights and responsibilities as an employer.

You have to provide the essential pay package commensurate with the responsibilities, health and insurance benefits. Bonuses can be used as an incentive and should be contingent on revenue and surplus. It is difficult to provide much else because human resource is a major component in your operating costs and *cash flow*.

When your company is more developed you can consider share-options, but do not kick it in too early, as the value of share-options will not be easily comprehensible to the average person you bring on board. And they have to earn the offer by performing well in the company for a minimum number of years.

10.5 PLACE OF OPERATIONS

To establish your operating base is a massive undertaking from a *runway* enterprise or SME viewpoint. The space you require has to be sufficient to accommodate your needs, but small enough to meet your costing. Do not rush into getting a space. You have time.

In the ensuing sections, the general essentials that a typical medical device facility requires to be operational are presented as an example. This is based on a combination of the BRASS experience, observations of several medical devices manufacturing operations, and insights gained from founders of two small medical devices manufacturing outfits. One founder was from the medical device industry who branched out on his own, and the other is a physician (still practicing in 2010) turned entrepreneur.

10.5.1 Do you Need an Address?

You can and should start virtually. When you register your company, it could be months before you require a physical location. You can use your home, lawyer's, accountant's or company secretary's office as the correspondence address. This obviates paying rent and all other associated costs such as utilities for a few months.[i] During this phase, you may still be trying to raise funds, licensing the IP and organizing and finalizing your plan. Stretch your dollar now as the money you save will be useful later.

A virtual place of work (e.g. your home) will usually have the following costs:

1. Lawyer fees – company registration, contracts, IP (if any).
2. Accountants' fees – taxes, annual statements, bookkeeping.
3. Telecommunications fees – Internet, phone and fax.
4. Office administrative costs – printer, copying, postage, courier, etc.
5. Travel.

From the above, you note that most of the costs are fixed except for IP and travel. Your cash can go a long way.

If you have chosen the sub-contractor route, you probably can maintain the virtual workplace for a prolonged period. If you require setting-up at a physical location, this virtual office provides you approximately a 6-month spending sparingly cushion while confirming all your needs, searching and settling on a place and hiring your first staff.

10.5.2 Settling on an Operations Location

Some universities have incubator facilities that will help provide your company specific space, as well as common shared facilities at a reasonable price, and should be considered if available. BRASS's service lab started in such facilities. Manufacturing companies can be accommodated in such incubator spaces.

If you are going to manufacture, you may wish to have your own space from the start because of quality system considerations. When possible look for a facility that permits you to start with the size you want, with an option to expand within a couple of years. Typically such arrangements are plausible for a new or vacated building, and during an economic downturn.

Real estate agents will tell you that location, location, location is everything when it comes to finding a place to commence operations. Today, many national, state and local governments tend to earmark specific locations for a particular industry group that include both physical and financial incentives. The "theme park" concept rests on the premise that clustering similar businesses in one location creates synergy and vibrancy, as well as economies of scale. These are important

---

[i]Depending on the country's company tax laws, you can charge a fraction for the costs of using your own home to the company. Check with your accountant.

considerations because of certain advantages. If you are a products company, easy access for receiving your raw materials and shipping your goods may be better. If you are a service that supports manufacturers, proximity to your customer base is a plus for access, communications and cutting down travel.

The industry also dictates some requirements. For the biomed businesses, possible restrictions could be a cleaner air environment (so that your HEPA[ii] filters are not overloaded). Therefore, locating a facility in the middle of an oil refinery zone or a quarry would not work. There may be other zoning restrictions such as keeping industries with certain types of wastes, e.g. biohazard wastes, in a specific area so that in the event of an incident or accident, containment can be more readily achieved.

Whatever the sales pitch, you must take care of number one, your business costs. It is unlikely you will have the capital to buy a plot of land and build to specifications. Therefore, leasing or rental would be the most probable channels open to you. Remember, rental is a fixed monthly cost to your overheads and must be kept as low as possible. Some of the questions you should ask would be whether the facilities are already outfitted for your needs? Normally, buildings for specific industries are designed, and outfitted to meet a particular industry segment's general requirements. Are utilities fees included as part of the rental? What are the hidden charges that you may not be aware of (e.g. parking, security)? Look for opportunities that meet your needs and budget. Do as much research and homework to get the best offer and deal, but set a deadline to make a decision on a site.

Finally if you lease or rent, do note that whatever renovations you carry out in the facility, you are normally obligated to return it back to "as received" condition, i.e. there is a cost involved. Thankfully, this can be deferred to a time when finding funds to do this should not be of concern.

10.5.3 Facility Layout Requirements and Renovations

If you are able to find a place that is fully outfitted and ready to get underway at the right price for your outfit, awesome. You are one step ahead and closer to success. If not, let's talk renovations.

You have to get the place, laboratory or production floor (likely controlled or clean room specifications) to do the things in a workflow sequence (from dirty to clean) suitable for your biomed venture. Layout your facility based on functionality to maximize the area,[iii] but keep an

---

[ii] HEPA: high efficiency particulate air.

[iii] You pay minimum rent by settling for the smallest square footage you need. A proper layout will squeeze the most useful workspace for what you have.

eye on details as the finished look should be professional and easy to clean and sterilize (experimental/production area) for operational work to be carried out properly.

For a simple medical device assembly facility, you probably require a Class 100K and at best, a Class 10K clean room with access doors between the clean, intermediate and outside areas, and change/gowning rooms.[iv] You also need a "goods receiving" area, preferably with storage, to check goods such as raw materials parts, boxes, packaging, etc. until checked and passed. You would also have a quarantine area when goods are ready to be sent for sterilization and/or storage. You also have to work out how to transfer materials into and out of the clean area. The complexity increases if you are including some manufacturing such as molding or machining as the space and workflow considerations are more demanding.

You will also need to estimate the ratio of office space to lab/production space.[v] For office, outfit staff workspace where paperwork is done. You should assign a table for yourself and not a separate office. You will need at least one discussion room (that sits four persons),[vi] and probably a conference room where you hold staff meetings and give presentations to clients, vendors and other guests. Locate these rooms near the entrance. You want to keep the office area separate so as not to disrupt on-going work and also avoid confidential documents being chanced on. You will also require an archive room to store your quality and operations documents (locked), a server room (locked as well) and printer/photocopy space. Laboratory/production space should be restricted access areas that visitors (including auditors and clients) enter only under supervision.

Furthermore, all safety rules and emergency measures will have to be identified and incorporated into your facility plan. A most important component would be that your manufacturing or laboratory space also meets the requirements of quality systems such as ISO, GLP or GMP requirements. These all require careful thought for incorporation so that you do it once and at the best price possible.[vii]

The contractor you choose must be knowledgeable with the biomed industry and preferably be a clean room specialist. There are specific

---

[iv] The Class refers to the maximum number and size of particulates permissible per volume of air.

[v] A 30/70 split for office to lab is typical.

[vi] This will be required during audits by certification and accreditation bodies and clients. Auditors require a private room to discuss and put a preliminary audit report together.

[vii] You may require a consultant here if you have no prior experience. Alternatively, there are biomed equipment vendors that have experience in some of these aspects, and there is no harm in getting some "free" consultancy when you purchase their equipment. Free means you still have to assess whether their recommendations will work for you.

requirements in this industry, e.g. special ceiling materials that minimize your particulate count, special paints and flooring materials. Your power supply needs have to be customized depending on the equipment you plan to bring in. Go through the layout on site before renovation commences and ascertain that the production and workflow can really work by confirming the appropriate siting of equipment. Make relevant changes to your renovation plan before beginning actual work.

I have never known a renovation to be on budget and completed on time. Be hands on in supervising your contractor and agree to changes (and cost increases) only if you are very sure the recommendations make sense. Furthermore, many details that appear reasonable in the plan may be impractical when you renovate. Others may require re-routing and equipment re-siting. You need to be there when the issues crop up, look it over so that you make decisions and avoid delays. Be patient, the finished product is usually worth the trouble you put up with.

10.5.4 Telecommunications: Internet, Phone, Fax and Photocopier

Communication is the basis for your clients to reach you and *vice versa*, and it is most conveniently done through the phone. How many phone lines does it take for your customer to get to you? You need at least one landline to be in business, two if you anticipate your volume to be high. Remember that no one can get through to your company when the line is busy (for a one phone line company) and that translates into business opportunities lost. There are many phone models, but ensure that you have a messaging system. Pay special attention to long distance calling rates, as this is not a fixed cost. Once you've got the line connected, you should also instruct your staff to be prudent in usage. Cell phones can be a mobile alternative when you are on the move.

A fax machine I suppose is now a necessary evil. You can share the line with your telephone, but this may be a bit tricky if you are a service company since you may want a dedicated talk line and another for fax. But do get a machine that prints out on plain paper instead of thermal paper as you need to archive documents (quality system) and thermal print fades after a while. A combination photocopier, fax, scanner and laser printer machine is an option if your usage is heavy.

Do you need a website? Maybe. What does a website do for you? People can find you and you can post information about the company, a useful marketing tool. Is it necessary at the start? My opinion is that it is unlikely for a service company and even less so for a products company to need a website in the first 6 months. It is important to have a website only if your marketing or part of your service relies on electronic means, for example filling out an electronic sample submission form or for clients to track the status of their work order remotely without asking one of your staff. But that occurs only when you are operational and have obtained the necessary accreditation or certification. Other than for purely business transactions, having a website is an unnecessary overhead expenditure at this early phase. You also do not want to turn clients off by not being able to service them during your setting-up stage while alerting your competition to your existence.

Do you need an e-mail account? Absolutely! These days, so many messages related to answering queries, keeping in touch and transferring information (electronic file attachments, saves fax time therefore money) occur via e-mail that having at least **one** account makes sense. Again the emphasis is on **one**, i.e. minimal to be operational for a start-up company if you have to pay for it. And you can piggyback access to your ISP via the fax/phone line on this if possible.

While you may think that a couple of phone lines and an e-mail account do not set you back much, it all adds up. Remember, many wise men (and of course wise women) would say "a dollar saved is two dollars earned". The operative aphorism is to maximize what you have while keeping your overheads low until absolutely necessary.

10.5.5 Equipping your Office

This is the lowest priority item of all your contemplations. How do you go about furnishing an office? First, since you are not furnishing for appearance, avoid anything extravagant or fancy. Second, impressions do count. When a client walks through the door, she must get the feel that you are an outfit serious about what it does that can do the job. The operative term here is functionally presentable, in other words not too grungy but not overly ostentatious either. There are a lot of bargains that may be attractive, look for them. Try a fire sale, sheriff's sale, going out of business sale, i.e. buy used and good quality when possible. You can always upgrade when the money comes in (even then, spend wisely).

When BRASS first started, the laboratory was already outfitted with chairs, tables and stools. At BRASS' second facility, the option was for a more presentable look as the client pool was increasing and there were to be more audits of the facility. The office was adjacent to the laboratory facilities and had to look the part. In the present facility, the laboratory area is larger and is in a standalone section. The office could revert back to a more utilitarian feel.

10.5.6 Equipment Purchase and Leasing

For the office, how many computers and other related electronic doodads such as video player, TV, slide projectors (these may now be a historical item), audio-visual projectors do you need? This depends on your staffing level and what you do for a business. Desktops are cheaper than notebooks, etc. and you know the tradeoffs with these electronic devices that I need not elaborate. The only advice I would give here is that you may think about buying quality rather than cheap. A computer crash is not a bargain for a start-up. Finally, purchase legal software and ensure you have virus protection and firewalls. Servers and associated security and backup are a must. Again you do not have to purchase all at once.

For the laboratory and/or manufacturing components, you need to furnish your company with the proper type of equipment to get the work going. You have a list of must have, nice to have and frills. You do not have a big equipment budget. Buy instruments and equipment that meet the need.

To equip your clean room, you need to acquire equipment such as HEPA filtration units, laminar flow hoods and stainless steel tables for assembling your products in controlled areas. Equipment to maintain positive pressure in clean and change rooms, and humidity and temperature monitoring and recording systems are also needed.

Do you require plastics molding equipment, package sealing equipment or automated packaging equipment?

One pertinent point to be aware of is that equipment manufacturers these days produce GMP/GLP-ready equipment such as ovens, autoclaves and analytical balances. These units include additional hardware and software and cost more, but consider their purchase because having regulatory compliant equipment is a necessity rather than a luxury. One other consideration is choosing industrial grade versus research grade equipment. This depends on usage. For production and manufacturing, the rugged industrial grade may be better. For accurate laboratory analysis, research grade is preferred.

10.6 FINAL INSTRUCTIONS

"Don't just do something. Stand there" is a catchy play on the phrase "Don't just stand there; do something". Both quotes have been around, and even used as the title of a book. While you prepare and execute (Chapter 11) your *action plan* you have to do both. There are instances you have to *stand* or wait, evaluating the situation thoroughly before acting. Other times you have to act or *do something* instead of waiting around for more data that leads into "analysis paralysis". Whenever you get yourself into such situations, recall the prolog segment on what *runway* means and you hopefully will be encouraged.

Real World Lessons Learnt

General

1. You must know what, how and when you execute specific tasks, i.e. establish milestones.
2. Plan according to cash-in-hand, not funds forthcoming.
3. A plan should be 100% achievable but must be executable to at least 50%.

Specific

1. Focus on the activities that lead to completion to generate revenue.
2. Hire the right people.
3. Virtual or real, depends on what your plans are. If real, has to be utilitarian not flashy.

Quote for the Chapter

"Fail to plan, plan to fail".

Hillary Diane Rodham Clinton (67th United States Secretary of State; US Senator-State of New York, 2001–2009; US First Lady, 1993–2001)

When the Rubber Hits the Road

From Academia to Entrepreneur.
DOI: http://dx.doi.org/10.1016/B978-0-12-410516-4.00011-2

11.1 CHECKPOINT #2: EXECUTION

You have finally got the cash to start-up, your *action plan* is all worked out, and momentum has built to a crescendo so that nothing can stop you now. No more toying with all sorts of possibilities in the head. You are ready for BIZ-NESS. What you do now either makes or breaks the venture.

Before the excitement overcomes you, it is pragmatic to recognize biomed start-ups have a propensity to falter, lapse into living dead and finally disintegrate. Below I propose six common reasons why I think they fail:

a. Improper implementation.
b. Financial imprudence.
c. Over focus on S&T.
d. Poor business decisions especially over-extending.
e. Inflexibility to adapt.
f. Competition appreciation neglect.

11.1.1 Implement Wisely

Once the euphoria of opening for business dies down, the reality that you have a lot to do will set in. You are probably impatient to get going and show your mettle. Emotions can get the better of you, for example being rushed into making a major dollar purchase because a salesperson made an offer that should not be refused but turned out badly, or facing a delay in one of your work schedules. These are some episodes that can lead you to make further poor decisions and responses that are inappropriate, upsetting the implementation of your *action plan*. Mistakes are easy to make and you are human. But getting out of such situations may not be easy because you may go through self-denial, justify your actions, or come up with some other excuse. Therefore, you may leave it too late to take corrective measures and the consequences may be an unrecoverable lapse into ruin.

The implementation of a plan requires strict discipline. So, in order to go forward, you need to first ensure any *elation hangover* is curtailed immediately. Reel in your bravado and check it at the door of common sense. Next follow your *action plan* because that was thought out at a time when you were sensible, emotion-neutral and thorough. If you are a business novice or virgin, do not permit the business theories you may have come across and all the advice you have been bombarded with to date to crowd your thoughts.

Implement accordingly. As stated in Chapter 5, "real-time" situational awareness takes precedence over the plan *once the rubber hits the road*. Assess, evaluate and respond as the situation dictates. Most decisions do not require a nanosecond response. Seek counsel from your advisors, ask for more pertinent and updated information, discuss with your team before making an informed decision. Then act. It may be a simple matter of buying a few laboratory stools for your staff to sit on when doing an assay in the clean room or controlled area. Sometimes cheap does not mean a good buy. How heavy is the stool or can it be cleaned easily, and can the stool's material withstand constant contact with the cleaning agents? Making a poor choice could mean replacement of the stool frequently that may impact on work progress. Little things matter.

11.1.2 Exercise Financial Prudence

The key to survival and growth for a start-up (or for any business, even mature ones) is to spend sparingly, or as the *seasoned entrepreneur* who helped BRASS make the connection with NAMSA puts it, "exercise asset parsimony". An observation I also made and learnt from Khoon Seng when he was operations manager at SVM was how carefully he utilized company funds even though he was not a shareholder of SVM. All spending had to have some reasonable justification that contributed to the company's interests, be it directly or indirectly. Whenever research grants or barter trade in terms of facilities or equipment were available, that was used first.

Succinctly, spend wisely in setting-up your company with the limited cash resources at hand. Continue this way of spending even when you succeed and resist the enticement to do a grand overhaul when you arrive business-wise and financially.

11.1.3 Focus on Your Product not S&T

This has been touched on in Chapters 1 and 6, and cannot be stressed enough. The practical aspects of product development must be your focus. You have to manage your scientific team well to continually direct their attention on the product. When valid reasons occur for necessary sidetracks into science for addressing an issue that impacts on the product, support it and monitor it. This is why you have to be hands-on and not let the scientific team handle the product development unsupervised. At times you will have to play referee between science and manufacturing. Do not rush, listen to both parties, make the decision and *explain thoroughly* on how you arrived at that position, especially to the side that has to compromise the most.

11.1.4 Make Good Business Decisions Especially Checking Overextension

Business decisions come in all imaginable permutations. They impact short-term, long-term, financial wellbeing and the survival of your enterprise. While I preach a lot about financial prudence, and in truth all decisions will eventually be financial ones, do not let that be your only reference when making a business decision.

For example, when BRASS was planning to relocate to a new facility, 8000 square feet was the planned space requirement. The new location met that requirement but an additional 2000 square feet of space was also available. The additional space could be utilized for new developments in the pipeline (at least 1 year down the road).

Prudence would dictate BRASS stick to the original plan of 8000 square feet. A *calculated risk* would prescribe BRASS to take up the additional square footage that would probably be idle for 2 years. BRASS settled for the *calculated risk* since paying the cost for the space was financially manageable.

The other caution about poor business decisions is again on S&T. A piece of science is a wonderful thing that can go in many directions. Settling on one product to develop may be your focus, but trying out other pipeline products simultaneously can be at the back of your mind since my comment about *one hit wonders* may nag at you constantly. If you permit this to gnaw at your subconscious, it can unwittingly lead to "starting" little exploratory "product" projects, leading to overextending your capabilities, resources, and loss of focus. Product development can relapse into further research with undefined outcomes resulting in a financial overstretch and eventually to business demise. Get the main, single job done first. Monitor all other activities. Curtail, halt and cancel all exploratory work when you have to.

11.1.5 Yet be Flexible

It has been said, "in adversity there is opportunity". Let's not get philosophical. When you open for business, you can be confronted with opportunities that you did not anticipate regardless of whether it's an economic downturn or upturn, where you are in the product lifecycle, or whether the science is in vogue or not. Do not be rigid and stick to your *action plan* disregarding "easy pickings" right in front of you. Your job as the entrepreneur is to be constantly on the lookout for unanticipated circumstances or opportunity and *act on what others do not see, cannot find, don't do or won't do.*

Let me use another BRASS example. The initial plan was to set up our capability to offer testing and consulting services. Once we obtained our ISO9001 certification and IEC guide-25 accreditation, we were ready for business. The first BRASS-accredited test was the endotoxin test. The target clientele was dialysis centers, as Singapore by law required dialysis water to be tested for endotoxin and chemistry on a regular basis. We spoke to the dialysis centers in Singapore. One dialysis center chain had a regular tests service provider and was change averse. A smaller dialysis center chain and other dialysis clinics had an issue of liaising with two service providers, one for endotoxin testing the other for chemistry, impacting their already busy workload. BRASS had no chemistry capability at the time. But we knew we could sub-contract. Consequently, BRASS tied-up with an accredited chemistry testing laboratory and presented our bundling solution to the smaller dialysis center chain and the dialysis clinics. The nurses in charge readily accepted the *gift from heaven*, and we were off to the races.

Removing the task of liaising with two service providers may appear insignificant to most, but from the clients' staff perspective it was, because priority was for patient care and ensuring that the dialysis equipment was operational. BRASS also reminded its clients a week ahead when the next test was scheduled, a value-add service for them. Eventually, BRASS converted most of the dialysis clinics in Singapore to use its service. You will also notice that BRASS did not disparage the small size of this business and continued to provide the best service it could.

A year later the SARS (Severe Acute Respiratory Syndrome) crisis descended on Singapore and other parts of the world. All the medical labs were overloaded with clinical testing. No prizes for guessing who was there (by referral from the dialysis clinics BRASS serviced) to take up the slack in non-critical but still essential endotoxin and chemistry testing.[i] This one opportunity also led BRASS to be noticed by industry players for our endotoxin and other subsequent tests offering, permitting BRASS to grow.

Being alert and amenable in customizing a solution to a need led to the way forward. Be a ferret. Continually be on the lookout. Others may let *status quo* rule but it's a great friend of the *runway* entrepreneur.

11.1.6 Be Alert

Described in Chapter 4, competition for BRASS was effectively non-existent in Singapore at the time of conception. But that did not last forever. After the Singapore government announced the biomed initiative in 2000, BRASS still had a relatively comfortable local environment to maneuver in. BRASS continued to focus on building its tests offerings, client base, and regionally representing two Global companies. As time passed, BRASS also began to be attractive as a mid-term sub-contractor to several clients. Due to one of the quirks of the biomed industry, once a sub-contractor is qualified, changing to another sub-contractor

---

[i]To this day, I remain indebted to these dialysis centers. *Gifts from heaven* can go both ways!

is difficult, as it would involve additional costs and time. Being "the first kid on the block" was an advantage to BRASS. But once you make inroads, you begin to get noticed. This is where concerns about competition can start to become a preoccupation. Rather than be obsessed, BRASS decided to continue its own growth plan and let the competition "fire the first salvo".

In recent times, two heavyweights operating in Singapore dealing in other areas of testing and regulatory matters woke up to the increasing local activity in biomed. With bigger wallets, they rival BRASS's offerings with a more comprehensive and cost-attractive range. Others with similar types of business are exploring laboratory testing to diversify their portfolio. You can sigh, get upset, be annoyed, but this must only be momentary. Ultimately, you have to react, the sooner the better. BRASS's response was to re-invent itself by focusing on its core capabilities. BRASS's business continues to grow, even in economically tough times. For BRASS, the decision to stay its course even though it is a frigate in a sea of battleships and cruisers was correct.

The lesson here is that you have to be realistic that others will come into your space. Don't be overconfident and never underestimate competitors, known and yet to emerge. Be aware of their expertise and the resource potential these challengers may have and can muster. The key to managing competition is to continually improve and innovate yourself in order to be ready to respond instantaneously.

In summary, beware that the scales are tipped against you as a *runway* start-up. Be vigilant to the six possible causes for enterprise tailspin described above and others I am sure you will encounter.

11.2 SAND THROUGH THE HOURGLASS

The *hourglass* analogy is apt for a start-up. Like the grains of sand that start trickling down into the lower half the moment the hourglass is set on a level surface, the countdown for your start-up enterprise commences the moment you sign the first check. The cash will seem to you as depleting exponentially from then on. Its not how many checks you sign, it's what's in the company's bank account. A list of expenditures you never anticipated uncomfortably appears. As there is only so much sand in the upper half trickling down to the bottom half, so is the amount of funds you have. Utmost in your mind is that you cannot run out of funds before your product is on the market or your first service generates revenue.

In Chapter 7, I related how the (low) six-figure start-up capital for BRASS was assembled. Total only the rental and the salary of three staff for 1 year, and you immediately realize that more than half of those funds had already been accounted for. Include the purchase of supplies to carry out the lab work and you could well use up all your start-up capital quite quickly. This is a sobering awareness.

To reiterate, the key to successfully maneuvering through the initial 6 to 12 months is:

1. Implement your *action plan* well, making adjustments at regular intervals as inputs indicate. Manage all the tasks you have to execute well.
2. Act and make decisions like you have no money in the bank! Use the funds you do have properly.
3. Continue to source for funds. That way, if you receive a new injection of funds, you can turn your *hourglass* over, i.e. you "buy" more time.

For BRASS, this was achieved by:

1. Implementation of the *action plan:*
   a. Revised and improved existing quality manual with the assistance of a consultant (with government funding). Implemented and practiced the procedures to demonstrate competency followed by applying to be certified and accredited.
   b. Hire staff, train and assign duties. Getting the first test on-line.
   c. Make contact with physicians and industry for possible consulting jobs.
2. Incubator: Where possible, leveraged on resources available at the incubator facilities instead of purchasing own equipment.
3. Continued trading activities.
4. Continued to source for new investors.

The above example for a service can be (and was) achieved within a year. For a product, executing a plan similar to Figure 10.1 can also bring you quite far along in 12 months. Get going intelligently.

11.3 OPERATIONS

Operations are about managing day-to-day activities, taking into account your strategic goals. List the important activities and prioritize them. Let's focus on a products example.

Product development is your key priority. Sub-contracting was discussed in Chapter 10 and requires no further elaboration. For the own facility option: if you had opted to develop, test and pass your prototype with a sub-contractor, this should be completed by the time your facility is ready. If you had chosen to wait and develop the prototype in-house, your first concern is very project management oriented, setting up your facility. Following the order developed in Figure 10.1, this equates to settling on the site, renovating and equipping the facility to bring it operational. Again, site considerations, renovations and equipping the facility were addressed in Chapter 10.

Once your facility is commissioned, there will a period of "settling in" as you develop a routine for all components of manufacturing to be "fully operational". Many issues will definitely arise when you develop your prototype in-house and/or your first product line goes through a pilot production run. This process may take up to 18 to 24 months to achieve, after which your operations should settle down to a more routine workflow. At that stage, you probably will begin revising your operational workflow to include a second product line as the first product is in the testing and regulatory submission process. If prototyping for the second product is to be carried out, you will have to isolate this work in order not to interfere with the main production activities of the first product line.

Setting up and implementing your QS that incorporates manufacturing will take time. Start running through and practicing as many of the activities that will be carried out once your facility is ready. Only after an initial break-in period is over and work becomes streamlined will you be able to finalize and harmonize all activities. You will also need to figure out raw materials purchasing, inventory control, shipping, sales tracking, post-market surveillance, etc. All are requirements of most regulatory compliant certification systems. This should get you ready for audit to be certified.

A facility and accompanying QS is both a burden and an asset. It costs, and it takes a lot of effort to maintain the facility operational and the QS current. But you have direct control in manufacturing your own products, and you can also become a sub-contractor for others who want to develop medical devices, opening you to business opportunities that can improve your *cash flow*, turning a burden into an asset. Ensure no conflicts of interest exist between your own and the contractee's products.

On the administrative side, the major matters you will have to sort out are finance, marketing, sales, IT and HR.

For finance you have to implement some form of *cash flow* automated monitoring for you to keep track of accounts receivable, as well as your monthly payment commitments. Your marketing and sales activities should parallel your product's progress. Your HR matters are chiefly payroll, health plans and workman's compensation. Finally, ensure you keep up with changing industrial and labor laws, and other issues pertinent to your industry.

Business insurance, particularly product liability insurance, has to be active when your product enters the testing or regulatory submission phase.

Determine the bank where you plan to have your account. You may already be using a local bank and that is fine for routine stuff. However, you may wish to consider a more global bank that can assist you in international transactions, especially when dealing with foreign currency and other trade conditions specific to individual countries. A bank with branches or active business in the country where your products are sold can facilitate many transactions.

11.4 CASH FLOW IS KING

A company operates on the following equation:

$$Cash\ flow\ = \text{Cash in Bank} + \text{new funds} + \text{revenue} - \text{expenditure}$$
$$= \text{Survival (and later growth)}$$

If you have ever balanced a checkbook you are qualified to manage *cash flow*. *Cash flow* is about having enough money in your bank account on a regular basis. DO NOT subscribe to an overdraft facility. You start with cash in the bank from your first round fund raising, but that depletes quickly as you have many expenditures to cover. You have to continue soliciting for new funds and collect invoices (revenue) due.

Your primary goal is never to let the cash in the bank go below the minimum sum that you will have to pay for the monthly service fees that can add up to be quite hefty for a small outfit. For example, many banks require a balance of $10,000.00 below which a service fee of $25.00 per month is charged. While $600.00 annually may appear nominal to you, it is $600.00 you don't have to pay for what you need. Furthermore, what you should be doing is working to increase that minimum balance to a point where you no longer need to be concerned about it.

BRASS was spending rapidly at the outset. I had to seek a periodic injection of funds from my shareholders. I was always concerned about meeting monthly payments in the first 2 years. As business picked up, the monthly payments to suppliers also increased, adding stress. Only in the third year did the situation stabilize to the point where collection of revenue (that is different from generating revenue) matched the expenditure. In year 4, the monthly collection amounts coming in surpassed the monthly expenditure and that was a relief. Today, the present team manages the funds differently. Suffice to say that they no longer experience the monthly desperation I felt in the early years. The *take home* lesson is for you to be prudent with the cash you have from the first check you sign. You achieve this by the following three actions.

11.4.1 Spend Like a Pauper, Hoard as a Miser

As an academic, utilizing funds from research grants is straightforward. You use research funds relatively freely according to the budget until the limit is reached; you do not pay salary for yourself, your students and staff. The institution also takes care of the upkeep of facilities such as paying for utilities and maintenance. In a *runway* enterprise, you must change that mindset immediately. To maintain positive *cash flow*, watch your spending. Ensure that any expenditure is necessary and you have the best of three quotes (you need not settle for the lowest as long as you justify). This often restricts you to settle for practical rather than fancy.

The other aspect is when funds, especially revenue, start flowing in, to not be extravagant. Your primary goal during this stage is to build your cash reserve. This is because there will be poor revenue months. The economy could also slip into a recession. You want to have reserves that can pay for salaries, rental, utilities and other expenses for at least 1 year. Remember the famous Morton Salt statement "When it rains, it pours®". Conserve your funds.

11.4.2 Debt Collection

Invoices have a stated payment due date that is normally 30 or 45 days from the date of invoice. There are clients who pay ahead of time, those that pay on time, others who delay until reminded, and the ones who default. You will have to learn which of your clients belong to which group and respond accordingly.

Some of the payment trends that I noted about BRASS clients were:

1. Big companies are usually good paymasters as they have a payment process that they follow. The only time there are hitches is when their accounts department do not receive the invoices by the cut-off date. To avoid this, you have to follow up with the recipient of service in that organization to approve the payment for work completed by you and forward your invoice to their accounts department. This observation applies to some big companies in nearby countries as well, and in this instance you can be more flexible in collection; but if the sum is large, it is still wise to collect upfront.
2. Smaller companies and lower invoiced amounts are generally slower to be collected. They may face a *cash flow* challenge themselves and place a priority in paying off the larger debts first as those are normally more critical to their operations.
3. Defaulters tend to be first and one-time clients.

Some of the practices that were instituted in BRASS as we learnt the reality of debt collection were:

1. Require first time customers to pay upfront prior to release of test reports or goods until they build up their credibility (usually a 6-month period), i.e. pay on time and in full.
2. Overseas customers pay in full before test reports or goods are sent. No exceptions.
3. Once an invoice is created; you are entitled to the money.
4. No amount is too small NOT to collect.
5. Request, persuade and, finally, demand. Legal action is not a last resort unless the fees (usually cumulative) you pay your lawyer are significantly less than what you can collect (a threshold factor is at least 10 times).
6. Review on a constant basis. This is why the monthly statements especially the accounts receivables (AR) are vital.

The practices, observations and rules came about over an extended period. Some were straightforward to realize, others took time to evolve. For example BRASS only got serious about debt collection when *cash flow* became increasingly difficult after the first round of funds was almost depleted. BRASS began focus on debt collection from an unexpected incident.

My staff Marie Chan sustained a hairline fracture in an ankle on a sales call. Once the medical matter was settled, she had to rest at home for 3 months. Knowing we were short staffed (only two in the lab), she asked how she could help from home. I gave her the AR and she started calling our clients to pay our invoices. She was so good at it that when she returned, I turned all finance matters over to her and she did a fantastic job until she left the company.[ii] She controlled our spending, negotiated for great deals in purchases, and managed our own payments well. She trained as an applied chemist, but definitely her talent and skills were elsewhere.

In hindsight, it was obvious, but as a scientist paying attention to setting up and running operations, obvious was not as apparent as supposed. I recommend you pay close attention to debt collection at least in the first 2 years, and subsequently monitor on a regular basis.

11.4.3 Paying Your Creditors

The flip side of debt collection is paying your creditors.

[ii] She left BRASS after 5 years of service to join a couple of friends in starting-up a finance related business.

Some of the practices that were instituted in BRASS as we learnt the reality of paying our creditors were:

1. Some creditors had to be paid on time, period. I struggled at times to meet this and used my own funds or persuaded a shareholder to meet a few deadlines. In these instances, the client's payments were coming in but did not meet the invoice deadlines of our creditors. Reimbursement of the short-term "loan" was immediate upon receipt of funds.
2. Government agencies were straightforward. They imposed fines automatically when the deadline was reached. They are however flexible and at times compassionate. Let me recount one episode.[iii] When your staff number exceeded 10 persons, the rule was you had to switch from hardcopy to electronic submission. Ignorance is not supposed to be an excuse but I went in to discuss with an officer of this agency who was kind enough to waive the penalty fee and gave me a *grace* period to rectify the issue as it was the first occurrence for BRASS.
3. Some creditors were flexible (that you could stretch) in payment time.
4. On rare occasions, you delay payment and hope for the best.

What I eventually worked out was a detailed monthly projection of the expenses I had to pay and revenue that could be reasonably expected to be collected in the month. It is good to pay according to a fixed procedure exemplified as follows.

1. Have all payments passed (document trail to verify the expenditure that is normally checked during an annual audit) and checks prepared a week before the end of the month.
2. Send out on or before the due date.

Another lesson learnt was to build goodwill in good times to see you through lean spells. In the early days, many local creditors insisted on payment within 30 days with no compromise. When BRASS became more *cash flow* stable, BRASS established a history of paying on time. Subsequently, on rare occasions when BRASS had a big expenditure to meet, I sought their understanding for a 1 or 2 months' delay in payment. Other times, I offered to pay the invoice partially until our mini crisis was over. This was amicably accepted. The caveat is that you have to make good and resume to being a good paymaster when your short crisis is passed.

Finally, some recommended practices about handling money:

1. Check all payment claims are in order and correct.
2. Before you sign a check or make payment, ensure the payee and amounts match the invoice or claims form. This is very important when only a single signatory is required for payment approval.

[iii] This was with the Central Provident Fund Board (CPF Board), Singapore.

3. When you pay yourself, have the payment claim approved by another director and have the alternate signatory sign the check when possible. A company's funds are not yours unless and until paid to you in the proper way.
4. Similarly, when you extend funds to the company on a short-term basis, have a photocopy of your check indicated as such, the purpose recorded and approved by another director.
5. All financial records are confidential, accessed only by authorized personnel and kept locked similar to the archive practices in a quality system.

11.5 MANAGING HR ASSETS

This is probably the trickiest aspect of running a business. In almost all other aspects of a business, you can size up the situation quickly, respond appropriately and promptly. Human resource is different. It takes time to recruit, train, and for a person to fit in and get into the groove of an operation. Handling human beings is difficult at best and can be exasperating at times. With experience you may get better, but by then you will have an HR manager to handle that for you.

11.5.1 The No One is Indispensable Rule

My first rule of managing HR assets is what I learnt as an 18-year-old recruit in the Singapore Armed Forces (SAF). You are trained that in battle, casualties will occur. Who that casualty was, what the casualty's rank was, is insignificant. You or someone else on the ground must take over the role of the casualty and continue the mission. My SAF lesson #3 is: *no one is indispensable.*

From the CEO down to the lowest ranked staff, be prepared to replace. Never be held ransom by anyone who believes the organization will fold without their participation. Be decisive. It is never a pleasant task, but as the boss, you have to remove staff when the action is right and for the good of the organization. A staff that does not fit will also affect your morale, the team's morale, and the work performance of the team may suffer and you cannot afford that. I have asked loyal staff to leave when their continued employment was detrimental to the organization, and dismissed senior hires when they don't fit. Some staff may develop a *prima donna* complex after some time in the organization that can be toxic. Such is a possible consequence of a small organization. If you can no longer manage them, you have to remove them. Make your own judgment. At times you may have to be patient until what you have noticed is confirmed, but when the opportunity arises, do it immediately.

Know your staff's capabilities and limitations. If you cannot find good and competent staff and must settle, ensure that the deliverables are listed and are met within a time line.

Realize also that most staff will be with you for between 3 and 5 years, especially the younger ones (Singapore context). Today, most people are about chasing and fulfilling personal dreams and goals. Prepare for this. Build a system that takes into account that there will be regular changes in staffing. This does not mean redundancy in job scopes, but it does mean that another staff can cover duties for a period of up to 3 months to give you time to hire and train a new person.

11.5.2 Lead

When you are the *runway* entrepreneur, you lead, you command and you manage your staff. At times you have to motivate them with bonuses, opportunities, and by training them to do their job well. Before promoting your staff, confirm that they not only can perform well, but they can also lead others and be good team players. There are those who are uncomfortable or reluctant to lead and only want to do the job well. Find alternate ways to credit the contribution of staff who do not want to be promoted. Keep your pulse on the morale of the team. Know when to step in and when to let matters handle themselves.

When you empower your staff, they must have the assurance that you will back them up. Mistakes will be made, and how you handle them will determine whether your staff will improve and grow or become a drain on your organization.

Sometimes you are the complaints or counseling bureau to your people. Make yourself available to listen to work or personal concerns and issues. You cannot solve every matter and you must make decisions based on the welfare of the whole organization and all staff, not just the person who brought up the problem. You have to be seen to be fair by all and to all, at all times.

11.5.3 About Interns and Student Attachments

One form of "cheap labor" is to have students from universities and technical colleges attached to your facilities for several months, either as interns or attachments (they differ in degree of commitment in time and allowance). I list some of the following points for consideration.

The good:

1. You have "hands" to augment your small HR force.
2. You help train the "workforce" from which some could become your future staff.

3. You build relations with other institutions.
4. Some of your "trainees" who join the workforce after graduation may be your future clients.

The bad:

1. Your staff may be further stretched if they have to supervise "transient trainees".
2. You may have "duds and troublemakers". Pre-selection interviews do not always guarantee you get good trainees. Other times, you accept any student as part of professional relationship management.
3. Confidentiality is an issue that requires careful compartmentalization.
4. Some of your "trainees" could eventually end up working for your competitors.

You will have to weigh the value of these programs to your organization. You have flexibility in the number you take in and their scope of duties. It also depends on where you are in your execution plan. If at a critical stage, it is wise not to take on a responsibility that will distract your staff. It is best to discuss with your team, since they are likely to supervise the trainees.

11.6 HANDLING VENDORS AND SUB-CONTRACTORS

Apart from the financial aspect discussed earlier, vendors and sub-contractors must be managed constantly. For example, whether they deliver services or goods for your operations on time, repair or calibrate your instruments and equipment well, etc. all impact on your overall operations and performance. Keep the good, discard and find replacements for the bad. Listen and understand what the market says about your vendors and sub-contractors. Discern that the information is credible, because sometimes rumors abound to discredit competition. Ensure you continue to receive competitive pricing. Accept reasonable price increases year on year. You should not accept an agreement you cannot terminate with appropriate notice.

You can change unresponsive vendors. There was a logistics company that was adamant that BRASS paid upfront for every shipment generated. I felt at the time this was an inconvenience, as I had to sign a check every time BRASS wanted to ship an item. We had already demonstrated for over a year that we could pay and requested a consolidated monthly invoice. A couple of weeks later, the regional vice-president for sales of their rival showed up and agreed to accept those terms. This alternate vendor got BRASS's business despite the subsequent persistent efforts of the original vendor to accept my proposed terms to retrieve the business.

I was really unhappy about their adamant attitude in not accommodating a reasonable request. The lesson is to not let policies be so inflexible that your people forget that goodwill may be beneficial for business.

11.7 ESTABLISHING ENTERPRISE CREDIBILITY

Your aspirations can only be fulfilled by first having a reliable operation in place. Forget about all else. If you do not get this right, the rest does not matter. You do not survive long without building your enterprise's credibility. You do this by adopting some or all of the following practices and adding more to the list yourself.

1. Practice until near perfect. If manufacturing, make the process flawless. Your goal is to ensure all your procedures give you a good product. For example, keeping your bioburden (potential contamination) to a minimal in your facility.
2. Refine towards perfection. Know that you never reach perfection, so keep refining.
3. Pace yourself. You have finite resources, and you are in a marathon, not a 100 meter sprint.
4. Fix things that go wrong immediately.
5. Address all inquiries and complaints within 24hours and no more than 48hours.
6. Do not take on more than you can handle. Overloading will show eventually in substandard products or services and can be the beginning of your downfall.
7. Maintaining expectations is harder than getting there. Find ways to challenge your people and yourself.
8. Build your own identity that separates you from your competitors. In marketing terms this is called differentiation.

11.8 MANAGING EXPECTATIONS

This is perhaps the most challenging aspect of running an enterprise. Everyone has needs, wants and goals. I believe you cannot prioritize any category, i.e. they require equal attention. The best you can do is to systematically cater to all as evenhandedly as you can. Staff has been addressed earlier. Two other groups require comment: customers and shareholders.

11.8.1 Customers

The maxim "the customer is always right" has to be treated with caution. Clients want the best at the least cost. Clients can move on if you cannot satisfy their wants. Where possible you should try and satisfy your customers. But there may be situations when going all out to please your customers is not in your best interest.

You are in the biomed business. For a product, remember that your product was created to meet needs, not wants. You have to explain well the difference your product makes to patient care. Always focus on the virtues and merits of your product, do not talk down your competitor's. You should set a limit on the amount of training you will provide on your product and the number of trial samples you supply. You also have to know the extent you can drop the product price.

The recurrent client issue that BRASS has faced the most is on test failures. Most times it is easier to fault sub-contractors. You have to accept this fact and be patient in walking your client through why their tests failed and demonstrate that the problem source was at the origin and not at BRASS. Because BRASS's operations follow an accredited way of working, there is enough evidence to support this assertion. But you still have to handle every incident well with tact. You are unlikely to be 100% faultless all the time.

Where possible, build client loyalty with your work or product performance, not on pricing or other gimmicks.

11.8.2 Shareholders

Your shareholders have rights because they gave you the funds. They support you and you are obligated to keep them informed. You can do this by keeping in touch informally when possible. Most times, a formal setting such as at AGMs (Annual General Meeting) or quarterly briefings is appropriate. On such occasions, provide an update, explaining the financial status and progress forthrightly.

As time progresses and as the venture is progressing well, you may have to change your style. This is when you have to cater to expectations of dividend payout and update them on your plans for their exit, if they so wish.

11.9 BOARD OF DIRECTORS AND SCIENTIFIC ADVISORY BOARD: A REVISIT

As stated in Chapter 6, you are most likely the only director of the company. But as your company grows, the needs will change. As you build your company, you should consider assembling a board of directors that can help you both in running the growing business, as well as in building the image of your company. Good directors can help you achieve bigger goals. Look for candidates you can trust from various backgrounds and experience. Ask around, seek recommendations and invite referrals. Persuade them if you have to, anyone good will have a busy schedule. Making it worth their while is not just about money as people at that level have more than enough. Some may wish to make a positive contribution to local businesses. Others may like to champion a cause for perhaps national pride or to give back to society. You may offer share options, but keep the director fees and claimable expenses modest.

For example, the present BRASS board consists of two members. The chairman of the board is a seasoned businessman in the construction industry. The in-country director is a retired CEO who successfully ran the Asian operations of a large engineering company for many years and was also involved in a successful start-up venture. A financial expert oversees the finance of BRASS, reporting to the directors. Both board members and the financial expert are paid fees that are well below market rate. All are paid an annual profit-linked bonus. The in-country director also brought in a prominent local businesswoman who was once in charge of the Singapore operations of an international IT company to be a mentor to the BRASS general manager. She insisted on a *pro bono* arrangement. The point is, sincere people who want to make a difference are available. Your job is to seek out established people who are looking for opportunities to make a difference.

Working with a board may not be straightforward. The board may not agree with you in some instances. If you retain a seat on the board, you will have to lobby and persuade your board members to get their support, especially in major decisions. Conversely, a board that rubber-stamps your wishes may be detrimental to your endeavors. In my case, I stepped down from the board because I was confident the board members would look after BRASS's interests. My main role is to inform and at times explain the board's decisions and actions to the shareholders. This leaves me to pursue new challenges without conflicts of interest.

You only set up a Scientific Advisory Board (SAB) if the science in your organization grows and there are funds (usually partially sponsored by government grants) to commit to R&D. Until your outfit is financially strong enough to sponsor up to 75% of any R&D and begin to do interesting and better still, pioneering science, resist the desire or pressure from others to create a SAB. Setting up a SAB can be intense. You want to have leaders in the research field, and they are difficult to recruit. Why would they want to lend their reputation to a small outfit unless you know them personally? Even then it has to be in their interest to come on board. If you continue as a private entity, my recommendation is not to bother. Only if you consider listing your company should you toy with a SAB.

11.10 TOWARDS SUCCESS

When you are operational, there are more issues to handle on a daily basis. As you move from a less than five-person operation to a greater than ten-person entity, the amount of attention you have to place on activities will become intense. You will have to identify those to whom you can delegate responsibilities to help you run the company. The good news is that you are more than on the way to success. The bad news is that this is where many falter and commence a downward spiral they do not recover from. Why?

1. The *initial success bug* bites you and the "I can do all things now" mode infects you. Overconfidence is an enemy of success. It does not hit you all at once; it eases itself in and is hard to spot. It may cause you to abandon the cautious methodical process you have adopted that got you through the first stage. You need to maintain this all the way to true success (refer to Chapter 13).
2. By now you are used to leading, i.e. telling everyone else what to do. You know what's best. Don't kid yourself! This is when you are in more danger of lapsing into arrogance. Everybody loves a winner, but not too many will have the same sentiment for an *obnoxious winner*.
3. The consequence of growing is specialization. Compartmentalization is unavoidable when you are transiting from start-up to a corporate mode of action. The best thing I did for BRASS when it started making good profits was to remove myself from the company and let a seasoned businessman hold the reins. He set a structure in place. When I returned in 2009, there was an admin department with an HR executive and a finance clerk. A sales department interacted with operations. Operations had various sub-units organized around the work done. Today, that structure has been further refined. You require structure when you grow, the extent depending on the pace of growth. This pace has to match your cash position.
4. You are known for one product, and when you grow, one product type. If you change category, or add new categories, your fortunes can change in an unfavorable direction. People know you for who you are. Stick with your identity and learn how to capitalize on it. This is about establishing and maintaining your business differentiation.[1] Remember who you are. My task in 2009 was to revitalize the science in BRASS. I changed the logo from a medical device theme to a more bio-based (a DNA double helix strand adorns the logo) format. Call this intuition because I had no idea BRASS would be more bio-pharmaceutical focused today. BRASS continued to progress because old and new clients know and rely on BRASS's foundation, science.

Your focus can shift from medical device to bio-pharmaceuticals as long as you ensure your base maintains its strength and heritage.
5. Finally, always remember that you are only as good as your last sale (the business equivalent of the academic "you are as good as your last publication"). You have to grow your business. But in a manner that makes sense for your business as suggested above.

In conclusion, initiative in starting a business is necessary, but getting the business to the point it is on the world stage is the final goal. There is some way to go yet.

Real World Lessons Learnt

General
1. Take care of your bizness.
2. Micromanage at the start.
3. Manage expectations.

Specific
1. The clock is ticking, do not slack or rest on any laurels.
2. Manage your *cash flow.*
3. Execute to meet milestones.

Quote for the Chapter

"With time and patience, the mulberry leaf becomes satin.
With time and patience the mulberry leaf becomes a silk gown".
Chinese Proverb

Reference

[1] For an in depth appreciation of this topic, please refer toTrout J, Rivkin S. Differentiate or die. NY: John Wiley & Sons; 2000.

12

A Few Additional Lessons from the Battle Front

12.1 SITUATIONAL ASSESSMENT

For all intents and purposes, if you have adopted some of the suggestions presented in the preceding chapters in starting your own company on a tight budget, you already are a biomed *runway* entrepreneur. Although you may not be where you plan to be, you have surmounted your self-doubt and reservations, worked through the type of business

From Academia to Entrepreneur.
DOI: http://dx.doi.org/10.1016/B978-0-12-410516-4.00012-4
215

you wish to start-up, raised some funding, are implementing your *action plan* and hopefully on your way to success. You have learnt a thing or two about continued existence, a few crafts and tricks of the trade to help you. You also realize that what has brought you thus far may not get you all the way. Are there more skills that you can equip yourself with to help you continue to confront what waits around the corner? You can always do with more assistance and counsel.

The lessons presented here were learnt from experience and hindsight. The following segments were distilled over years of hitting my head against many a brick wall and realizing that brain damage need not be a permanent condition, with recovery indicated by amazing yourself on how well you can toughen your resolve to keep going. In no particular order or rationale, the headings are based on individual questions or situations that I have confronted or pondered.

12.2 CHARACTER

There is a popular story (probably myth by now) of a wealthy Chinese businessman who started off his #1 son in his organization as a janitor. The boy rose through the ranks, learning the ropes and tricks of the trade the hard way. By the time he took over from his father, he was a thorough and shrewd businessman because he had to learn the family business from the ground up (sound familiar?). This process takes time (in years, i.e. cannot be hurried), and builds a character based on humility, hard work, perseverance and developing resilience along the way.

These approaches to learning appear to be less common nowadays. The trend is to pursue and finish study or training programs in the shortest time so as to begin employment. The path to advancement preferred is by going for further training in "specialty" programs, rather than building understanding on the job. This "rule of the day" may be a handicap in many situations, since knowledge tempered with experience provides insight. Therefore, I recommend that you do not shortcut the lessons you have to learn in the first 2 or 3 years of your *runway* entrepreneur's "learning" program.

One of the more important skills to acquire is character building. What is presented here will get you started, but the endpoint is left for you to determine.

The first lesson in building character is *runway* entrepreneur math. The probability of starting and bringing an enterprise to success in most estimates is greater than one in a million, i.e.: **1**: 1,000,000

Note the number of zeros following the second 1 digit (i.e. after the *colon*). It really does not matter how many zeros follow, whether it is 6 zeros (as above), 9 zeros (billion) or more. One in a million is not good odds. The entrepreneur determined to succeed is biased in only visualizing the first number digit **1** (in bold). They defocus all digits after the *colon* punctuation mark. *You are the **1** who is going to succeed.* This kind of focus can be termed a winner's focus. Relearn this math since you probably have forgotten about it. When did you learn this? When you won a biological competition that became you.[1] You were born a winner, but life has made most of us forget that fact. **Recall and reassert your winner's attitude.**

The second lesson is *runway* entrepreneur vocabulary. Among the many other lessons I learnt in the SAF (Singapore Armed Forces) is that the SAF never **retreats**. *Tactical withdrawal* is the only course of action permissible in an unfavorable situation. What a positive attitude to adopt when "the stuff hits the fan". As an academic, there are times when students who had failed my tests would try to change my mind about their marks. I used this SAF lesson to formulate my reply. I tell them they had not earned the right to use the term *fail*. The term fail or failure is a privilege extended to those who have succeeded;[i] they could only use the word *setback*. They never came back to dispute again. Change your vocabulary. Remove negative words when confronting challenging conditions.

Third is balancing your passion and drive. You are passionate about your undertaking. You are driven with determination to get it done. You must find a **balance** between your passion and drive, **and control** both for your *runway* enterprise. Otherwise, you may get ahead of those around you, leaving them frustrated as they cannot catch up or understand you at the first pass of what you propose next.

Fourth, regardless how entrepreneurs come about, there is one three-course diet for a start-up *runway* entrepreneur that I know will help you to succeed: **handling adversity, more adversity and total adversity.** The best training method is to face the challenges, endure, overcome and prevail. You will always have doubt! You will always ponder whether you have made the right decisions. Even when things turn out right or are going well, you will wonder what's next up the bend that is going to hit you. Face it and get on with it.

Finally, learn from worthy examples. When I lived in the USA in the late 1970s/early 1980s, one of the privileges was watching American football during the fall of each year. I liked watching the Dallas Cowboys play. A key reason was their quarterback, Roger "The Artful Dodger" Staubach. I observed that he had the trust of his coach and teammates, the leadership quality he used to propel the team through sometimes hopeless situations and win the game, especially the brilliant "Hail Mary" passes. The poise and determination that he showed on

---

[i]Of course you can succeed without ever having failed.

the playing field was worth watching.[ii] American football may be far removed from science and entrepreneurship, but the method for winners and those who become successful transcends the career that an individual chooses. Observe and learn from those whom you see as good role models to follow.

The lessons continue. You set the remaining agenda.

12.3 BS AND SAVING FACE

There is no other dignified way to title this segment, so I make no apologies. The context of the terminology is as commonly applied. Dealing with BS and their originators is a skill you must master to be a true success.

Situations will always arise where you find no matter what you say or do, you will meet people who will give you the response you do not need to hear. Harry Beckwith in his book *Selling the Invisible* couldn't have put it more precisely when he called these people "intelligent people".[2] These people have a way of coming onto the scene, delivering their pearls of wisdom in the most sincere and logical manner possible and in the process, making a miserable time for you **if you let them**. They are either genuinely well intentioned, having your best interest at heart or they are downright mean, not wanting you to succeed and have any success. You should immediately conclude that seriously accepting what they say is counterproductive.

In my struggle to get BRASS launched, I met many a persons who conveyed the notion that I was so full of BS that I should have a long shower preferably using a ton of disinfectant topped off with fragrance. Most were polite and brushed me aside. However, I relate two incidents to illustrate what you can be up against.

A senior administrator once accosted me in the late 1990s. He had caught wind that I was in the process of starting and implementing the BRASS concept. With two of his lieutenants flanking either side of him, I was informed in no uncertain terms that a chemist dabbling with life sciences was illogical. This monologue was delivered in a very solemn tone and almost sounding concerned for my academic scientific career. It was a most thought provoking encounter.

One of the benefits of having served in the SAF during its infancy where sergeants and corporals screamed at recruits for no reason whatsoever except to inform them that they were superior beings prepared me well. I was suitably *immunized* to such censure.

[ii]Of course there were "bad days at the office" as well. Even then there was poise in handling disappointment.

It took a little while, but it dawned on me that I once heard about the poor in an Asian country picking these droppings once they had hardened and using them as fuel for their stoves. One thing led to another and I came up with my own solution for handling these matters. When people inform me my ideas are full of BS, I smile and think *manure*. Not because the real stuff tastes anywhere near palatable, and certainly BS if left on its own will stink as it putrefies and in the end is washed away with the rain or whatever. But the same material if *industriously utilized* can produce a harvest of plenty. And it takes a while to take effect and must be properly handled. Ask any farmer, she knows the benefit of organic fertilizer, how cash crops are produced. Care and patience must be the companion components. Therefore, in the hands of a wonder that is you, BS can turn into *manure* that eventually turns into a start-up company with a bright future!

So next time anyone says to you, hey buddy (or gal) you're full of BS, think *manure*. It will make you smile, they'll think you're a fool and you can have the last laugh, provided of course, that what you have are real plans and that your action will turn into a profitable reality.

The second incident was a somewhat more formal full-face encounter. BRASS once presented to a funding source in 2002, a time when a resource such as BRASS was evidently relevant for Singapore.[iii] The memorable comment from this episode was "your numbers are not sexy enough"! How do you "save face" when you are told you have no "sex" appeal? I suppose you can console yourself that you live in an age where there is nothing the wonders of modern cosmetic surgery can't revise, and you'll be fine. And of course note that sex appeal is not a criterion for a *runway* entrepreneur.

Through the years, I have learnt that the best response when handling BS and need to "save face" encounters is to smile and say thank you under these disparaging circumstances, especially in the face of the most "intelligent people". After all, I have also come to realize that such experiences could be looked at as blessings in disguise because they made belief in my pursuits stronger and further motivated me. But, even though my critics may not have the same opinions as me, I believe there is no necessity to act or speak disrespectfully to them. Just chalk these as one of the many lessons and do not let such remarks upset or deter you from the path to your success. And if you recall the quote in Chapter 1, in the scheme of things, it is you who are "in the arena" that matters.

12.4 ROSE

There are two core issues that matter for a biomed *runway* enterprise. The first, we have already discussed, patient safety. The other is ROSE.

[iii] This was my assertion. Obviously, the opinion in this situation was contrary.

We're not talking about a wonderful lady I know. ROSE is the acronym for Return On Shareholder's Equity.

ROSE is what must motivate you to look after all the details that will set your business apart: marketing, operations, hiring and keeping good staff, impeccable business ethics, etc. Your staff and shareholders demand it; your survival depends on it. All other niceties do not matter in the scheme of things. Take care of number one and two, and the rest will fall in place. Ignore either or both, and you're finished. This is not a once and for all exercise, it is constant, and you cannot stop.

Why is ROSE so important? A business as stated is set up for a single purpose, PROFIT. You are not in business to look good in your résumé or do perfect science. You are there to earn cold hard cash, i.e. revenue. You put in effort and money as your personal investment. But in a biomed business, as we now know, it is unlikely you do it all on your own. Furthermore, when you set up a business, not only your co-investors, but your staff and clients (in a sense) become your shareholders. You, presumably, are committed in your responsibility to them and therefore, making and increasing your company's value must be the focus of your attention. Instead of having a list as long as your legs, all you need to remember in every encounter, every decision, every thought you make on behalf of your company, is ROSE. As you are guided by ROSE you will respond and decide according to what will benefit your shareholders, and that includes you. Enough said.

12.5 THE KISS PRINCIPLE

This acronym has been around and is still worth repeating. "Keep it simple, stupid". The biomed industry, as has been stated *ad nauseam*, is a knowledge-based activity. The basis for your product (or service) commanding a high price is the use of knowledge to solve a biomed need. If you are a medical device manufacturer you will know that the sophistication of your product is in the concept and design. The features of the product are "locked-in" by the time prototyping completes. While you may have required the services of PhD scientists and high-powered engineers in these *brainpower* phases, the same is improbable when you go into production.

The actual manufacturing of a medical device can be at times rather labor intensive and mundane. Therefore, staffing your production line human resource with the same caliber workforce would be absurd. If you did, you'd have a high wage bill, your bookkeeper will faint and your accountant will be a candidate for a triple bypass. Translated, the science has to be viable in a production line handled by proficient and hardworking staff that may not be scientists and definitely will not possess the high-power qualifications, only the manual skills and dexterity to assemble the product. This is the cost reality in manufacturing. Therefore, whatever the product, it must be simple enough to realize at the production level. This is of more importance when you outsource manufacturing, especially to a less developed country.

If you were a service company, the client is most interested in the support that you provide especially the technical part. Your ability to translate, at times, complex scientific terms and procedures into structured high school science that does not come across as condescending is expected. This is because some of your clients may not have the scientific background and even if they do, you know that science is a wide field. The same and even more care should be exercised where regulatory matters are concerned, even though regulators have the requisite qualifications and experience. Stating in plain terms what your product is, what tests were performed and the pass criteria all facilitate easier progress for approval. That is why at BRASS, we have scientists who handle the technical aspects and technologists who carry out the actual lab work, i.e. assays. This way there is a balance in wage costs that translate as affordable pricing for our clients.

At the other end of the scale is the user. Don't forget that physicians, skilled and educated as they are, have a patient's life on their hands and the need to learn how to use your product may delay its adoption. Even if you can convince the physician to use the device, your other hurdle, the support staff, especially the surgical nurse-in-charge, have to be convinced as well. If the packaging is too difficult to separate to access the device, troublesome assembly or user safety while handling is not well thought out in the preparation stage, their resistance will make your product's rejection potential high.

Simple is simple. It performs the required function with little fuss, is easy to produce, easy to handle and use. Think it through, KISS can be a make or break factor in your product's adoption.

12.6 CREDENTIALS

Knowledge-based implies that an individual should have the right academic qualifications as a foundation to exploit the science. For many, this equates to a PhD in *something* as a prerequisite for a biomed entrepreneur. This has been discussed and is not disputed. But having the right credentials is not so much about whether you have the appropriate three alphabets after your name, the right piece of paper, or several pieces of paper. Most times, pieces of paper facilitate you a foot in the door at best. How you make use of the opportunities that piece of paper provides is what matters. After all, I know of individuals with only a high school background but with 20 years' industry experience leading a team that included several multi-papered individuals. It is what is in your "DNA", i.e. personal make-up, which really determines your worth. Therefore, a PhD is good to have but not essential.

I contend that more important is to decide that you want to be a biomed entrepreneur before pursuing a course of study. This gives you a head start and as the quote for Chapter 6 indicated, preparation is half the component to success. Preparation in this instance would include taking a course of study (and choosing the most suitable modules) and searching for other non-academic exploits such as skydiving (that requires daring, training and discipline) to build up your portfolio of experiences. Therefore, in my opinion, a good first degree in science, engineering, medicine or dentistry is sufficient. Individuals with a sense of adventure, ready to defy convention and the status quo (within legal and ethical boundaries) are what make for good *runway* entrepreneurs.

The other academic qualification that comes to mind when entrepreneurship is mentioned is the MBA. In my opinion, to have an MBA or not is a personal choice. Obtaining an MBA is normally a costly undertaking financially, as well as time-wise, even if done on a part-time basis. The recipient of an MBA gains from a formal program, insights that are definitely not readily garnered on the streets. My perception is that the knowledge gained from an MBA can be very useful in many right situations especially when applied to *jet-stream* entrepreneur situations. For start-up *runway* entrepreneur purposes, be judicious as what is learnt in an MBA program may not be readily adapted to a style that is more informal and at times, resorts to *guerilla warfare* tactics for survival. Certainly, when you enter the growth phase, I believe that a lot of what you learn in an MBA program would be helpful. Make your choice, go study for an MBA or hire an MBA graduate, whatever works for you!

12.7 DAYLIGHTING

Moonlighting is a term used to refer to a person with a primary (daytime) job having a secondary job, usually outside normal office hours (at night or very early in the morning). Moonlighting most often is motivated by personal financial circumstances.

The definition (this book only) for *daylighting* is a situation where a person holding down a full-time job finds latitude to pursue their dream pre-occupation, oftentimes with the full knowledge of their employer. The purpose of *daylighting* has to do with satisfying an unfulfilled calling while not compromising personal financial circumstance. The *daylighter* uses in-between spare time in the day, evenings and weekends towards achieving the dream while not neglecting their duties in the full-time job. This was the situation I found myself in, once BRASS was officially launched in 1999. It was legal in the sense that NUS gave me (written) permission to be a non-executive director in BRASS, as well as one day a week away from my academic duties to tend to BRASS.

However, nothing is straightforward, as your *daylight* job must take overriding precedence. Academic duties are still duties you have to fulfill, and they do not come in neat time pockets. For example, lectures for a normal module are twice or thrice a week for 12 weeks at a stretch, and you have to show up for them. Usually the timing is not in your favor, i.e. not at the start or end of the day but somewhere in the middle. You also have to prepare for lectures. The days of using one set of lecture materials for 20 years were over when I started as an academic. With the progressive use of IT and the constant appearance of new science, you have to update your lecture materials every year. At NUS, your lecture materials had to be uploaded onto the university's intranet for your students to download before the lecture. Furthermore, you have administrative duties that means you at least have to show up when meetings are called. Since I was senior enough to chair committees, this meant time spent on preparation as well. And you are running a research program that cannot be neglected. You cope. The upside was that as long as these duties were taken care of, you had a lot of liberty to pursue your dream relatively unimpeded. Therefore, one day a week was up to one's interpretation of how to utilize those 8 hours.

Daylighting is not an inconvenience; it is a lifeline towards accomplishing the opportunity of a lifetime. Use it well.

12.8 BALANCING ACT

One of the more challenging matters you will face as a budding *runway entrepreneur* is where to draw the line between your institution and your enterprise. You normally start out at the institution you are working at and leverage every advantage you can. This was advocated in Chapter 3. But this applies only as long as it remains your own applied research because you, the PI, control all activities. When you register a company, immediately transfer all activities to your enterprise under the terms you have worked out with your institution. Once transfer is complete, keep what you do in your institution and company separate. Why?

If you continue to work within the confines of academia on an extended basis, you may encounter problems down the road. For example, if your research becomes known to industry, a patron may be interested in ascertaining the worth of what you have initiated. You obtain "research" contracts from this industry sponsor and perform the work in your research space, intending to "transfer" some or all of the work to your enterprise gradually as your facility comes on-line. Doing the "industrial research" past a certain stage can be problematic. How do you separate what is done in the institution and what is carried out in the enterprise? You may have an agreement with your industry office to permit you to do this, but your institution also rightfully has a claim to a "piece of the action" since you utilized their facilities and resources. How do you sort this out? Balancing activities at this stage is arduous, as a convenience can get messy pretty quickly. This situation is a disaster in waiting. Decouple as early as possible, because leaving until later can be a nightmare to sort out.

The day BRASS was out, it remained out. The situation was easier because all the incubation staff from IMRE joined BRASS. My department of chemistry research and students were kept separate. It is my recommendation that you do the same as early as possible.

12.9 READ, CUSTOMIZE AND APPLY

"Knowledge is power" is a common phrase and even a proverb used by many for a variety of occasions. For the *runway* entrepreneur it would be more appropriate to rephrase to *knowledge is the beginning of power*. Knowledge is the starting point for you to get better. Only when you utilize it appropriately does knowledge have power to get you where you plan to go.

Information is vital. Meet people by attending trade shows, exhibitions and conventions, and talk to your clients. Listen to the anecdotes, opinions, insights, descriptions, etc. that come your way. Ignore gossip and never pass that on. Passing on gossip is a poor reflection of your judgment and that is an impression you do not want others to form of you.

But you obtain the most **information** by reading extensively according to topics (breadth) as well as by specialization (depth). Hoard books and revisit them often. Visitors to my university office were often curious at the titles on my bookshelves, as more than half had nothing to do with chemistry. Don't bother explaining. The effort is for your own benefit and that is all that matters. Purchase books and read them at least three times. The first is to get a general overview, the second is to highlight the details that jump out at you, and the third is to extract the points that caught your eye for consolidation into your resource notebook or electronic files and folders. And of course do not leave them there for aging or archiving purposes. Review the extracted information thoroughly because there must have been a reason you were drawn to those words, lines or passages.

Imbibe, ponder, digest, process and assimilate the information, ideas and suggestions you encounter. **Customize** to suit your own style by defining what is suitable for application and incorporation, what to discard, or store for later retrieval and future use. Customization of the information you gather permits you to *apply*, i.e. turn that information into a knowledge reservoir that you can access to suit each crucial situation you will confront. This is not a one-time exercise.

Finally, there are those who feel that hoarding information, and keeping or exercising when to disseminate knowledge, is power. You are not in business to stagnate, move at a snail's pace, or to be the only focus of success. Of course you must retain proprietary information that you do not want competitors to access, but you want to disseminate information and know-how to your staff and your team so that everyone can act on it for the betterment of your organization. Share, teach, coach and define boundaries of information exchange at all levels.

12.10 ROCK AND ROLL INSPIRATION

There will be times when you will face disappointment, feel discouraged, or be overwhelmed. Willpower is essential to continue, persist and prevail. For the ultimate in *pick you back up* inspiration I have always found the best source is in rock and roll music. If one discounts the silly love songs and other noise associated with rock and roll, there have been many well-scripted songs whose lyrics are worth playing over and over in one's head for comfort, endurance and encouragement, especially when you confront a rough patch.

Examples I've found useful include:

Justin Hayward's (The Moody Blues) line stating "it's easier to try then to prove it can't be done" from the song "Blue World" is the straightforward reply (equivalent to "why not?") to addressing "prophets of doom" pronouncements of why your "brainy" ideas won't work.

And my all time favorite is Jeff Lynne's (ELO or electric light orchestra) lyrics in "Hold on tight to your dreams" (especially when the French part "accroche-toi à ton rêve" comes on) that can only inspire to get you to the finish line.

I am sure you can find your own inspirational songs to suit your own situations, so rock on.

12.11 EPITAPH OR GLORY?

Whether your company succeeds or succumbs to market forces can never be predicted. *Staying the course* is the only given. The last lesson to be aware of is perhaps the toughest, but has to be stated for completeness.

As you progress, continue to evaluate your own performance as well as your team members. Who is asking the right questions, proposing the right solutions and leading the fight? There may come a time when your effort may not be great in comparison to some of the people on your team. Discuss with your board and close friends. Perhaps you are more suited for the science function after all, and it was only your initial enthusiasm that got the enterprise this far, but it will not get the company to the finish line. As noted in Chapter 5, it's easy to start but very hard to finish, and finishing well is extremely difficult. If you reach this point, reflect and offer to follow. The best person must lead, not necessarily the founder. Therefore, if such a circumstance occurs, do not let your pride rule over business reality. The main goal is to succeed. Do not get in the way of your company's glory by writing its epitaph with your refusal to step aside.

Looking back, BRASS was a good idea before its time. There were a lot of bumps in the road because I was most times clueless. The only thing going for BRASS in the first three years was my stubbornness in not giving up. BRASS turned out well because everyone else in and related to BRASS filled in the places where I was wanting. I was willing to:

1. Continue to beg for funds and periodically "top up" personally in rough months in the first 3 years.
2. Take responsibility for each month's results and not "pass the buck" onto my manager or take it out on my three or four team members. I had good people working for me. Most were recent graduates without the grades some employers seek. But they were hardworking and went more "extra miles" than I had the right to expect that made a tremendous difference.
3. Not let my pride stand in the way of doing what was most appropriate (a "saving face" issue).
4. Learn financial prudence. Pleading with suppliers to cut you a break was very humbling for an active academic in my environment (another "saving face" issue).
5. Resisting the temptation to start an animal facility when business started getting brighter. Many parties were asking me about this aspect in 2005. This would have been a serious over-extension that probably would have led to BRASS's demise.
6. Stepping aside and letting others take the lead at various junctures on BRASS's path forward.
7. Continuing to stay focused on BRASS's strength "propelled by science" on my return in 2009.

8. From BRASS, I realized my talent in start-up, growth and sustainment of an enterprise was primarily as a *troubleshooter*. Each time BRASS needed some sorting out, I was there to right side up BRASS.

Identify your talents and strengths. Use it for the good of the *runway* enterprise you started. The bottom line is you serve everyone else in the undertaking, not the other way round. And I wish you all the best on your business achieving the glory it deserves.

Real World Lessons Learnt

This chapter has only specific lessons.

1. You were born a winner never doubt that.
2. You will have *anti-fans*.
3. Do what you must (legally and ethically) to succeed.
4. It's not how smart you are but what you are and do.
5. Be practical: a lifeline is a *gift from heaven* to use well.
6. Learning is continual.
7. Rock and roll inspires.
8. Make or break depends on you.

Quotes for the Chapter

"Your attitude, not your aptitude, will determine your altitude. Expect the best. Prepare for the worst. Capitalize on what comes".

Zig Ziglar

References

[1] Mandino O. The Greatest Miracle in the World. : Bantam Books; 1975 [Chapter 9].
[2] Beckwith H. Selling the Invisible: a Field Guide to Modern Marketing. New York: Warner Books; 1997. p. 67.

13.1 CHECKPOINT #3: FACING REALITY

There are only two possible outcomes for your enterprise once you have set up shop and opened for business: your venture will succeed or it will not. There is possibly a third state termed *living dead*, a situation where you suspend activity and wait for *things*[i] to turn in your favor. This situation usually never works, so it is best to bypass this phase and revert immediately to the flop appraisal. The primary reasons your venture can stall or turn awry are:

(1) THE SCIENCE AND/OR PRODUCT ARE SUPERSEDED BY SCIENTIFIC ADVANCEMENT OR COMPETITION.

This is the real world. That science is advancing at a breakneck pace and you are not alone has already been dealt with. If others have gotten to market quicker than you, admit it and deal with it. If others have got a better product than you and you can see no way around it, find a way to close. And if the science is superseded, start on new science. An example from my research area of chitin[ii] illustrates advancing science surpassing a present product concept.[1]

Heparin is a natural glycosaminoglycan[iii] extracted from animal sources that has been in clinical use as an anti-clotting agent for several decades. The chemical structure of chitin resembles heparin except for one distinctive feature. Dating back to the 1970s, there has been a lot of reported research on adding this distinctive feature to chitin, making modified chitin better resemble heparin. From these studies, modified chitin has been demonstrated to exhibit the anticoagulant effect to be similar to, or better than, heparin. Conceptually, the modified chitin can be an alternative to heparin. Commercially this has not happened and may no longer be viable to attempt. In the interim, heparin has been produced by chemical synthesis. The pharmaceutical form has already been approved for clinical use. From the regulatory perspective, the chemical method of producing heparin is preferred over modified chitosan, as the molecular identity is easier to define and the substances are purer. Should work continue in the exploration of chitin as an alternative to heparin? A proponent would have to do a thorough evaluation as to the worthiness of continuing exploring modified chitin as a heparin substitute.

My recommendation was for research to continue, since as long as funding was available, the possibility of generating something new or interesting that was not related to the application as a potential heparin replacement exists. However, extending to commercial exploitation as

---

[i] Because perhaps you "don't want to" or "would rather not" deal with a possible flop. This is no way to treat yourself, your staff, clients and investors.

[ii] The term *chitin* is taken to represent both *chitin* and its popular chemical derivative *chitosan*.

[iii] Ignore the scientific terminology if you do not comprehend. It doesn't affect "the price of tea in China" so you should not be overly distressed.

a heparin alternative is not sensible in light of the demonstrated chemically synthesized equivalent.

This is what you must confront and come to terms with. The scientist in you can continue, but the entrepreneur must *bite the bullet* and stop. End of story!

(2) THE BUSINESS HAS HIT A FINANCIAL WALL.

When the cash runs down with no more forthcoming to get to the finish line, what can you do? As explained in both the IPT and ARM episodes, the funds just could not be raised. The contributing scientific and technical reasons supporting the decision to discontinue were straightforward. This may not be the situation you encounter. When the scientific and technical reasons are still positive, due diligence obligates you to evaluate why funding continues to be the issue and whether there are new channels to pursue. I recommend a further 6, but no more than 12, months to find alternate funding because your product cannot wait forever. If it was never meant to be, it is best to realize sooner, pull the plug, and regroup to try a new endeavor.

(3) YOUR CUSTOMERS FOUND THE PRODUCT TOO COSTLY AND/OR THE PRODUCT UNDERPERFORMED.

Your product, despite being superior, may not be well received because of its cost compared to existing alternatives. Your pricing may have arisen from production costs overrun that can occur despite all you have done to keep every expense on or below budget. The flip side is that you can only squeeze your margin that much. You may get away with selling below costs in the short-term, but if you objectively evaluate from a longer-term perspective and cannot see getting out of this impasse within 12 months, you really have to make a decision.

Or, your product may have scored well during prototyping and trials, but run into usage issues when fully launched. You will have to conduct a full review and look for fixes that do not impact your finances and timeline too much without compromising patient safety. You may also have to consider the negative effect of the setback. Admittedly, as a *runway* venture, your resources may not permit a new campaign to counter the negative image that may have set in, leaving you no choice but to close down.

In summary, when you have exhausted every avenue, and all indications are for you to terminate, delay no longer. The only foolish act at this juncture is to continue to hope things will turn around. They seldom do.

The legal manner to wind up a business is governed by the laws of the country where your business is registered. Those are details your company secretary or lawyer should be able to assist you. More important is to end professionally and ethically:

1. Pay all your staff. Scrounge the funds if you need to, but pay them their due. The ones who stayed with you to the end deserve their pay. You may even have to take that bank loan based on your 2 months salary limit.
2. Pay all your creditors with whatever is left over. You may have to work out a deal to pay off the invoices over a few months, but you will gain their respect. Keeping your reputation and integrity is important. You may want to do this again down the road and you want them to remember how you settled accounts. You may be talked about for some time after you leave the scene and you might as well let them have something nice to say about you (there is of course no guarantee they will do this).
3. Archive all documentation for the requisite time period (usually 7 years). Tidy up as many details that you can. Finally, take at least a week off before you ponder over what next. You earned the rest.

Now that we have dispensed with the flop; the rest of this chapter is about success.

13.2 FROM START-UP TO PROFIT AND BEYOND

In your action plan, you would have set the milestones you need to achieve along the way to success. These are important to get your product manufactured, tested, submitted for and obtain regulatory approval, and finally start selling. Do these well, maintain and improve on the operational aspects continually. However, your focus will inevitably be from the financial standpoint and you have to be on top of this. Business milestones are measured by revenue and profit, while your stress relief is obtained by a positive *cash flow* and cash in the bank.

13.2.1 Revenue Landmarks

These are your landmarks and indicators of progress and success:

1. First revenue month.
2. First profit year.
3. Paying taxes even after factoring in tax breaks.

Your first revenue month is a watershed to aspire to. This will be your first **credit** entry (all others were debit) since the day initial funds were put into your company's bank account to start the venture. This source of funds is also different. The message you receive is that others have assessed your effort and found it worth paying for what you have created. Savor the moment but do not get carried away. You have a long way to go before removing the minus sign accompanying several digits after it from your company's annual statement of accounts, i.e. your financial position is a net loss.

BRASS was generating trading revenue from the beginning and that was welcomed. When the first testing fee payment was received, that was a significant event. Subsequently, every month has been a revenue-generating month. This is the goal; revenue must come in on a constant basis. Still BRASS's overall financial position was a net loss for many years, despite a positive *cash flow*.

Your first profit year indicates you are established, no longer a novelty but accepted by your customers as reliable. This is also when your first warning bell must sound. The tendency is to expand capacity in anticipation of increased sales because you now have momentum. Do a business potential survey and evaluate the results. The data may not support your perception. This is the period you must exercise the utmost caution in flexibility. Balance the need to grow with greater financial prudence. Constantly remind yourself that at this stage, the financial year may be a profit but the accounts will still be overall negative because of the accumulated losses (all the money spent to get the product out). Aspire to continue maintaining net profit.

Probably the best news will occur when your enterprise has to pay taxes! This sounds absurd, who looks forward to paying taxes? The simple fact is that when you have to pay taxes your enterprise's annual statement of accounts will indicate a net profit that does not contain accumulated losses. In other words, you are out of the financial "woods". And the more taxes you have to pay, the better is the growing profit.

13.2.2 Growth Milestones

Corresponding to revenue landmarks are the many phases of growth to look out for. There are many ways to measure growth: size of the organization in space and/or staff number, sales figures, and others that can be used. The most appropriate is of course revenue, as it is the least biased. The following are important milestones with regards to revenue.

1. Breakeven.
2. $1 million.
3. $5 million.
4. Beyond $5 million.

There are many ways to define breakeven, but the simplest is when your profit covers what has been put in. Take the hypothetical situation when $2 million was put in. This will probably be difficult to recover in profit within 5 years, since accumulated net profit may not have reached $2 million. Therefore realistically, when you hit revenue targets of $1 million and $5 million, they are good growth milestones because they indicate that revenue is headed in the right direction, upwards.

Making your first profit and maybe reaching the target of $5 million is awesome but the game is not over yet, there are decisions to make. Recall in Chapter 5, the first goal was to reach $5 million in revenue. To go beyond that mark, there are two main choices. First is to consider activating your exit plan. This is the subject of the next sub-section, 13.2.3. Second is to take your company beyond this $5 million point, an undertaking that more likely requires you to abandon the *runway* mode. This is the subject of sub-section 13.2.4.

13.2.3 From Profit to Exit by IPO or M&A

Recall that technology-based ventures including biomed enterprises are set up to create value for its *founding* investors. When the venture begins to perform consistently and starts to make steady profits year on year, your *founding* investors will probably indicate their desire to exit, and perhaps you will as well. The options presented in Chapter 5 are restated, IPO,[iv] M&A[v] and carrying on by buying out the majority or all of your shareholders. M&As and IPOs are direct mechanisms to exit, while purchasing the company from your existing shareholders is obviously financially more challenging. M&As may require the guy in charge to stay on for a while but typically not for long. Once the organization adopts the new owner's way of running, you will quickly find that you have surpassed your *use by date*. IPOs may also require the guy in charge to stay, depending on the situation and how you have structured your future role in your company. Be informed that in a public company, you can be removed from office more readily than in a private company.

I have never been fond of IPO even though that was put in front of my face before I started BRASS and again in 2009. In 2009, I had an offer of up to $5 million to grow BRASS in preparation for IPO. My reluctance eventually was picked up and the preliminary discussions led nowhere. The chief downside to my reluctance was the consistent pressure to meet the listing requirements, such as achieving quarterly targets for stock performance. The second is the increased number of shareholders you have to be responsible to. Doing an IPO does have its attractiveness to many, principle among them is the funds that can be brought in that permits doing more, leading to growing at a faster pace that increases the

---

[iv] Initial Public Offering: listing your company on the stock exchange. It depends on the country and the intended stock exchange's listing requirements. Some do not require profit to list.

[v] Mergers and acquisitions.

value of your organization. It also permits founding shareholders a way of exiting reasonably well if they so choose because they can sell their shares publicly. If you revel in this type of environment, can handle these affairs, and your organization is a candidate for IPO, this is certainly a choice worth considering. I prefer the M&A option.

M&A requires an interested party (the acquirer, normally the bigger and cash-able outfit) to express an interest to the target (frequently the smaller outfit). The reasons for acquisitions are diverse such as increase market share, acquire an externally developed technology, enter a new market, etc. Your job if you plan M&A as an exit is to make and grow your company to be a suitable target for acquisition. When an interest is expressed to acquire, my recommendation is for you to first obtain an independent appraisal of your company.[vi] This will provide you a ball-park idea of your company's value that prepares you for the negotiation of the sale price. According to a banking source, a LOI (letter of intent) stating other terms such as non-competition by key personnel and reten-tion of a fraction of the sales funds for a fixed time period (to clear out-standing accounts and related finance matters) normally follows after agreement of the sale price. Realize that you may not have any say in staff retention. Note also that the LOI can precede negotiations on price.

Discuss everything openly with your board members to obtain a con-sensus. This is one instance you do not want to act alone. You do not have to revert to your shareholders, as the board has the authority to act on this matter. Finally, there is a sales agreement that is circulated among the shareholders to vote on. The majority vote required to pass the M&A motion is normally stated in the company's Memorandum of Articles and Association. Usually this is not a simple 51%, but more towards 75% to 90% and even 100%. This is because M&A is a major event and per-suading a majority of shareholders to accept is to safeguard the interests of individual minority stakeholders who may have objections to the deal.

What is a good sale price? The buyer of course wants the lowest, the seller the highest. Valuation is another one of those items in the "beholder's eye" domain. Let me recount to you two cases. The first is a 10% shareholder who actively participated in starting a company with several partners. After several years the company was valued at around $20 million. A new investor wanted to come in and the company was re-valued to $50 million. Unfortunately, the 10% shareholder and the new investor did not see eye-to-eye. The 10% shareholder was offered $2 mil-lion (10% of the previous valuation) to exit. Rationale dictated that she should have negotiated for somewhere near $5 million. Nevertheless, the 10% shareholder took the $2 million and left. The company increased to

[vi]You will have to pay a fee for this. Use an accounting, banking, or legal contact to refer you to a suitable valuator (appraiser).

a value of $100 million the next quarter. Shortly after, a new competitor appeared and wiped out the $100 million company's business overnight and the remaining shareholders were left with pennies per share value. The second case relates to another promising start-up that was offered $1 million plus 5% annual royalty payments for 20% of the company. This company was top of a shortlist of three companies for the potential acquirer. The founders of the start-up held out for more. The potential acquirer refused to compromise and went on to the second candidate on the shortlist who took up the offer. The start-up subsequently folded. I leave you to decide who was pragmatic.

The third option is to take over the reins completely. After some time, your original shareholders who helped you by putting money in may want to exit for their own reasons. If this is expressed, you should find a way of accommodating this request. As stated, this can be financially challenging but those who want to exit often times would likely settle for a reasonable proposition. I caution exchanging them for new shareholders unless the incoming shareholders are willing to buy in at a higher price and also provide a value add in the transaction. As you grow, for a private entity, the fewer shareholders you have may be the better recourse.

13.2.4 From *Runway* to *Jet-stream*

If you choose to stay on and run the show after buying out most or all of your shareholders (or through staying on in an IPO), the game gets bolder and definitely more interesting. This is when you have to consider becoming a *jet-stream* entrepreneur. This is not a course of action for everyone. Recall the *runway* entrepreneur analogy is about a small propeller-driven aircraft that has its limitations, for example service ceiling (how high the aircraft can ascend) and speed, and that may be yours as well.

Jet-stream is about progressing to a bigger stage and a comparatively humongous step-up in all departments. This requires a different mindset and embracing a new culture. You will have to acquire new skills to be a *jet-streamer*, and your organization's potential has to match the ambitions. You may also have to discard most of the bad habits of a *runway* entrepreneur. Discuss taking this action with your advisors. Their support would confirm that you have the capability, mentality and stamina to make the change. A good business consultant can assist you to transit to the new level.

The other aspect is breaching the $5 million mark. For a biomed enterprise, $5 million for most people is very much a cottage industry existence. To expand significantly and grow astronomically is a necessary ingredient to strive to the $100 million level and beyond. Apart from requiring big money, you need a bold plan either by increasing your market-share across borders, acquiring complementary businesses, or developing good revenue-generating products. Some of these possibilities you may already have had in your original business plan. Revisit and update. You are about to do it all over again, but this time you have a track record and your plans will be viewed differently. You are believable and a better prospect for a buy-in.

13.3 REWARDS AND ACCOLADES

How do you measure success? Recall in Chapter 4 you were asked to determine your own measure of success. See if your present status matches what you defined. In general, I believe if you can meet the following, you are successful.

1. Survived and still operating well after 5 years and growing.
2. Continual real revenue stream with profits that are free from:

   a. Government grants funding.
   b. No more occasional top-up of funds by shareholders to continue the business.
   c. No debt. You may disagree on this one but I am firm that you should be able to be loan-free except for the odd lease for equipment you are paying off.

The best indicator is when shareholders smile and congratulate you at company AGMs. Do not go overboard when you receive compliments.

It is natural to seek some form of financial payback when your enterprise finally makes it. You are the one who made the most sacrifices; sweating the big and small stuff more than others, all the while enjoying the challenge but at little or no remuneration. Approach your board and shareholders to discuss this important matter. You earned it.

Since it's beginning until the end of 2010, I was paid director's fees only twice, in the two profit years before I left. BRASS did pay for some expenses, when I bothered to claim. At the 2010 AGM, BRASS shareholders unanimously voted to reward me for bringing BRASS to its present level that continues to improve. I agreed to a paid consultancy appointment with BRASS when I retired from NUS. Annual renewal of this arrangement by the board of directors protects BRASS from an open-ended commitment.

Finally, you must also let go of any baggage you brought along with you, preferably as soon as possible. Forget about the nasty things you heard behind your back and the folks who stood in your way. Holding grudges and worse, toying with revenge is for immature fools. Be magnanimous.

13.4 ACHIEVEMENTS

In the end it is important to keep score as well. What have you achieved? Permit me a little indulgence to summarize BRASS. It took 6 years for BRASS to achieve a first year of profit. On reflection, it should have been 3 or 4 if only I had not been left to my own devices and had accepted counsel from others more readily.

> Facility: From 500 square feet of lab space to its present facility of 10,000 square feet lab and office.
> Staff: Originally 3. Present number is around 18.

BRASS's present reputation in the industry and financial achievements are a source of pride for its board of directors, management team, staff and shareholders. One fact stands out. Our clients can sub-contract to anyone. But given a choice, they don't sub-contract to good enough. They sub-contract to PREMIER, i.e. BRASS.

My publications and other academic accomplishments aside, that BRASS is a financially successful NUS spin-off company that has helped to contribute to the Singapore economy for roughly 15 years, as well as providing increasing employment over the years, is my only real "return on investment" on the research funding extended to me.

13.5 LOOK AFTER YOUR SHAREHOLDERS

There are people in this endeavor who have cheered you on, encouraged you, backed you financially, opened "doors" for you, played their part for you by getting their part of the job done (well), and even prayed for you, an unending list. For the majority, your memory may escape you. But for those you do recall, you should do the necessary. Not out of a sense of duty, obligation or other practical reasons. Rather a genuine gesture of gratitude because as the English poet *John Donne* put it:

> No man is an island entire of itself;
> Every man is a piece of the continent, a part of the main;[2]

For many, a sincere *thank you* face to face, a card or e-mail, will suffice. Others you may want to take to an appreciation lunch or dinner.

There are two specific groups you should reward financially when possible. The first is your staff. They are the ones who assisted you to transform a tentative undertaking into the success before you. Use bonuses and other non-monetary means to acknowledge their contributions.

Second, your loyal first round shareholders who trusted you and were prepared to lose everything they *wagered* on you. As soon as is possible, pay dividends. Shareholders (rightly) pay attention and look forward to receiving dividends. Don't wait for one or a few to inquire or worse, demand dividends. Pay now. You should fight to at least cover their initial investment as quickly as possible, because business fortunes can turn awry instantaneously. Why do I use the term *fight*? Unless you own the company outright, the board of directors is the legal authority to declare dividends (this is standard in Singapore under the Companies Act Chapter 50). You are up against a board of directors who view retaining every last dollar possible in the company's coffers as their duty. In their mind, a business setback, economic downturn, an unforeseen big expenditure may "occur" tomorrow, and they must have the cash reserves to deal with the crises. I generally agree with this sentiment; you may be financially better off than before, but you still may have a long way to go. Therefore, find a balance between the board's caution and your shareholders' expectations.

13.6 MONUMENTS AND CORPORATE CITIZENSHIP

Once you are successful, do not let success get to your head. The tendency is to be freer with the funds, especially when the profit begins to build up as cash reserve in the bank. Always remember that the profit your company is accruing is not yours alone, but your shareholders' as well. You don't need a fancy office with the finest furniture. And if you crave for a few trappings of official luxury, bring it before your shareholders at the company's AGM. They may indulge you and approve the expenditure for the great job that you have done. When your shareholders have had their say and give their support, you do it with their blessings; that's a better way.

You don't have to build monuments such as an iconic company facility that is architecturally fanciful and a landmark. Abstain as well from using company funds to sponsor various community activities in the name of being a good corporate citizen.[3] These provide intangible benefits at best, but what you are really doing is locking in your shareholders to your causes; this is not playing fair to the people who have supported you. Note that this is different from marketing activities, for example when you sponsor conference events where you showcase your company's products.

This does not mean you should not be philanthropic. Do it with your own money, i.e. the bonuses and dividends that you will receive. In so doing, your shareholders can decide how they want to spend their own (dividend) money. Be true to business principles, how to use the profit due each shareholder is their prerogative. They know very well how to exercise the privilege.

13.7 VIEW FROM ABOVE: LOOKING BACK, GOING FORWARD

How does it feel to have made it or reached the point where all things are manageable? You should at least be satisfied with what you have accomplished and perhaps just a little disappointed because you could have done more or better.

Be real. If you don't know what you have attained and are feeling down on yourself, let me fill you in on your achievements, regardless of whether your venture turned out successful, mediocre, or ran into one set-back too many to recover from.

First, believe it or not, you have satisfied your stakeholders with regard to your having put in the best effort that they entrusted you with. For your shareholders, putting up money was one thing and for many, it was an easy thing. Some of your shareholders may express dissatisfaction at the results. Don't let that bother you. There will always be a few who will never be appeased regardless, even if you gave them an astronomical return on their investment. To your shareholders who are behind you and congratulate you, be gracious. Let them know they too contributed to where things are today because you didn't get there on your own. This sentiment should be extended to your other stakeholders, i.e. your staff, your clients, customers, suppliers and most of all, your family. They have overlooked your shortcomings in many situations and despite their reservations, backed you all the way. There will also be the many names and faces you won't remember or probably never even knew, who in their own way facilitated your passage. This is the true measure of success, to realize that along the way, you have managed to inspire, rally and lead others around you, and you have made a difference. No one gets there on her own efforts alone. Never ever let it get to your head that you were the only all important moron responsible for the final result.

Second, savor the moment. After all, there is always **only one winner**, you. There is nothing wrong with celebrating achievements. You earned it. Remember, this has been about you overcoming yourself, the greatest impediment. Enjoy your newfound status because everyone loves a winner. Just do not act like an *anal sphincter* about it.[vii] There is no need to be obnoxious and make a grand issue about it, especially if it belittles others. There are proper and dignified ways of going about these matters. **Remember, today's hero can easily be tomorrow's villain** and falling from grace is only a half step away.

Third, take stock. What has it really been about and what have you accomplished? An entrepreneur's achievement is more than satisfying

---

[vii] For those who are biologically challenged, please Google it or use a dictionary.

herself and her shareholders. Entrepreneurs are also contributors to their society. You have supported the economy of the country where you are located by providing gainful employment for some of its citizens. You have assisted your customers in achieving their goals and missions. You have also played a supporting role in the employment of others that deal directly or indirectly with your enterprise, for example telecommunications, banks, law firms, logistics and courier services, airlines and many others. The list is endless. And remember, all the fees and other taxes you pay to your government are just as important.

Give yourself a pat on the back, you have not only passed the test, you have done it in the best possible way, and you have helped others along the way. Don't let anyone tell you otherwise.

Finally, you have learnt something about yourself. What drives you, your tolerance and endurance levels. You now know your limitations and how you overcome them, and how you handle setbacks and compliments. What else could you ask for?

13.8 MOVING ON

Once you have achieved success the question will arise, what next? Even if you had chosen to move on to being a *jet-stream* entrepreneur, one day, the *end of the road* you are on will appear. This will probably also be the time when your bodily signals, long suppressed by self will, start hitting you. The long hours, the constant reacting to the countless situations you had faced, and the emotions that engulfed you each time, all will take their toll. You are drained and exhausted. You will look out at your company's landscape and realize that there is a team in place that can run the show and the need for your physical presence is slowly diminishing. You should be overjoyed when you sense this happening. Your organization had long ago left its start-up mode behind, the phase where you were the center of the universe. Now your burden is shared, and perhaps off-loaded.

At this point, you have one final important lesson you must learn, *how to let go*. Nothing lasts forever. Staying on would just postpone the inevitable and may even make you a liability. When an organization progresses way beyond the start-up phase, there are new goals, requirements, strategies and structures that are needed. The vision may still be the same, but the manner to achieve them will most likely be different. Your presence may still be required, but most probably in a reduced capacity. It is your imperative and duty to find and hand over the vision to a successor who can lead the company to new heights. This is because, unless you were born with the Midas touch, you will find that somewhere along the road, your ideas and ways of management may not be suitable in the next or subsequent phases of the company. Different people are suited for different seasons. Better to identify it yourself and find an honorable exit than to be told and voted out. So expect it. Prepare for it.

The key element I want to emphasize is *let go*. You don't own it. It was never your baby alone, and anyway, babies grow up don't they? Many others have a share in it. Never be sentimental. Do what is best for the company. Holding on can sometimes lead to a death spiral that you cannot pull out of. Do the smart thing, quit while you're ahead. The ultimate test of success is to be able to walk away from it all, gracefully and with dignity.

Recall, SAF Lesson #3 about indispensability.[viii] You are dispensable. So take care of #1, you. Moving on is about realizing that once you have made your contribution, others must take over. Moving on will also permit you time to reflect on the path you took, recall the good and bad times, savor the victories and appreciate the setbacks, and take stock of the milestones that you have attained. And maybe like me, write a book.

13.9 GONE FISHING

This book has described one way to look at starting a biomed enterprise, the *runway* style. It was not a straightforward way for me. I would even say a hard way. I trust you learnt a little from it. If not, let's talk fishing.

There is an eatery in Changi Village (Eastern part of Singapore) called Charlie's.[ix] This eatery serves an assortment of steaks, fish and chips, the best of the British colonial diet and of course a mixed bag of alcoholic beverages. A pleasant place to go to have a meal away from the city, but be forewarned, it can be quite crowded. The peculiarity is that Charlie's opens only in the evenings till late. I like the owner's philosophy of opening only from Mondays to Fridays. Weekends? Forget it! There is a sign that states unambiguously "Gone Fishing"!

Gone Fishing is about you being good to yourself. If you permit the enterprise, situations or others to dictate your pace, you end up the sucker and abusing yourself physically, mentally and emotionally. The entity that is you is a biological being that requires rest. Do not deny yourself the opportunity to relax, take a vacation and if blessed, enjoy the respite with your family and loved ones. The real world does not really need you.

[viii] In case you were wondering, I am available to consult for lessons #1 & #2.

[ix] To indemnify myself, I must admit I have not been there in years and do not know if Charlie's still exists. But it was there once. Believe me!

I have been telling everyone for a long time that when I retire I'll go fishing. Every time I state this, I conjure up the image of sitting on a canvas chair by a peaceful riverbank or a lake's edge somewhere in the wilderness of Canada, fishing line in the water, book on my lap. What a life that will be. No cell phone, no notebook computer, the absence of the Internet and therefore no e-mails. Just gazing at nature (even perhaps an occasional bear) and no deadlines to meet. Peace at last. Well, at least, for a couple of months.

Anyway, I am rambling. Thank you for reading my book. If the contents were in someway useful and you applied it, tell me about it via e-mail.

Guess who won't be reading his e-mail!

Real World Lessons Learnt

General
1. There will come a time when the party ends.
2. There will always be others who can take over.
3. There will always be something else to go to.

Specific
1. Don't be too hard on yourself.
2. Don't let life run you. Let go. Run your life.
3. The true meaning of life is to find contentment.

Quote for the Chapter

"And in the End,
It's not the years in your life that counts,
It's the life in your years".
  Abraham Lincoln (1809–1865; 16th President of the United States)

THE END

References

[1] Khor E. Medical applications of chitin and chitosan: going forward Kim S-W, editor. Chitin, Chitosan, Oligosaccharides and their Derivatives – Biological Activities and Applications. Boca Raton: CRC Press; 2011. p. 405–13.
[2] Donne J. *Meditation XVII. Devotions upon emergent occasions*, 1624.
[3] Al Dunlap puts the point across well and I leave you to glean it for yourself: Dunlap AJ. *Mean business*. Times Business Books-Random House 1996 [Chapter 13].

Index

Printed and bound by CPI Group (UK) Ltd, Croydon, CR0 4YY

08/05/2025

01864984-0001